£1.50

Mastering

German

Second edition

Antony Peck
*Senior Lecturer at the Language Teaching Centre,
University of York*

Betty Parr
Founding Editor

D1464947

MACMILLAN

© Antony J. Peck 1982, 1995

All rights reserved. No reproduction, copy or transmission of this publication may be made without written permission.

No paragraph of this publication may be reproduced, copied or transmitted save with written permission or in accordance with the provisions of the Copyright, Designs and Patents Act 1988, or under the terms of any licence permitting limited copying issued by the Copyright Licensing Agency, 90 Tottenham Court Road, London W1P 9HE.

Any person who does any unauthorised act in relation to this publication may be liable to criminal prosecution and civil claims for damages.

First edition 1982
Second edition 1995
Published by MACMILLAN PRESS LTD
Houndmills, Basingstoke, Hampshire RG21 2XS and London
Companies and representatives throughout the world

ISBN 0–333–61432–1
ISBN 0–333–61434–8 cassettes
ISBN 0–333–61433–X pack

A catalogue record for this book is available from the British Library.

10 9 8 7 6 5 4 3 2 1
04 03 02 01 00 99 98 97 96 95

Printed and bound in Great Britain by
Biddles Ltd,
Guildford and Kings Lynn

Acknowledgements

The author and publishers would like to thank the following for the use of photographs: J. Allan Cash Ltd, pages 154, 175; Photobank, pages 165, 184, 185, 197; Helen Tyler, pages 2, 14, 37, 49, 59, 68, 70, 132; Zefa, pages 25, 93, 94, 143.

Every effort has been made to trace all the copyright holders, but if any have been inadvertently overlooked the publishers will be pleased to make the necessary arrangement at the first opportunity.

The cassettes which accompany this book can be ordered from your local bookseller or, in case of difficulty, from Macmillan Direct, Houndmills, Basingstoke, Hampshire, RG21 2XS (telephone 01256 29242).

Contents

Introduction: how to use this book   *vii*

1   Guten Tag!   1
Greetings and introductions
     How to greet people; how to be polite; how to introduce
     yourself and others; how to take your leave

2   Wie komme ich ...?   13
Getting about
     How to find your way on foot and when driving; how to
     understand directions

3   Ein Doppelzimmer   24
Staying in hotels
     How to obtain a hotel room; how to make and confirm a
     booking

4   Hin und zurück   36
Travelling by train
     How to buy a train ticket; how to ask about times of trains

5   Taxi, bitte!   48
Travelling by taxi, bus or tram
     How to order a taxi; how to state your destination; how to
     ask the destination of public transport

6   Es tut weh   58
Illness
     How to make an appointment with the doctor; how to
     describe symptoms of illness; how to say how long
     symptoms have lasted; how to describe the type of pain

7   Was darf es sein?   68
Shopping
     How to go shopping; how to understand salespeople; how
     to ask to try on clothes; how to ask for something different;
     how to ask the price

8 Haben Sie Kinder?   82
   Families and nationalities
        How to ask about and state your own nationality; how to
        say where you come from; how to say whether you can
        speak a language; how to discuss family and marital status;
        how to ask about a job, profession

9 Wie ist das Wetter?   92
   Places and weather
        How to ask about the location of towns; how to ask about
        and describe places; how to ask about and describe weather

10 Revision tests   106

11 Ein Tisch für zwei   118
   Eating out
        How to ask for a table at a restaurant; how to call the
        waiter; how to ask for the menu; how to ask what someone
        would like to eat or drink; how to order a meal; how to ask
        for the bill; how to express the time

12 Kann ich hier parken?   132
   Asking permission
        How to ask permission; how to refuse permission

13 Was sind Sie von Beruf?   142
   Jobs and professions
        How to talk about what people do for a living; how to talk
        about where people work; how to talk about hours of work

14 Wo wohnen Sie?   153
   Accommodation
        How to ask where someone lives; how to describe your
        accommodation

15 Interessen   164
   Hobbies and interests
        How to ask about and say what you are interested in; how
        to express likes and dislikes

16 Wir müssen gehen   174
   'Want' and 'must'
        How to express what you want to do; how to express what
        must be done; how to express what doesn't have to be done

17 Können Sie singen? 183
   Suggestions and proposals
      How to make a suggestion or proposal; how to ask and
      say what one can do; how to say how well you can do
      something

18 Ich möchte reisen 196
   Dreams and wishes
      How to ask about and express what one would like to do;
      how to say that one would like to have something done;
      how to ask when services will be completed, and when
      articles can be collected

19 Gestern und vorgestern 204
   Talking about the past
      How to refer to past time

20 Revision tests 214

Pronunciation key 219

Answers to exercises 222

Translations of dialogues 238

Grammatical summary 261

Money, weights and measures 298

Some useful hints and tips 302

Signs on public display 307

Bibliography 311

Introduction: how to use this book

Learning aim

The aim of *Mastering German* is to enable you to acquire the ability to take part in everyday communication with native speakers of German. This means being able to take part in the following two sorts of language exchange:

- You need to be able to 'survive' in the language, and that means being able to take part in transactions which are necessary for your health and comfort. This includes such things as shopping, ordering meals, reserving rooms in hotels and finding your way around by public transport.
- The other sort of language which you need is the language for making social contact with speakers of German. The social language is particularly important if you are likely to meet German speakers at home or abroad and spend some time with them in a social setting. Businessmen and women, in particular, may find this sort of language of great use for helping to create a suitable social atmosphere in which business can be done.

The materials

Mastering German consists of a book and accompanying recordings. If you are beginning the study of German, you will find the recordings of particular use in helping you to acquire good pronunciation, intonation and stress. A guide to pronunciation is included in the book. If you already have some mastery of the pronunciation of German you will still find that the dialogues, using native speakers, will help you to speak not only with clarity, but with a good range of expression.

How to find your way about the book

Each chapter aims to help you with certain topics; these are listed on the contents page. If you wish to 'cash in' your study as soon as possible you should concentrate first on mastering these topics. The most important parts of the book for you are the dialogues, the notes on the dialogues, the vocabulary and the structures to learn, Section A of the exercises and the 'spontaneous' dialogues – the last exercise in each chapter. These are the communicative parts of the book, and will help you learn how to make an arrangement or meet somebody, how to request a service, how to make a suggestion or proposal, etc.

If you wish to acquire a grasp of German grammar, you should pay particular attention to the second section of the structural explanations in each chapter. This takes points of grammar arising in the dialogues, and explains them fully, so you are not left wondering how a structure works. A list of what grammar is explained in each chapter appears in the Grammatical summary at the back of the book, where you can also expand your grammatical knowledge.

Language for speaking and language for understanding

The main emphasis in this book is on the skills of speaking and understanding. Some parts of the language presented will consist of things you will want to say, and others will consist of things you want to *understand*. You will have a good idea of those things you are most likely to want to say, and should consequently concentrate on practising these parts of the language aloud. Do remember, however, that the better you become at speaking the language, the freer natives will feel in replying to you!

In choosing the topics to include in this book, the proposals of the Threshold Level for Language Learning, published by the Council of Europe, have provided a most useful point of reference.

How to get the best out of Mastering German

1 The following procedure is recommended for studying the dialogues
   (a) Look at the Contents list and study the *topic* of a chapter to see how it sets out to teach you to use German. This will inform you of what you should be able to do by the time you have got to the end of the chapter, and this in turn will help you to evaluate your own progress.
   (b) Read through the German text of the dialogue and listen to it simultaneously on the recording. Try to work out the meaning of each sentence as it occurs. Very often the common linguistic ancestry of

English and German will help you to find out the meaning. These similarities between English and German will sometimes be more apparent when looking at the spelling of words, and sometimes when listening to the way they are spoken. When you have predicted the meaning as far as you can, refer to the translation at the back of the book, so as to be quite sure that you understand the dialogue thoroughly before proceeding.

(c) If you are working with the book alone, work out the pronunciation of the sentences in the dialogue, using the pronunciation guide. If you are working with the recordings, speak the dialogue quietly while listening. By degrees increase the volume of your own voice, and decrease the volume of the recording. After two or three times, it should be possible to pronounce the dialogue accurately and with good expression. When you are beginning to establish a correct pronunciation of the sentences, it will probably help to stop the recording after each sentence, and to repeat it aloud several times before continuing to the next sentence.

2 For students with little language learning experience

(a) Having worked through the dialogues in the way described above, go on to the section labelled Structures to learn. With the help of the pronunciation guide, speak the sentences aloud, noting carefully which uses of the language they help you to master.

(b) It is probably best at this stage to omit the study of the grammatical section, and go straight to Section A of the exercises. Do the exercises as best you can without referring to the answers at the back of the book. Only when you have really thought about what you want to say, and tried hard to get it right, should you check with the answers.

(c) 'Spontaneous' dialogues are included at the end of every chapter. These are an introduction to German spoken at a natural pace and without a script. The intention is to practise understanding the *gist* of a conversation without concentrating on individual structures. This is very much like the situation you will find yourself in abroad, when understanding the sense of a conversation is the key to survival. Read the questions *first* to get an idea of the situation and then listen to the dialogue as many times as you like. There are answers at the back of the book.

(d) When you have worked through the whole book in this way, return to Chapter 1, and go through the book again as indicated below.

3 Intermediate students

If you have already mastered the rudiments of German, perhaps at school, but you have now become a bit 'rusty' on a lot of it, you should work first through the dialogues as indicated above, and run through the Structures to learn and the communicative exercises as indicated for beginners. In this way, you will be able to put to practical use elements of the language which you may previously have learned more formally and which was not based on immediately relevant situations.

You should then proceed directly to the grammar section, in order to consolidate what you have learned.

Then go carefully through the structural exercises (Section B) based on the grammar section, checking answers with the answer key at the back of the book. You will sometimes need to refer to the Grammatical Summary at the back of the book as well as the section in the chapter.

Vocabulary learning

Each chapter contains lists of the most important words which occur in the chapter. It is not a complete list of all the new words which occur, since these are given by the translation of the dialogues. The word list gives a basic vocabulary which you should be able to use actively.

Here are some suggestions, intended to help you learn new vocabulary items:

1   Cover up the English translation, and try to use your knowledge of German to guess the meaning of the German word. Then check whether you are right or wrong by uncovering the English version. Continue in this way until you can recognise all the new words.
2   Then go on to the more difficult way of learning vocabulary, and cover up the German version and try to remember the equivalent for each word. You should try to remember whether nouns are masculine, feminine or neuter, and how they make their plurals. If possible, work with a friend who can ask you the English words and check whether you have succeeded in remembering the German equivalent.

Revision tests

Chapter 10 and Chapter 20 consist of tests on the earlier chapters in the book and are intended to help you gauge your own progress.

The German alphabet

The German alphabet coincides with the English alphabet, except in one case. The symbol 'ß' is the equivalent of 'ss'. The rule concerning the use of 'ß' and 'ss' is a complicated one, and may safely be left until a more advanced stage in learning German. You simply need to know that the two symbols are pronounced identically. If you wish to learn the rule for using 'ß', you should consult *Hammer's German Grammar and Usage* (see Bibliography).

Alles Gute!!
All the best!!

Guten Tag!

Greetings and introductions

 Dialogues

Dialogue 1

Professor Hecht has called to return a catalogue which she borrowed from a business acquaintance, Herr Kirchhof.

```
 1  Sekretärin:   Ach, Frau Professor. Guten Tag!
    Prof. Hecht:   Guten Tag, Frau Hausmann.
       Ist Herr Kirchhof da?
    Sekretärin:   Ja, Moment bitte.
 5     Herr Kirchhof ...
       Professor Hecht ist da.
    Herr Kirchhof:   (at door) Guten Tag, Frau Professor!
    Prof. Hecht:   Guten Tag, Herr Kirchhof!
    Herr Kirchhof:   Bitte, kommen Sie herein.
10  Prof. Hecht:   Danke.
       Wie geht es Ihnen?
    Herr Kirchhof:   Sehr gut, danke.
       Bitte, nehmen Sie Platz.
    Prof. Hecht:   Danke.
15  Herr Kirchhof:   Eine Tasse Kaffee?
    Prof. Hecht:   Oh ja, gerne.
    Herr Kirchhof:   Frau Hausmann, zwei Tassen Kaffee, bitte.
    Frau Hausmann:   Ja, gern.
    Herr Kirchhof:   Nun, wie geht es Ihrem Mann?
20  Prof. Hecht:   Ausgezeichnet!
    Herr Kirchhof:   Und Andreas und Daniella?
    Prof. Hecht:   Auch sehr gut.
    Herr Kirchhof:   Und hier ist der Katalog.
    Prof. Hecht:   Ja, der Katalog.
```

Wie geht es Ihnen?

Dialogue 2

Elke Kustmann is having a party at her flat in the Fürstenstraße in Munich. She works at a smart dress shop in Munich and is celebrating a good month, with plenty of commission. Amongst her guests is a new friend and admirer, Fritz Löb.

(Front door bell rings)

1 Elke: Herr Doktor! Guten Abend!
     Doktor Neumann: Elke! Guten Abend!
     Elke: Wie schön.
      Kommen Sie herein.
5 Doktor Neumann: Danke.
      Darf ich meine Frau vorstellen?
     Elke: Guten Abend, Frau Neumann.
      Willkommen!
     Frau Neumann: Guten Abend!
10   Danke schön für die Einladung.
     Elke: Bitte, bitte.
      Das ist Fritz.
     Fritz: Guten Abend!
      Löb ist mein Name.

(Front door bell rings again)

15 Elke: Eckhard!
   Eckhard: Elke!
   Elke: Du hier!
      Das ist fantastisch!
   Eckhard: Elke, du bist noch immer so schön.
20 Elke: Ach, nein.
   Eckhard: Doch. Doch.
   Fritz: (Clears his throat)
   Elke: Ach, ja.
      Das ist Fritz.
   Eckhard: Becker.
25 Fritz: Angenehm.
      Löb.
   Eckhard: Angenehm.
(Front door bell rings again)
   Elke: Entschuldigen Sie!
...
(some hours later)
   Doktor Neumann: Auf Wiedersehen!
30   Vielen Dank.
   Elke: Nichts zu danken.
      Auf Wiedersehen!

Information

(a) Notes on Dialogue 1

1	Frau Professor	German titles are: 'Herr' (Mr), and 'Frau' (Mrs, Ms). 'Fräulein' (Miss) is now rarely used for adult women. In German you address people with a title such as Professor or Doctor as e.g. 'Frau Professor', 'Frau Doktor'. Similarly 'Herr Professor'.
1	Guten Tag	The greeting 'Guten Tag' applies to the whole day, where in English we would say 'Good morning' or 'Good afternoon'.
15	Eine Tasse Kaffee?	This is short for '(Would you like) a cup of coffee?'
16	Gern(e)	Here this means 'Yes please'. It can also mean 'My pleasure' (see line 19). You can use the word with or without the final 'e' as you choose.

(b) Notes on Dialogue 2

1	Guten Abend	This greeting is used from about 6 pm onwards.
11	Bitte, bitte	This emphatic repetition of the word 'bitte' is best translated as 'don't mention it'.
14	Löb ist mein Name	If you wish to state your name, you can begin by stating it in order to give it emphasis, but it is more usual to say 'Mein Name ist Löb'.
17	Du hier!	This is the familiar form of 'you', which you may hear used between family and close friends. The 'Sie' form is the standard form to use to adults, and all you need to learn for now.
18	fantastisch	Here are some other words which you might find useful for expressing enthusiasm: wunderbar großartig klasse You can use the first two in any society, but 'klasse' is slightly more colloquial.
21	Doch	This word means 'yes' when spoken emphatically, because the previous sentence has been in the negative. If, therefore, the previous speaker says e.g. 'no it isn't' and you wish to reply 'oh yes it is', you would use the word 'doch'.
24	Becker	Adults introduce themselves to other adults by giving their family name.
25	Angenehm	This word literally means 'pleasant' and is best translated by the conventional English phrase 'pleased to meet you'.
31	Nichts zu danken	'Don't mention it' is clearly not a literal translation, but is a good rendering of the meaning.

(c) Word list

Here is a list of the most important words in the dialogues. You should learn them by heart. They are given here in the order in which they occur in the dialogues. After each noun, the plural ending is given in brackets. (-en) means add the letters 'en': 'der Herr' (singular); 'die Herren' (plural). (-e) means add 'e'. (-er) means add an Umlaut to the vowel, thus modifying its sound (see page 20), and also add the letters 'er'. (-) means the plural is the same as the singular. For more information on the plural of nouns, see the Grammar section of Chapter 14. In German, certain syllables of words are stressed. This is shown in bold type.

die Sekretärin (-nen)	secretary
Frau	Mrs, Ms
Herr	Mr
da	there
bitte	please
kommen	to come
danke	thank you
sehr	very
gut	good, well
nehmen	to take
die Tasse (-n)	cup
der Kaffee	coffee
ja	yes
der Mann (-er)	husband or man
ausgezeichnet	splendid(ly)
und	and
auch	also/too
hier	here
der Katalog (-e)	catalogue
die Frau (-en)	wife or woman
vorstellen	to introduce
willkommen	welcome
die Einladung (-en)	invitation
fantastisch	fabulous
der Name (-n)	name
noch immer	still
schön	beautiful
nein	no
doch	yes (after a negative)

(d) Some phrases

Moment bitte	Just a moment, please
Kommen Sie herein	Do come in
Wie geht es Ihnen?	How are you?
Bitte, nehmen Sie Platz	Please sit down
Gerne	Yes please
Wie schön!	How nice!
Entschuldigen Sie	Excuse me
Auf Wiedersehen	Goodbye
Vielen Dank	Thank you very much

(e) *Further useful vocabulary*

These are words which occur later in the chapter. You will find it useful to learn them as well.

das Auto (-s)	car
der Schuh (-e)	shoe

Structural explanations

(a) *Structures to learn*

(i) How to greet people

Guten	Tag	Good	morning; afternoon
	Morgen		morning
	Abend		evening

Gute	Nacht	Good night
	Besserung	Get better soon
	Reise	Have a good journey

(ii) Other frequently used phrases

Guten Appetit!	Enjoy your meal. (Nearly always said by people sitting at the same table, before they begin to eat.)
Alles Gute!	All the best!
Prost! Prosit! Zum Wohl!	Cheers! Good health!
Viel Glück!	Good luck!
Viel Spaß! Viel Vergnügen!	Have a good time!

(iii) How to be polite

Bitte	People use these phrases when
Bitte schön	offering something to someone else
Bitte sehr	e.g. a customer handing money to a salesperson, or a waiter placing a dish of food on the table. It is a rather more polite equivalent of 'Here you are'.

Bitte Bitte schön Bitte sehr	The same expression means 'please'. 'Bitte schön' and 'Bitte sehr' are slightly more emphatic.
Gerne	Literally 'I'd like to', commonly used to mean 'yes please'.
Danke Danke schön Danke vielmals	All these expressions mean 'thank you'. They are arranged in order of degree of emphasis.
Bitte	'Bitte' can also mean 'don't mention it'. You use it when somebody has thanked you for something. Here is a possible exchange: Er: (offering something) Bitte sehr! Sie: (thanking him emphatically) Danke vielmals. Er: Bitte, bitte (don't mention it).
Grüß Gott	This means the same as 'Guten Tag', but is used in the south of Germany and in Austria.

N.B. The letter 'ß' is pronounced as if it were 'ss'.

Entschuldigen Sie	This means 'Excuse me', and can also be used to apologise for small mistakes.
Verzeihung	This is how to say 'sorry' for larger offences, accidents, etc.

(iv) How to introduce yourself

1   Say your family name e.g.   Freeman!
 Hardy!
 Willis!

2   Johnson
 Peterson } ist mein Name
 Davidson

3   Mein Name ist { Jones
 Smith
 Robinson

(v) How to introduce somebody else

1   Das ist { Mr Smith
 Dr Jones
 Prof. Pike

2

$$\text{Darf ich} \left\{ \begin{array}{l} \text{meinen Mann} \\ \text{meine Frau} \\ \text{Herrn Schmidt} \\ \text{Dr Jones} \end{array} \right\} \text{vorstellen?}$$

3 If you wish to make it known that you are about to introduce people to each other, you can use the phrase 'Darf ich vorstellen?' to indicate your intention, and then continue with:

$$\text{Das ist} \left\{ \begin{array}{l} \text{Mr Jones} \\ \text{Herr Schmidt} \end{array} \right.$$

(vi) How to take your leave

Auf Wiedersehen	This can be used on most occasions.
Auf Wiederhören	Reserved exclusively for ending a telephone conversation.

$$\left. \begin{array}{l} \text{Kommen Sie gut heim} \\ \text{Kommen Sie gut nach} \\ \quad \text{Hause} \end{array} \right\}$$ An expression of the wish that the person concerned will reach home safely.

(b) Grammar

(i) Nouns

The names of people, things and places are *nouns*. In the following sentences, the nouns are printed in italics. Note that some nouns can be abstract.

The *man* was drowning   We're going to *town*
She made some *coffee*   He felt great *happiness*

(ii) Pronouns

Pronouns are words which are used instead of nouns. These are known as *personal pronouns*. N.B. The familiar forms 'du' and 'ihr' are used when addressing children up to the age of about 15 or 16, and amongst members of the family. More in Chapter 15.

Singular		**Plural**	
ich	I	wir	we
du	you (*familiar form*)	ihr	you (*familiar form*)
er	he	Sie	you (*formal or polite form*)
sie	she	sie	they
es	it		

(iii) Verbs

Verbs are words, or combinations of words, which express states, actions or events. In the following sentences, the verbs are printed in italics.

He *is* ill	They both *jump* for the ball
She *lives* in Manchester	She *gets* a cheque every month
I *like* beer	They *are going* on holiday soon
He *has* a bad cold	I *buy* my shirts at Harrods

The above verbs are said to be in the present tense, that is, they refer to a state, event or action as it is now.

Each verb in German has six forms, three in the singular and three in the plural. These forms tell you who performs the action or event of the verb, or to whom or to what the state expressed by the verb refers.

Here are the present-tense forms of the verb 'sein' (to be) together with their relevant pronouns.

ich bin	I am
du bist	you are (*familiar form*)
er ist	he is
sie ist	she is
es ist	it is
wir sind	we are
ihr seid	you are (*familiar form*)
Sie sind	you are (*formal or polite form*)
sie sind	they are

(iv) Adjectives

An *adjective* is a word which *describes* someone or something. In the following sentences, the adjectives are printed in italics.

That is a *fat* man	*My* son is thirteen
This car is *old*	Beer is *best*

Possessive adjectives indicate to whom something belongs. They correspond to the *personal pronouns* given above.

Mein Name	my name
Meine Frau	my wife

You will find a complete list of *possessive adjectives* in the Grammatical Summary.

(v) Gender

All nouns in German are categorised in three genders: masculine, feminine, neuter. Gender only *partly* corresponds to male and female, and you should consequently learn the gender of each noun as you meet it.

'Mann' (man or husband) is masculine, shown in the vocabulary list thus: 'der Mann'.

'Frau' (woman or wife) is feminine, shown in the vocabulary list thus: 'die Frau'.

'Auto' (car) is neuter, shown in the vocabulary list thus: 'das Auto'.

(vi) Singular and plural

A singular noun is *one* person, thing or place. A plural noun is *more than one* person, thing or place.

(vii) Agreement

Agreement means that two words, e.g. a noun and an adjective, are both masculine, or both plural.

Possessive adjectives (the words for 'my', 'your' etc.), as all adjectives, must agree with the noun they describe. They show agreement by adding certain endings.

mein Mann	my husband	dein Mann	your husband
meine Frau	my wife	deine Frau	your wife
mein Auto	my car	dein Auto	your car
meine Schuhe	my shoes	deine Schuhe	your shoes

You will find a complete list of *adjective agreements* in the Grammatical Summary.

(viii) Capital letters

1 Capital letters are used at the beginning of sentences.
2 They are also used for all nouns.
3 They are used for 'you' in the polite form and also for possessive adjectives in the polite form.

Exercises

Exercise 1

1 What would you say to somebody who is just going to bed?
2 What would you say to somebody who is just going to take her driving test?
3 What would you say to somebody for whom you have just poured out a drink?
4 What would you say to your secretary first thing in the morning?
5 What would you say to your mother as she gets into the train to go home?
6 What would you say to your friend when you visit him in hospital?
7 What would you say to the head waiter as you go into a restaurant one evening?
8 What would you say to a friend who is just going off on holiday?
9 What would you say to an acquaintance you have met on the street in daytime?

Exercise 2

You are having friends round this evening to celebrate your birthday. The front door bell rings. Dr Schmidt and his wife are there.

1 What do you say to him?
2 He introduces his wife to you. What does he say?
3 You are very pleased to meet her.
4 Ask them to come in.
5 Ask them to sit down.
6 Frau Schmidt wants to thank you for the invitation. What does she say?
7 Ask them if they would like a cup of coffee.
8 He would like a cup. What does he say?
9 She doesn't want coffee.
10 The front door bell rings again.

Exercise 3

You have been corresponding with Herr Kunze of Siemens for some time. You have an appointment to see him in Düsseldorf, and he has invited you to his home for dinner. How would you reply to the things he says to you? Listen to the recording and give your responses in the pauses. You will be able to check your answer after the pause. Repeat the exercise as many times as you need to respond correctly.

Exercise 4: Eine Party: A party

This section appears at the end of each chapter and is specifically designed to accustom you to spontaneous, unscripted conversations spoken at a natural pace. The scripted dialogues you have heard so far highlight important structures and vocabulary which you will need to communicate effectively in

German. The aim of this dialogue is different – you should not try to understand everything, but to grasp the *gist* of the conversation. By practising this skill, you will be better prepared for your first experience in a German-speaking environment, and be able to extract the main information from a conversation without worrying about the detailed language and expressions used.

Read the questions below before you start listening and then listen to the conversation as many times as you like. You may find this difficult at first, but you can always come back to a dialogue later in your study. Soon you will find you become better at listening for specific information and understanding the gist of the conversations.

1 What is the name of the hostess?
    (a) Frau Beyer   (b) Frau Bauer   (c) Frau Becker
2 What are the names of the guests?
3 What does the hostess ask her guests to do?

2 Wie komme ich ... ?

Getting about

Dialogues

Dialogue 1

Frau Meyer is a widowed lady of 75. She has gone on a special cheap day-return train journey to Regensburg. She wants to revisit the house where she was born. She is looking for the post office in the Amalienstraße, where her parents used to have a flat on the third floor. However, everything has changed since she was a girl.

1 Frau Meyer: Entschuldigen Sie!
              Wie komme ich zur Amalienstraße, bitte?
    Fußgänger: Wie bitte?
    Frau Meyer: Die Amalienstraße.
5   Wie komme ich zur Amalienstraße?
    Fußgänger: Ja ... die Amalienstraße ...
    Frau Meyer: (interrupting) Furchtbar!
              Ganz furchtbar!
    Fußgänger: Wie bitte?
10 Frau Meyer: Hier ist alles neu.
    Fußgänger: Ja, das stimmt.
              Zur Adriastraße, nicht wahr?
    Frau Meyer: Nein, nicht zur Adriastraße, zur Amalienstraße.
              Wie komme ich zur Amalienstraße?
15 Fußgänger: Ach, ja.
              Gehen Sie hier geradeaus, nehmen Sie dann die erste Straße links.
    Frau Meyer: Die erste Straße links.
    Fußgänger: Das ist die Marktstraße.
              Gehen Sie die Marktstraße hoch, dann kommen Sie zur Amalienstraße.

Nehmen Sie die erste Straße links

Dialogue 2

Fritz Löb teaches English at a Munich school. He is an expert on Romanesque churches. He is separated from his wife, but has no children. He is friendly with Elke but can't really afford her tastes. Elke is driving Fritz to see a very beautiful baroque church in a small Alpine town called Mittenwald.

(Elke hoots her horn)
1 Elke: Entschuldigen Sie!
    Wie kommen wir nach Mittenwald?
  Junge: Wie bitte?
  Elke: Nach Mittenwald.
5 Junge: Ich weiß es nicht.
  Elke: Danke.
  (Under breath)
    Blöder Kerl!
  (Fritz sees a girl they can ask.)
  Fritz: Entschuldigen Sie!
    Wie kommen wir nach Mittenwald?

10 Mädchen: Nach Mittenwald?
    Fahren Sie hier geradeaus.
  Fritz: Geradeaus.
  Mädchen: Nach Garmisch.
    Dort biegen Sie nach links ab.
15 Fritz: Ist das weit?
  Mädchen: Nein.
    Zwanzig Kilometer ungefähr.
  Fritz: Danke.
  Mädchen: Fahren Sie Richtung Innsbruck.
20 Fritz: Richtung Innsbruck.
    Danke.
  Mädchen: Bitte.

Information

(a) Notes on Dialogue 1

2 Wie komme ich (zur) ...?

'How do I get (*literally* come) to ...?' The word 'do', used to make English questions, has no equivalent in German. Questions are formed by making the subject and the verb change places.

3 Wie bitte?

You can say 'wie bitte?' or just 'bitte?' if you do not understand what somebody says and you want them to repeat it.

6 Ja ... die Amalienstraße

It is typically German, when people ask you a direct question, to begin the answer with the word 'ja'. It is really just a way of getting time to think, but if you learn to use it, you will sound immensely authentic.

11 das stimmt

This is a very useful phrase for agreeing with what somebody else has just said.

12 nicht wahr?

In this sentence this expression means 'wasn't it?' The same expression, however, will do for 'don't they?', 'can't I?', 'mustn't we?', etc. It is consequently a very useful phrase which doesn't change and can be used to turn any sentence into a question.

(b) Notes on Dialogue 2

7 Blöder Kerl!   We know it's nice to know how to be rude to people, but beware! In Germany you may have to pay a fine for saying something like this. The expression translates literally as 'stupid chap'.

(c) Word list

Here is a list of the most important words in the dialogues. You should learn them by heart. They are given here in the order in which they occur in the dialogues.

wie?	how?
der **Fuß**gänger (-)	pedestrian
kommen	to come
furchtbar	terrible
ganz	quite
hier	here
alles	everything
neu	new
nein	no
nicht	not
gehen	to go
ge**rad**eaus	straight on
nehmen	to take
dann	then
die **Straße** (-n)	street
links	left
der **Junge** (-n)	boy
das **Mäd**chen (-)	girl
fahren	to go (by car, bus, etc.)
ab__**bieg**en	to turn (information on verbs with two parts in Chapter 4)
weit	far
zwanzig	twenty
unge**fähr**	approximately
die **Rich**tung (-en)	direction

(d) Some phrases

Nicht wahr?	Isn't it? etc.
Gehen Sie die **Markt**straße hoch	Go up Market Street
Ich weiß es nicht	I don't know

(e) Further useful vocabulary

These words occur in the rest of the chapter. You will find it useful to learn them as well.

das **Krank**enhaus (-er)	hospital
das **Kur**hotel (-s)	spa hotel
der **Bahn**hof (-e)	station
der **Sport**platz (-e)	sports ground
die **Spar**kasse (-n)	savings bank
rechts	right
nächst-	next
erst-	first
zweit-	second
dritt-	third
das **Hall**enbad (-er)	indoor swimming pool
das **Frei**bad (-er)	open-air swimming pool
die **Grund**schule (-n)	primary school
die **Kir**che (-n)	church
der **Camp**ingplatz (-e)	camping ground
der **Kind**ergarten (-)	nursery school
die **Reit**halle (-n)	riding hall
das Restau**rant** (-s)	restaurant
der **Markt**platz (-e)	market place
die Post	post office
das **Rat**haus (-er)	town hall
der **Park**platz (-e)	car park
die **Werk**statt (-en)	service station

Structural explanations

(a) Structures to learn

(i) How to find your way in town

Wie komme ich   How do I get

zum	Krankenhaus (*n*) Kurhotel (*n*) Bahnhof (*m*) Sportplatz (*m*) ?	to the	hospital Spa Hotel station sports ground ?	
zur	Sparkasse (*f*) Amalienstraße (*f*)	to the	savings bank Amalienstraße	

You use 'zum' with all masculine and neuter words, and 'zur' with all feminine words.

(ii) How to understand some of the directions which people may give

1 Gehen Sie (hier):   Go:
    geradeaus   straight on
    links   to the left
    rechts   to the right

die Marktstraße { hoch / entlang } { up / along } Market Street

2 Nehmen Sie die: Take the:

nächste ⎫
erste   ⎬ Straße { rechts / links }   next ⎫
zweite ⎪   first ⎬ street { on the right / on the left }
dritte ⎭   second
                              third

(iii) How to find your way when driving

When you are driving the places you want to get to are usually some distance away, and you must use the word 'nach' for 'to'.

Wie { komme ich / kommen wir }   How do I/we get

nach { Perlach / Rothenburg? / Dasburg }   to { Perlach / Rothenburg? / Dasburg }

(iv) How to understand some of the directions you may hear

Fahren Sie (hier) { links / geradeaus / rechts }   Go { left / straight on / right }

Biegen Sie nach { rechts / links } ab   Turn { right / left }

(b) Grammar

(i) Cardinal numbers

The numbers 1–30 are as follows:

1	eins	11	elf	21	einundzwanzig
2	zwei	12	zwölf	22	zweiundzwanzig
3	drei	13	dreizehn	23	dreiundzwanzig
4	vier	14	vierzehn	24	vierundzwanzig
5	fünf	15	fünfzehn	25	fünfundzwanzig
6	sechs	16	sechzehn	26	sechsundzwanzig
7	sieben	17	siebzehn	27	siebenundzwanzig
8	acht	18	achtzehn	28	achtundzwanzig
9	neun	19	neunzehn	29	neunundzwanzig
10	zehn	20	zwanzig	30	dreißig

N.B. There is no 's' in 16. There is no 'en' in 17.
You will find further numbers in the Grammatical Summary.

(ii) Ordinal numbers

Numbers indicating the order of things.

1st (first)	der, die, das erste
2nd (second)	der, die, das zweite
3rd (third)	der, die, das dritte
4th (fourth)	der, die, das vierte
5th (fifth)	der, die, das fünfte

You will find further such numbers in the Grammatical Summary.

(iii) 'Fahren' and 'gehen'

The words 'fahren' and 'gehen' both mean 'to go'. You use 'fahren' when you are mobile with a car, bike, motorbike, or train and you use 'gehen' when you are on foot.

(iv) 'Zu' and 'nach'

You use 'zu' for the names of streets, or places or buildings in town which are a comparatively short distance away. You use 'nach' for greater distances, for the names of suburbs of towns, e.g. Perlach, or when asking how to get to other towns, e.g. Mittenwald.

(v) Verbs

The most frequently used forms of verbs are:

I	e.g.	I go, I have
he	e.g.	he goes, he has
she	e.g.	she goes, she has
we	e.g.	we go, we have
you	e.g.	you go, you have

Remember that German verb forms have endings which agree with the personal pronouns they accompany.

Regular verbs follow a regular pattern of agreement which, once learned, can be applied to other regular verbs of the same type.

Here are two examples of *regular* verbs:

- *The verb 'gehen'* *(to go)*

Personal pronoun		Stem	Ending
ich	(I)		e
er	(he)		t
sie	(she)	GEH-	t
wir	(we)		en
Sie	(you)		en

ich	gehe	I go
er	geht	he goes
sie	geht	she goes
wir	gehen	we go
Sie	gehen	you go (*formal or polite*)

● *The verb 'kommen' (to come)*

Personal pronoun		Stem	Ending
ich	(I)		e
er	(he)		t
sie	(she)	KOMM-	t
wir	(we)		en
Sie	(you)		en
ich	komme	I come	
er	kommt	he comes	
sie	kommt	she comes	
wir	kommen	we come	
Sie	kommen	you come (*formal or polite*)	

The verbs 'gehen' and 'kommen' are *regular* in the sense that:

1 the stem is unchanged for each part of the verb,
2 the endings are identical for each verb.

Remember that the *polite* or *formal* 'you' has a personal pronoun 'Sie' with a capital 'S'.

● *The verb 'fahren' (to go, or to travel – by car or public transport)*

This verb is *irregular*, because the spelling and pronunciation of its stem change from one person to another.

		ich	fahre	I go
Vowel	→	er	fährt	he goes
changes here	→	sie	fährt	she goes
		wir	fahren	we go
		Sie	fahren	you go (*formal or polite*)

You will find tables of the most common German verbs in the Grammatical Summary.

(vi) Accents

The only accent in German is called the Umlaut. It is written with two small dots. They occur from time to time above the letters 'a', 'o' and 'u'. Where the letters 'a' and 'u' come together, any Umlaut goes on the 'a': 'Häuser'. The Umlaut has the effect of changing the sound of the vowel beneath it. Whenever you see a word with an Umlaut in one of the dialogues, you should pay particular attention to the pronunciation.

Exercises

Exercise 1

Imagine that you are in the small town of Brakel and really want to find out what it has to offer. How would you ask the way to the following places ?

1	The hospital	Krankenhaus (*n*)
2	Savings bank	Sparkasse (*f*)
3	Station	Bahnhof (*m*)
4	The sports ground	Sportplatz (*m*)
5	The indoor swimming-pool	Hallenbad (*n*)
6	The open-air swimming-pool	Freibad (*n*)
7	The primary school	Grundschule (*f*)
8	The old people's home	Altenheim (*n*)
9	The Capuchin church	Kapuzinerkirche (*f*)
10	The campsite	Campingplatz (*m*)
11	The nursery school	Kindergarten (*m*)
12	The riding hall	Reithalle (*f*)
13	The mini golf course	Minigolfplatz (*m*)
14	The Forest Restaurant	Waldrestaurant (*n*)
15	The market place	Marktplatz (*m*)
16	The post office	Post (*f*)
17	The town hall	Rathaus (*n*)
18	The car park	Parkplatz (*m*)

m – masculine
f – feminine
n – neuter

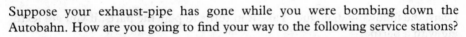

Exercise 2

Suppose your exhaust-pipe has gone while you were bombing down the Autobahn. How are you going to find your way to the following service stations?

1	The Audi service station	Audi-Werkstatt (*f*)
2	The Volkswagen service station	Volkswagen-Werkstatt (*f*)
3	The Opel service station	Opel-Werkstatt (*f*)
4	The Ford service station	Ford-Werkstatt (*f*)
5	The Rolls-Royce service station	Rolls-Royce-Werkstatt (*f*)

 Exercise 3

You are on holiday travelling by car in Germany (possibly in your Rolls-Royce). You are by yourself and you want to find your way. Listen to the names of the places on your recording and then ask for directions. You will hear the correct answer following the pause.

 Exercise 4

Learn the following dialogue. Take it in turns to play the parts, if you are learning with a partner.

SALZBURG   6 km

A: Wie weit ist es nach   How far is it to Salzburg,
   Salzburg, bitte?   please?
B: Sechs Kilometer ungefähr.   About 6 km.

1	DESSAU 21 km		6	KUFSTEIN 9 km
2	HALLE 52 km		7	ZÜRICH 56 km
3	JENA 101 km		8	TÜBINGEN 71 km
4	LINZ 23 km		9	ANSBACH 56 km
5	KITZBÜHEL 39 km		10	FULDA 45 km

Exercise 5 Im Auto: Finding your way by car

Don't forget to read the questions below before listening to this dialogue, and remember: you do not have to understand every word, just listen for the information you need.

1 Where does the man want to go?
   Is it (a) Zirnstadt (b) Zirndorf (c) Miendorf?
2 Is it far?

③ Ein Doppelzimmer

Staying in hotels

Dialogues

Dialogue 1

Antonio Raggi came from Naples when he was five years old, went to school in Germany, and consequently speaks perfect German. He studies at a fashion school in Munich and is currently doing some practical work in the business where Elke works. Antonio's uncle and aunt have written from Naples to say that they want to come and see him in Munich. They have asked him to book a room for them.

1	Antonio:	Guten Abend!
	Empfang:	Guten Abend!
	Antonio:	Ich möchte ein Zimmer reservieren.
	Empfang:	Ja, für wie lange?
5	Antonio:	Für fünf Nächte.
		Von Montag bis Samstag.
	Empfang:	Ja. Ein Einzelzimmer oder ein Doppelzimmer?
	Antonio:	Ein Doppelzimmer.
	Empfang:	Mit Bad oder Dusche?
10	Antonio:	Mit Dusche.
		Ein ruhiges Zimmer bitte.
	Empfang:	Ja, ja. Das Zimmer ist schön ruhig.
	Antonio:	Gut.
	Empfang:	Auf welchen Namen bitte?
15	Antonio:	Raggi. R-A-G-G-I.
	Empfang:	Vielen Dank.
	Antonio:	Was kostet das Zimmer?
	Empfang:	Es kostet 120 Mark.
	Antonio:	Ist das mit Frühstück?
20	Empfang:	Ja, das ist mit Frühstück und Mehrwertsteuer.
	Antonio:	Danke.
	Empfang:	Bitte.

Ihr Zimmer ist im fünften Stock

Dialogue 2

Elke has decided to go north to Hamburg for the weekend, and try to see an old boyfriend of hers. She hopes that, if she sees him again, it may help her to get her emotions sorted out with respect to Fritz.

1   Elke: Guten Tag!
  Empfang: Guten Tag!
  Elke: Haben Sie ein Zimmer frei bitte?
  Empfang: Jawohl.
5   Was für ein Zimmer?
  Elke: Ein Einzelzimmer.
    Mit Bad.
  Empfang: Für wie viele Nächte, bitte schön?
  Elke: Ich bleibe zwei Nächte.
10   Empfang: Ein Einzelzimmer mit Bad.
    Ja, das ist möglich.
  Elke: Was kostet das Zimmer?
  Empfang: Das kostet pro Nacht 95 Mark mit Frühstück.
  Elke: Ich nehme es.

15 Empfang: Bitte, tragen Sie sich ein.

...

Ihr Zimmer ist im fünften Stock.
Elke: Hat das Zimmer einen Ausblick?
Empfang: Jawohl, es hat einen schönen Ausblick.
Über die Alster.
20 Elke: Wie schön.
Empfang: Haben Sie Gepäck?
Elke: Ja, mein Gepäck ist hier.
Empfang: Portier!

Dialogue 3

Fritz has been wanting to see the Petrikirche in Bad Reichenhall for ages. Elke
won't be in Munich next weekend, so that will give him just the opportunity he
needs. Anyway, Elke is not so interested in churches.

(On the telephone)
1 Empfang: Hotel Bayerischer Hof.
Fritz: Guten Tag!
Haben Sie ein Zimmer für nächsten Samstag, bitte?
Empfang: Für den zwölften?
5 Fritz: Ja, für Samstag den zwölften.
Empfang: Nein, es tut mir leid, wir sind völlig ausgebucht.
Fritz: Danke schön.
Empfang: Bitte sehr.

Information

(a) Notes on Dialogue 1

6 Samstag

There are two words for 'Saturday' in
German. 'Samstag' is used predomi-
nantly in the south of Germany, that
is to say south of the river Main,
and in Austria. The other word is
'Sonnabend', which is used more frequently in the north.

14 Auf welchen Namen?

German uses this expression to
enquire the name of the guest.

20 Mehrwertsteuer

You have to pay VAT in Germany,
just as you do in the UK. Usually,
however, the VAT is already included
in the price.

(b) Notes on Dialogue 2

3	Haben Sie ein Zimmer frei?	Remember that questions are formed in German simply by putting the verb before the subject: 'Sie haben ein Zimmer' – 'Haben Sie ein Zimmer?'
4	Jawohl	Although familiar to many English speakers from old war films, this word now sounds rather formal, and is used much less frequently than the simpler 'Ja'.
7	Mit Bad	Although only a bath is mentioned, this nearly always means that you have a private bathroom.
15	Bitte, tragen Sie sich ein	'Please sign the register' is naturally not a word-for-word translation of the German, but it does give the meaning.
19	die Alster	The Alster is a lake in the centre of Hamburg, which is one of the main attractions of the city. Several steamer routes criss-cross the lake. In the winter the Alster often freezes over, and becomes a vast skating rink.

(c) Word list

Here is a list of the most important words in the dialogues. You should learn them by heart. They are given here in the order in which they occur in the dialogues.

gut	good
der Abend (-e)	evening
das Zimmer (-)	room
reservieren	to reserve
die Nacht (-̈e)	night
von	from
Montag	Monday
bis	to
Samstag	Saturday
das Einzelzimmer (-)	single room
oder	or
das Doppelzimmer (-)	double room
mit	with
das Bad (-̈er)	bathroom
die Dusche (-n)	shower
ruhig	quiet

was?	what?
kosten	to cost
das **Früh**stück	breakfast
die **Mehr**wertsteuer	VAT
frei	free; available
wie **viel**e?	how many?
bleiben	to stay
möglich	possible
nehmen	to take
der **Stock** (¨e)	floor (of a building)
der **Aus**blick (-e)	view
schön	beautiful
über	over
das **Gepäck**	luggage
für	for
völlig	completely
ausgebucht	booked up

(d) Some phrases

Ich **möch**te	I'd like
Für wie **lang**e?	For how long?
Schön **ruh**ig	Nice and quiet
Auf **wel**chen **Nam**en, **bitt**e?	What name, please?
Vielen Dank	Thank you very much
Was **kost**et ...?	What does ... cost?
Was für ein ...?	What sort of a ...?
Im **fünf**ten Stock	On the fifth floor
Es tut mir leid	I'm sorry
Das geht in **Ord**nung	That's all right

(e) Further useful vocabulary

These are words and phrases that occur later in the chapter. You will find it useful to learn them too.

leider	unfortunately
das **Zwei**bettzimmer (-)	twin bedroom
ohne	without
die **Wo**che (-n)	week
wann?	when?
heute	today
lange	a long time
morgen	tomorrow
ein **biß**chen	a bit

Structural explanations

(a) Structures to learn

(i) How to establish whether there is a room available

What you need to say

Ich möchte ein Zimmer
  reservieren
  I should like to reserve a room

Haben Sie ein Zimmer frei?
  Have you got a room available?
Haben Sie ein Zimmer für heute
  abend?
  Have you got a room for tonight?

What you need to understand

1 Ja, das ist möglich
   Ja, das geht
   Ja, ein Zimmer habe ich noch
     There is a room available

2 Nein, leider, alles ist ausgebucht
   Nein, wir sind völlig ausgebucht
   Nein, es tut mir leid
     There is no room available

(ii) How to describe the sort of room you want

What you need to say

(Ich möchte)
  ein Einzelzimmer   a single room
  ein Doppelzimmer   a double room
  ein Zweibettzimmer   a twin bedroom
  mit/ohne Dusche   with/without shower
  mit/ohne Bad   with/without bath

(iii) How to say how long you want it for

What you need to understand

Für wie lange,   For how long?
  bitte?
Für wie viele   For how many
  Nächte?   nights?
Von wann bis   From when
  wann?   to when?

What you need to say

Für eine Nacht   For one night
Für zwei Nächte   For two nights
Für eine Woche   For a week
Von heute   From today
  bis Montag   until Monday
Von Montag   From Monday
  bis Samstag   until Saturday

1 Ja, das ist   Yes, that is
   möglich   possible.
  Ja, das geht   Yes, that is OK.
   in Ordnung
2 Nein, es tut   No, I'm sorry.
   mir leid
  Nein, das ist   No, that is
   nicht möglich not possible.

(iv) How to confirm the booking

Gut, ich nehme das Zimmer   Bitte, tragen Sie sich ein
Good, I'll take the room   Please sign the register

(b) Grammar

(i) Days of the week

You will find a complete list in the Grammatical Summary.

(ii) Months of the year

These are in the Grammatical Summary, too.

(iii) Dates

When you want to say '*On* a certain date', the ordinal number for the date ends in '-en'. The English word 'of' is not translated.

Am ersten Januar   On the first of January
Am zweiten Februar   On the second of February
Am dritten März   On the third of March
Am vierten April   On the fourth of April

See Chapter 2 for information on ordinal numbers.

When you want to say '*For the* (a certain date)', the ordinal number for the date ends in '-en'.

Haben Sie ein Zimmer
{
für den ersten Januar
für den zweiten Februar
für den dritten März   ?
für den vierten April
für den fünften Mai
}

Have you got a room
{
for the 1st of January
for the 2nd of February
for the 3rd of March   ?
for the 4th of April
for the 5th of May
}

(iv) Dates continued

Der wievielte ist heute?   What is the date today?

When you want to say '*It is* (a certain date)', the ordinal number for the date ends in '-e'.

Es ist	der erste Januar	It is	the 1st of January
	der zweite Februar		the 2nd of February
	der dritte März		the 3rd of March
	der vierte April		the 4th of April
	der fünfte Mai		the 5th of May

(v) More verbs

● *The verb* 'bleiben' *(to stay or remain)*

This is a *regular* verb. Its stem is unchanged throughout and its endings are also regular.

ich		e	ich	bleibe	I stay
er		t	er	bleibt	he stays
sie	BLEIB-	t	sie	bleibt	she stays
wir		en	wir	bleiben	we stay
Sie		en	Sie	bleiben	you stay (*formal or polite*)

● *The verb* 'haben' *(to have)*

This is unfortunately *irregular*, but it is one of the most important and frequent verbs in the whole language, so you had better learn it.

ich	habe	I have
er	hat	he has
sie	hat	she has
wir	haben	we have
Sie	haben	you have (*formal or polite*)

● *The verb* 'nehmen' *(to take)*

This is *irregular*, too. Notice how the spelling of the stem changes.

ich	NEHM-	e	ich	nehme	I take
er	NIMM-	t	er	nimmt	he takes
sie			sie	nimmt	she takes
wir	NEHM-	en	wir	nehmen	we take
Sie			Sie	nehmen	you take (*formal or polite*)

You will find a table of the most common verbs in the Grammatical Summary.

(vi) How to express duration

Questions about duration	*Statements about duration*
Wie lange?: How long?	Sehr lange!: For a very long time
Für wie lange?: For how long?	Nicht lange: Not for long
Wie lange bleiben Sie?: How long will you be staying?	Von Dienstag bis Freitag: From Tuesday until Friday
	Bis morgen: Until tomorrow
	Bis Dienstag: Until Tuesday
	Nur bis Mittwoch: Only until Wednesday
	Ein bißchen: For a little while
	Noch ein bißchen: For a little while longer

Exercises

A

Exercise 1

Ask for the types of hotel room shown for the length of time indicated opposite. The first one is done for you. If you are studying with a partner, take it in turns to play each role.

Guest: Haben Sie ein Zimmer frei?
Hotel: Jawohl. Was für ein Zimmer?
Guest: Ein Einzelzimmer.
Hotel: Für wie lange?
Guest: Für eine Nacht.

Exercise 2

Take the role of Herr Schmidt. If you are studying with a partner, take it in turns to play the roles. You will find the complete dialogue in the Answers to the Exercises.

Schmidt	Empfang
1 Greet the receptionist.	
	2 Guten Tag, der Herr.
3 Ask if there is a room available.	
	4 Ja, ein Zimmer habe ich.
5 Ask whether there is a single room available.	
	6 Für wie lange, bitte?

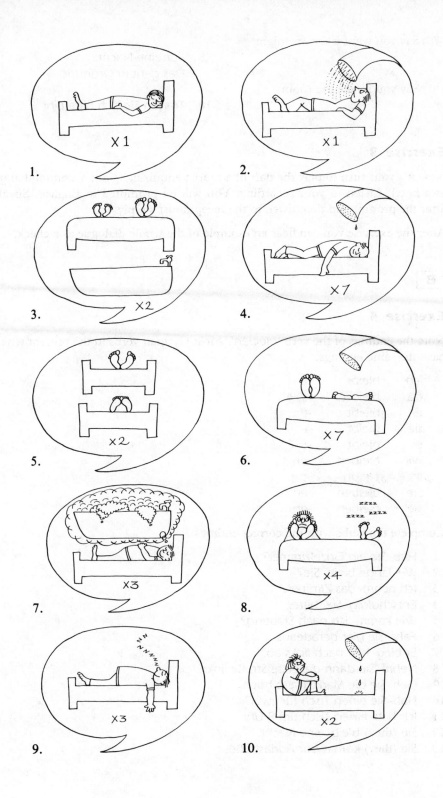

1.

2.

3.

4.

5.

6.

7.

8.

9.

10.

7   Say you want it for one night.

        8   Für eine Nacht.
           Das geht in Ordnung.

9   Say you'll take the room.

      10   Tragen Sie sich bitte ein!

 ## Exercise 3

Now it's your turn to play the part of a tourist enquiring about accommodation at a hotel. Listen to your recording. You will be prompted in English. Speak after the prompt and then listen to the receptionist's reply.

After the exercise you can hear an example of the whole dialogue as a check.

B

 ## Exercise 4

Note the endings of the verb 'bleiben'. Most German verbs in the present tense have the same endings.

ich	bleibe	-e
du	bleibst	-st
er	bleibt	-t
sie	bleibt	-t
es	bleibt	-t
wir	bleiben	-en
ihr	bleibt	-t
Sie	bleiben	-en
sie	bleiben	-en

Complete the verbs with the correct endings:

1   Hab- Sie ein Einzelzimmer?
2   Wie lange bleib- Sie?
3   Ich nehm- das Zimmer.
4   Entschuldig- Sie, bitte.
5   Wie komm- ich nach Stauting?
6   Fahr- Sie hier geradeaus.
7   Er bieg- hier nach links ab.
8   Nehm- Sie dann die erste Straße links.
9   Geh- Sie die Marktstraße hoch.
10   Hab- Sie einen Tisch für zwei?
11   Ich hab- einen Tisch um 8 Uhr.
12   Sie (they) bleib- eine Nacht.
13   Sie (they) komm- zur Adriastraße.

Exercise 5

This is how to express the year:

> 1933 – neunzehnhundertdreiunddreißig
> 1956 – neunzehnhundertsechsundfünfzig
> 1981 – neunzehnhunderteinundachtzig
> 1995 – neunzehnhundertfünfundneunzig

Now state the following dates (see ordinal numbers in Chapter 2):

1   2.5.1978.
2   16.6.1982.
3   31.12.1999.
4   11.8.1982.
5   27.3.1983.
6   17.5.1985.

Exercise 6   An der Hotelrezeption: Reserving a room in a hotel

Don't forget to read the questions below first, before listening to this dialogue, and remember: you do not have to understand every word, just listen for the information you need.

1   What sort of room does the tourist want?
2   For how long?
3   What does the receptionist ask the tourist to do?

4 Hin und zurück

Travelling by train

 Dialogues

Dialogue 1

Frau Meyer is going to see her great friend Mitzi, who lives in Augsburg, about 50 km from Munich.

1 Frau Meyer: Grüß Gott!
  Angestellte: Grüß Gott!
  Frau Meyer: Einmal zweiter Klasse nach Augsburg, bitte.
  Angestellte: Einfach oder hin und zurück?
5 Frau Meyer: Hin und zurück, bitte.
    Was kostet das?
  Angestellte: Zweiundfünfzig Mark, bitte sehr.
  Frau Meyer: Was? So viel?
  Angestellte: Tut mir leid.
10 Frau Meyer: Das ist ja unerhört!
  Angestellte: Ich kann nichts dafür.
  Frau Meyer: Sechzig Mark.
  Angestellte: (counts) 53, 54, 55, 60, bitte.
  Frau Meyer: Danke.
15 (still grumbling) Zweiundfünfzig Mark.
    Das ist ja unerhört.

  Frau Meyer: Entschuldigen Sie, bitte!
  Information: Ja, bitte?
  Frau Meyer: Wann fährt der Zug nach Augsburg?
20 Information: Augsburg ... Augsburg ....
    Der Zug fährt um 9 Uhr 27.
    Und kommt um 10 Uhr 13 an.
  Frau Meyer: Danke.
    Muß ich umsteigen?

Einmal zweiter Klasse, bitte

25 Information: Nein. Der Zug fährt direkt.
     Frau Meyer: Danke.
     Information: Bitte.

Dialogue 2

Antonio wants to go with his uncle and aunt as far as Innsbruck. They will go on to Rome, and he will return alone to Munich.

1 Antonio: Guten Tag!
     Angestellte: Guten Tag!
     Antonio: Zweimal zweiter Klasse nach Innsbruck, bitte.
     Angestellte: Einfach oder hin und zurück?
5 Antonio: Einfach, bitte.
     Angestellte: Zweimal einfach nach Innsbruck.
        Achtundneunzig Mark, bitte schön.
     Antonio: Moment.
        Dann auch einmal nach Innsbruck.
10 Angestellte: Einfach?
     Antonio: Nein.
        Hin und zurück.
     Angestellte: Zweimal einfach.
        Einmal hin und zurück.

15 Stimmt's?
    Antonio: Ja, das stimmt.
    Angestellte: Das macht 196 Mark, bitte schön.

    Antonio: Um wieviel Uhr fährt der Zug nach Innsbruck?
    Information: Um 9 Uhr 31.
20 Antonio: Danke.
    Auf welchem Gleis?
    Information: Auf Gleis 3.
    Antonio: Danke.
    Information: Bitte.

Information

(a) Notes on Dialogue 1

3	Einmal	In German you draw attention linguistically to the fact that there is only one person travelling. Compare with line 3 of Dialogue 2.
4	Einfach	Literally this means 'simple', but in this context it means 'single'.
5	Hin und zurück	This means literally 'there and back'.
7	Zweiundfünfzig Mark	'Fifty-two marks.' For the cardinal numbers from 30 onwards see p. 262 in the Grammatical Summary.
9	Tut mir leid	This is short for 'Es tut mir leid' (I am sorry) and so slightly less formal.
19	Wann fährt der Zug ...?	Notice the question word order again.
22	Und kommt ... an	The English verb 'to arrive' is rendered in this sentence in German by a verb which has two parts to it.

(b) Notes on Dialogue 2

3	Zweimal	This indicates that there are two people travelling.
15	Stimmt's?	Short for 'stimmt es?' (is that right?) This more colloquial form is usually used.

(c) Word list

Here is a list of the most important words in the dialogues. You should learn them by heart. They are given here in the order in which they occur in the dialogues. N.B. Verbs with two parts are shown thus from here on: **an__kommen**.

die **Angestellte** (-n)	female employee
einmal	one (i.e. person travelling)
einfach	single
oder	or
hin und zu**rück**	return
was?	what?
uner**hört**	terrible
fahren (fährt)	to go (of transport)
der Zug (-e)	train
an__kommen	to arrive
um__steigen	to change (trains)
di**rekt**	straight through
zweimal	two (i.e. people travelling)
dann	then
auch	also/too
welch-	which
das Gleis (-e)	platform

(d) Some phrases

So viel?	As much as that?
Ich kann nichts da**für**	There's nothing I can do about it
Um 9 Uhr	At nine o'clock
Muß ich ...?	Must I ...?
Das stimmt	That's right
Um **wie**viel Uhr?	At what time?

(e) Further useful vocabulary

These are words which occur later in the chapter. You will find it useful to learn them too.

wo?	where?
ab__fahren (fährt ab)	to leave
ab__waschen (wäscht ab)	to wash up
ab__trocknen	to dry up
auf__räumen	to tidy up
an__rufen	to ring up (i.e. telephone)
ein__kaufen	to do the shopping
ab__schließen	to lock up
auf__geben (gibt auf)	to give up
aus__gehen	to go out
auf__stehen	to get up
zu__machen	to close

ein_treffen (trifft ein)	to arrive (of trains etc.)
der **Teller** (-)	plate
die **Spiel**sachen (plural only)	toys
die **Lebensmitt**el (plural only)	groceries
der **Laden** (-)	shop
die **Arb**eit	work
der Bus(-se)	bus
das Kind (-er)	child
das Haus (-er)	house
der Chef (-s)	boss
die **Mutt**er (-)	mother

Special note

Eine Angestellte	A female employee
Ein Angestellter	A male employee
Eine Reisende	A female traveller
Ein Reisender	A male traveller

Structural explanations

(a) Structures to learn

(i) How to state how many tickets you want

(in other words how many people are travelling)

Einmal:	one person is travelling
Zweimal:	two people are travelling
Dreimal:	three people are travelling

(ii) How to state the class you are travelling

Erster Klasse	– 1st class
Zweiter Klasse	– 2nd class

(iii) How to state your destination

Nach Augsburg
Nach Innsbruck

(iv) Single or return?

Einfach	Single
Hin und zurück	Return

Note the similar construction of the following sentences:

1   Einmal erster Klasse nach München, hin und zurück.
2   Zweimal zweiter Klasse nach Bremen, einfach.
3   Dreimal erster Klasse nach Regensburg, hin und zurück.
4   Einmal zweiter Klasse nach Reutlingen, einfach.
5   Zweimal erster Klasse nach Fürth, hin und zurück.
6   Zweimal erster Klasse nach Feuchtwangen, einfach.

If you miss out any of these elements when you ask for your ticket, you will be asked about it.

| Einmal zweiter Klasse | This phrase is really an abbreviation of: 'a ticket of the second class'. The idea of a ticket belonging to such a category is conveyed by using the genitive case. See Grammatical Summary pages 283–5. |

(v) How to ask what time a train leaves

Wann fährt der Zug nach { Hamm / Münster / Höxter / Bielefeld / München }   ?

(vi) How to ask what time the train arrives

Wann kommt der Zug in { Hamm / Münster / Höxter / Bielefeld / München } an ?

(vii) The 24-hour clock

In German-speaking countries the 24-hour clock is used for all formal expressions of time and in particular for travelling in order to express times of arrival and departure, etc. As long as you know the cardinal numbers up to 60, it is very easy (see Chapter 2).

13:00	dreizehn Uhr
12:00	zwölf Uhr
09:05	neun Uhr fünf
18:15	achtzehn Uhr fünfzehn
16:25	sechzehn Uhr fünfundzwanzig
21:30	einundzwanzig Uhr dreißig
11:10	elf Uhr zehn
06:20	sechs Uhr zwanzig

| 21:30 | einundzwanzig Uhr dreißig |
| 14:45 | vierzehn Uhr fünfundvierzig |

(viii) How to ask if and where you have to change trains

(Wo) muß ich umsteigen?
  (Where) do I have to change?

(b) Grammar

● *Observe how these sentences are formed:*

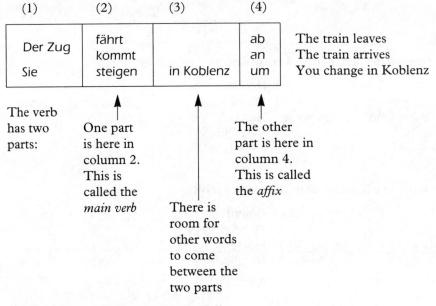

	(1)	(2)	(3)	(4)	
	Der Zug	fährt		ab	The train leaves
		kommt		an	The train arrives
	Sie	steigen	in Koblenz	um	You change in Koblenz

The verb has two parts:

One part is here in column 2. This is called the *main verb*

There is room for other words to come between the two parts

The other part is here in column 4. This is called the *affix*

Observe how these sentences are similar:

What do all good husbands do?
  Sie waschen ab.   They do the washing up.
What do wives do afterwards?
  Sie trocknen ab.   They do the drying up.
What do (some) children do before they go to bed?
  Sie räumen auf.   They tidy up.
What does grandma do on Sunday?
  Sie ruft an.   She rings up.
What does mother do on Friday afternoon?
  Sie kauft ein.   She goes shopping.
What does the boss do before going home?
  Er schließt ab.   He locks up.

What does Peter do if he is very discouraged?
Er gibt auf.   He gives up.
What does Mary do every Saturday night?
Sie geht aus.   She goes out.

personal pronoun + main verb + affix

And these:

What does the good husband wash up first?
Er wäscht die Teller ab.   He washes up the plates.
What do wives dry up first?
Sie trocknen die Teller ab.   They dry the plates.
What do children tidy up?
Sie räumen ihre Spielsachen auf. They tidy up their toys.
When does grandma ring up?
Sie ruft am Sonntag an.   She rings on Sundays.
What does mother buy on Fridays?
Sie kauft Lebensmittel ein.   She buys groceries.
What does the boss lock up?
Er schließt den Laden ab.   He locks up the shop.
What does Peter give up when he is discouraged?
Er gibt seine Arbeit auf.   He gives up his work.
When does Mary go out?
Sie geht am Samstag aus.   She goes out on Saturdays.

personal pronoun + main verb + another word/expression + affix

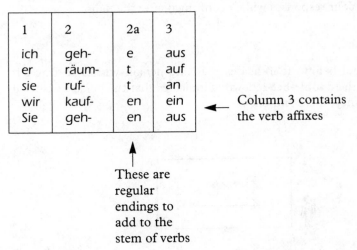

1	2	2a	3
ich	geh-	e	aus
er	räum-	t	auf
sie	ruf-	t	an
wir	kauf-	en	ein
Sie	geh-	en	aus

← Column 3 contains the verb affixes

↑ These are regular endings to add to the stem of verbs

The most common affixes are: 'an', 'auf', 'aus', 'bei', 'ein', 'her', 'hin', 'mit', 'nach', 'vor' and 'zu'. The affix is put last in the sentence.

Note the formation of the verbs used in the sentences below:

ich trockne ab	wasche ab	schließe ab	gebe auf
er trocknet ab	wäscht ab	schließt ab	gibt auf
sie trocknet ab	wäscht ab	schließt ab	gibt auf
wir trocknen ab	waschen ab	schließen ab	geben auf
Sie trocknen ab	waschen ab	schließen ab	geben auf

● *Looking up verbs with separable affixes in the dictionary*

If you want to look up one of these verbs in the dictionary, or a vocabulary list, you must look up the right form of the verb. For example, you will not find 'wäscht ... ab', or 'trocknet ... ab'; you must look up 'abwaschen' or 'abtrocknen'; these forms are called the *infinitive*. Here are some more examples:

steht auf	aufstehen	infinitive
macht ... zu	zumachen	(When the infinitive form
trifft ... ein	eintreffen	of the verb is used, the affix is stressed)

Exercises

A

 ### Exercise 1

You are travelling in Germany by train. Listen to the names of your destinations on your recording, and then ask the time of the next train to that destination in the pause. Your responses will be confirmed after the pause.

 ### Exercise 2

Look at the symbol below. It indicates that one person wishes to travel to Berlin, 2nd class; the double-headed arrow indicates that the person wishes to make a return journey, there and back.

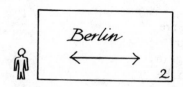

Reisender: Einmal zweiter Klasse nach Berlin, bitte.
Angestellte: Einfach oder hin und zurück?
Reisender: Hin und zurück, bitte.

Make up similar dialogues to match the following symbols. If you can work with a partner, take it in turns to play the parts of the 'Reisender' and the 'Angestellte'.

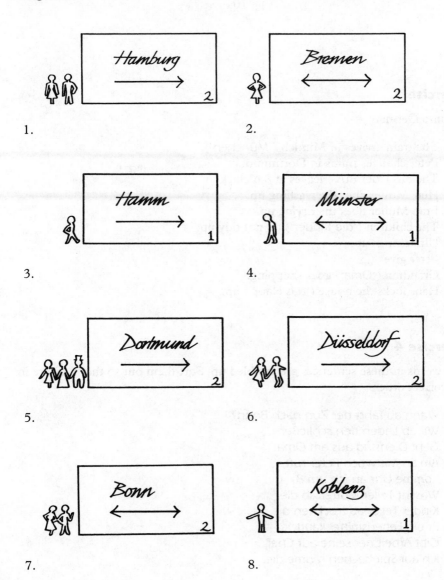

1.

2.

3.

4.

5.

6.

7.

8.

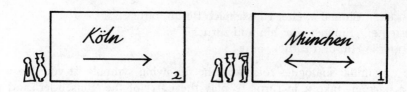

9.   10.

B

Exercise 3

Put into German:

1 The train arrives in Munich ('München').
2 Peter changes trains in Dortmund.
3 The bus ('der Bus') leaves at 8 o'clock.
4 Herr Müller does the washing up.
5 Frau Müller does the drying up.
6 The children ('die Kinder') do not tidy up.
7 Ulrike rings up.
8 Peter gives up.
9 Grandma ('Oma') goes shopping.
10 Hans locks the house ('das Haus') up.

Exercise 4

The words in these sentences are jumbled up. Sort them out so that they are in the correct order.

1 Wann ab fährt der Zug nach Bonn?
2 Wir ab Laden den schließen.
3 Geht Dienstag aus am Oma.
4 Am an Mittwoch Peter ruft.
5 Komme Uhr an ich um 8.
6 Wäscht Teller Mutter ab die.
7 Kinder Teller ab trocknen die die.
8 Er ein Lebensmittel kauft.
9 Gibt Arbeit der seine auf Chef.
10 Ich auf Spielsachen räume die.

Exercise 5   Im Hauptbahnhof: Buying a ticket at the station

Don't forget to read the questions below before listening to this dialogue, and remember: you do not have to understand every word, just listen for the information you need.

1   Where does the traveller want to go?
2   What sort of ticket does she want?
3   How much does the ticket cost?
4   When does the train leave?
5   When does it arrive?
6   Will she have to change trains?

⑤ Taxi, bitte!

Travelling by taxi, bus or tram

 Dialogues

Dialogue 1

Elke is late for her appointment with Fritz, and in order to avoid having another row with him about punctuality, she decides to take a taxi.

1 Elke: (dials taxi number) Ich möchte ein
   Taxi bitte.
 Angestellte: Ihr Name?
 Elke: Kustmann.
5 Angestellte: Adresse?
 Elke: Fürstenstraße 15.
 Angestellte: Wohin?
 Elke: Zur Nietzschestraße
 Angestellte: Das Taxi ist in 10 Minuten da.
10 Elke: Danke.

 Taxifahrer: (rings front door bell)
   Frau Kustmann?
 Elke: Ja.
 Taxifahrer: Ihr Taxi ist hier.
 Elke: (gets in) Zur Nietzschestraße, bitte.
15 Nummer 30.
 Taxifahrer: Ja, ist in Ordnung.

 Taxifahrer: (arriving in Nietzschestraße)
   So, bitte schön.
 Elke: Was macht das?
 Taxifahrer: Das macht 6 Mark 50.
 Elke: (giving him 7 marks 50)
20 Danke.
  Das stimmt so.

Ihr Taxi ist hier

Dialogue 2

Frau Meyer wants to go to the centre of Munich for her annual visit to the Christkindlmarkt during the week before Christmas. The Christkindlmarkt takes place on the Marienplatz in front of the town hall. There are many stalls selling fried sausages, hot punch, sweets, nuts, and Christmas delicacies of all sorts. There are also many stalls selling Christmas decorations and presents.

1   Frau Meyer: Entschuldigung!
      Fährt die Nummer 23 zum Rathaus?
   Mann: Nein, nicht die Nummer 23.
   Frau Meyer: Ach du lieber Himmel!
5   Welcher Bus fährt denn zum Rathaus?
   Mann: Sie brauchen die Nummer 18.
      Sie fährt zum Rathaus.
   Frau Meyer: Ach, vielen Dank.
      Die Nummer 18.
10 Mann: Ja, sie fährt zum Rathaus.
   Frau Meyer: (to herself)
      Das ist ja unerhört!!
      Das war immer die 23!!

Information

(a) Notes on Dialogue 1

6 Fürstenstraße 15	In German you say the name of the street first and the number afterwards.
9 Das Taxi ist in 10 Minuten da	Here German uses the present tense to indicate future time.
21 Das stimmt so	Literally: 'that is correct'. The customer indicates that he or she requires no change with the phrase 'Das stimmt so'. It is common to round taxi fares and meal bills up about 10%.

(b) Notes on Dialogue 2

2 Fährt die Nummer 23 ...?	Remember that there is no equivalent to the English 'does' in a German question. The verb simply comes before the subject.
12 war	This is the past tense of the verb 'sein' (to be) and translates as 'was'.

(c) Word list

Here is a list of the most important words in the dialogues. You should learn them by heart. They are given here in the order in which they occur in the dialogues.

das **Taxi** (-s)	taxi
der **Name** (-n)	name
die **Adres**se (-n)	address
wo**hin**?	where to?
die **Minut**e (-n)	minute
da	there
der **Taxifahr**er (-)	taxi driver
hier	here
Ent**schul**digung	excuse me
die **Numm**er (-n)	number
nicht	not
welch-?	which?
der Bus (-se)	bus
das **Rathaus** (-er)	town hall
brauchen	to need
immer	always

(d) A phrase

Ach du **lieber Him**mel!   Good Heavens!

(e) Further useful vocabulary

These are words which occur later in the chapter. You will find it useful to learn them too.

der **Haupt**bahnhof	main station
der **Flug**hafen (⸚)	airport
das **Zen**trum	centre
die Stadt (⸚e)	town
das Schloß (**Schlöss**er)	castle or palace
die Stadt**mitte**	town centre
die **O**per (-n)	opera or opera house
die **Quitt**ung (-en)	receipt
die **Straß**enbahn(-en)	tram
das **Frei**bad (⸚er)	open-air swimming pool
der **Profess**or (-en)	professor
die Sekret**ärin** (-nen)	secretary
der Freund (-e)	friend (male)
das Geld	money
das Bier	beer
der Zug (⸚e)	train
das The**ater** (-)	theatre
der Hund (-e)	dog
der **Gart**en (⸚)	garden
groß	big
der **Vat**er (⸚)	father
alt	old
jung	young

Structural explanations

(a) Structures to learn

(i) Ordering a taxi (how to state your address)

Hindenburgstraße 17   The name of the street is stated
Mozartstraße 25   first. The number comes after.
Nietzschestraße 30
Oskar von Müller Ring 129
Neue Straße 6
Kennedy Allee 43

(ii) How to state your destination

zum
{
Hauptbahnhof
Flughafen
Rathaus
Stadtzentrum
Schloß Nymphenburg
}
(all these words are masculine or neuter)

zur
{
Hindenburgstraße
Kennedy Allee
Stadtmitte
Oper
}
(all these words are femi-

'Zum' is used with masculine and neuter nouns, 'zur' with feminine nouns. These expressions are used in the directions which the customer gives when streets or buildings are named, particularly when they are within the town where one takes the taxi.

nach
Perlach
Wedding
Wellingsbüttel
Zirndorf

'Nach' is used when the customer names an area or district or another town.

(iii) How to pay the taxi driver

Was macht das?   How much is that?

(iv) How to get a receipt for the taxi fare

Eine Quittung über
elf
neun
zwanzig
} Mark

A receipt for
eleven
nine
twenty
} marks

(v) How to ask where a bus or tram goes to

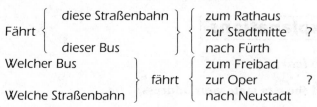

Fährt
{
diese Straßenbahn
dieser Bus
}
{
zum Rathaus
zur Stadtmitte   ?
nach Fürth
}

Welcher Bus
Welche Straßenbahn
} fährt
{
zum Freibad
zur Oper   ?
nach Neustadt
}

(b) Grammar

(i) The indefinite article

As we saw in Chapter 1, all German nouns can be categorised in one of three genders: masculine, feminine or neuter. When you want to say, for instance, *a* boy, or *an* apple, these words, which are called *indefinite articles*, vary according to the gender of the noun they accompany. Here are some examples:

Masc.	Fem.	Neut.
ein Professor	eine Sekretärin	ein Zimmer
ein Zug	eine Straße	ein Taxi

We can summarise this rule by tabulating the *indefinite articles* alone.

Masc.	Fem.	Neut.
ein	eine	ein

N.B. If you think about it, there can be no plural of 'a', or 'an'.

(ii) The negative

If you want to say 'not a', or 'not an', then the word is 'kein'. It behaves just like the *indefinite article*.

Masc.	Fem.	Neut.
Der ist kein	Sie ist keine	Das ist kein Taxi!
Professor!	Sekretärin!	

We can summarise this rule thus:

Masc.	Fem.	Neut.	Plur.
kein	keine	kein	keine

The word for 'not' is 'nicht'. 'Nicht die Nummer 13': 'Not the number 13.'

(iii) Subjects and direct objects

1 The subject of a sentence is the person or thing which *does* the action or event indicated by the verb. All the forms of the indefinite and negative article described above are the subjects of sentences. In German, the subjects of sentences are said to be in the 'nominative case'. We can summarise this rule thus:

	Masc.	Fem.	Neut.
	ein	eine	ein
nominative	kein	keine	kein

2 Consider the sentence 'The dog bit the postman'. We know who did the biting. It was the dog: the subject of the sentence. We also know who shouted 'Ouch!' It was the postman! We can say that whatever is bitten, bought, kicked, liked, etc., is the *direct object* of a verb. In the following sentences, the *direct objects* are printed in italics. Note that verbs describing states, as well as actions, have direct objects.

Peter kicked *a ball*
We bought *a house*
I have *a room*

He likes *beer*

She has not got *a cheque book*

Here are some German sentences with the *direct objects* underlined.

> Der Professor hat <u>eine Sekretärin</u>
> Sie hat <u>keinen Freund</u>
> Ich habe <u>kein Geld</u>
> Frau Meyer braucht <u>eine Tasse Kaffee</u>

In German, the direct objects of sentences are said to be in the 'accusative case'. We can summarise this rule thus:

	Masc.	**Fem.**	**Neut.**
	einen	eine	ein
accusative	keinen	keine	kein

N.B. It is the *masculine* form of the *indefinite article* which is different in the *accusative case*. The difference is the letter 'n'.

N.B. There is no direct object after the verb 'sein' (to be).

(iv) The definite article

1 When you want to say *the* professor, *the* street, or *the* house, these words, which are called *definite articles*, vary according to the gender of the noun they accompany. Here are some examples:

Masc.	**Fem.**	**Neut.**
der Professor	die Straße	das Haus
der Zug	die Sekretärin	das Taxi

We can summarise this rule by tabulating the definite article alone:

	Masc.	**Fem.**	**Neut.**
nominative	der	die	das

2 If you think back to that postman who got bitten a little while ago, you will remember what *direct objects* are. They are said to be in the 'accusative case'. Now, we can summarise the rule about the *definite article* as we did for the *indefinite article*:

	Masc.	**Fem.**	**Neut.**	**Plur.**
nominative	der	die	das	die
accusative	den	die	das	die

Notice the definite article has a *plural form*, because we can talk about 'the dogs', or even 'the postmen'. Notice, too, that the difference between the nominative and the accusative case in the masculine is again the letter 'n'.

You will find a full list of definite and indefinite articles in the Grammatical Summary.

(v) Personal pronouns

Where the object of the sentence is a *personal pronoun*, the accusative form of the pronoun is used. Here are the most common pronouns; there is a complete list of accusative pronouns in the Grammatical Summary.

Nominative	Accusative
ich	mich
er	ihn
sie	sie
es	es
wir	uns
Sie	Sie
sie	sie

(vi) 'Some' or 'any'

These words which are so important in English are generally not required in German:

Haben Sie Geld?	Have you any money?
Nein, ich habe kein Geld	No, I haven't got any money
(at a party:)	
Herr Müller, Sie haben kein Bier	Herr Müller, you haven't got any beer

(vii) 'Not'

'Not' simply translates into 'nicht', which usually follows the verb:

Die Nummer 23 fährt nicht zum Rathaus.	The number 23 does not go to the town hall.
Sie müssen nicht umsteigen.	You do not have to change (trains).

(viii) Prepositions

Consider the following sentences, taken from the dialogues:

Zur Nietzschestraße	To Nietzsche Street
Die Nummer 18 fährt zum Rathaus	The number 18 goes to the town hall

As we saw earlier, 'zum' is used with *masculine* and *neuter* nouns, 'zur' is used with *feminine* nouns.

Each of these two words is in fact a contraction of two other words:

zum = zu dem
zur = zu der

The two words 'dem' and 'der' are examples of our old friends, the definite articles. Here, where they accompany the *preposition* 'zu', they are said to be in the *dative case*. Another case! There will be more about this in Chapter 9.

Some prepositions accompany the *accusative case*, and others accompany the *dative case*. (Some prepositions may be used with both cases!) You will find a list in the Grammatical Summary.

Exercises

A

 ### Exercise 1

See how many questions you can make.

$$
\text{Fährt}
\begin{Bmatrix} \text{dieser Bus} \\ \text{diese Straßenbahn} \\ \text{die Nummer 15} \end{Bmatrix}
\begin{cases} \text{nach} \begin{cases} \text{Egersdorf} \\ \text{Steinach} \end{cases} \\ \text{zum} \begin{cases} \text{Stadttheater} \\ \text{Rathaus} \\ \text{Flughafen} \end{cases} \\ \text{zur} \begin{cases} \text{Stadtmitte} \\ \text{Goethestraße} \end{cases} \end{cases} ?
$$

 ### Exercise 2

You are a traveller in Germany, and you are trying to find your way around by bus and tram. You will be prompted in English on the recording and told where you are and what you are thinking. You have to convert these thoughts into requests for information about the buses or trams. An example answer will be given after each pause.

B

 ### Exercise 3

Convert the following sentences into the negative. The first one is done for you:

Example: Ich habe ein Buch.
Ich habe kein Buch.

1 Er hat ein Auto.
2 Sie möchte einen Kaffee.
3 Er ist Professor.
4 Sie hat eine Einladung.
5 Wir haben einen Hund.
6 Das ist der Bahnhof.

7   Der Garten ist groß.
8   Der Vater ist alt.
9   Frau Meier ist jung.
10   Raggi ist in Hamburg.

Exercise 4   Taxi: Telephoning for a taxi

Don't forget to read the questions below before listening to this dialogue, and remember: you do not have to understand every word, just listen for the information you need.

1   What is the name of the taxi firm?
     Is it (a) Gastgeber   (b) Kußberger   (c) Hamburger?
2   Where does the customer live?
     Is it (a) Robert-Koch-Straße   (b) Richard-Loch-Straße
     (c) Robert-Schmidt-Straße?
3   Where does she want to go?
4   What is the customer's name?
     Is it (a) Sabine Wachmann (b) Sabine Wichtmann (c) Sabine Wichmann

6 Es tut weh

Illness

 Dialogues

Dialogue 1

Frau Meyer has had another very bad night, so she decides to go and see her doctor. She rings for an appointment.

1 Assistentin: Praxis Doktor Storm.
       Guten Morgen.
   Frau Meyer: Guten Morgen.
       Ich möchte den Arzt sehen.
5 Assistentin: Haben Sie einen Termin?
   Frau Meyer: Nein.
       Geht es heute vormittag?
   Assistentin: Nein.
       Es tut mir leid.
10   Heute vormittag ist nichts mehr frei.
   Frau Meyer: Ach nein!
       Ist nichts mehr frei?
   Assistentin: Nein.
       Es tut mir leid.
15 Frau Meyer: Geht es heute nachmittag?
   Assistentin: Ja. Kommen Sie um 16 Uhr.
   Frau Meyer: Gott sei Dank!
       Um 16 Uhr.
       Ja, das geht.
20   Danke schön.
   Assistentin: Auf Wiederhören!
   Frau Meyer: Auf Wiederhören!

Ich verschreibe Ihnen etwas für die Kopfschmerzen

Dialogue 2

Fritz Löb went out to his 'Stammtisch' at the Gasthaus Adler last night. It was his regular Wednesday night out and as sometimes happens he had too much to drink. The following morning he finds himself in Dr Storm's surgery explaining his symptoms.

1   Doktor Storm: Nun, was fehlt Ihnen denn?
    Fritz: Ich habe Kopfschmerzen.
    Doktor Storm: Ist das alles?
    Fritz: Nein, Herr Doktor.
5   Mein Bauch tut weh, und ich habe Durchfall.
    Doktor Storm: Seit wann haben Sie Durchfall?
    Fritz: Seit gestern.
    Doktor Storm: Ich verschreibe Ihnen etwas für den Durchfall.
    Fritz: Vielen Dank, Herr Doktor.

Dialogue 3

Antonio once entertained ambitions of playing for Inter Milan. He has had to settle for something less exalted, however, and he plays for a Munich club called TSV 1886. On Sunday afternoon he had a difference of opinion with an opposing goalkeeper and on this Monday morning he finds himself in Dr Storm's surgery.

1 Doktor Storm: Nun, wo tut es weh?
  Antonio: Hier.
    Es ist mein Rücken.
  Doktor Storm: Hier?
    (He pokes Antonio's back)
5 Antonio: Au!! Ja!
  Doktor Storm: Ist das ein stechender Schmerz?
  Antonio: Nein.
    In der Nacht war es ein dumpfer Schmerz.
  Doktor Storm: So, so.
10   Kein Fußball für Sie.
  Antonio: O weh!

Information

(a) Notes on Dialogue 1

5	Termin	'Der Termin' means a date or a fixed time for an appointment.
7	Geht es	The expressions 'Geht es?' and 'Es geht' are very useful expressions which can be used in many situations. 'Es geht' is the equivalent of English expressions such as 'It's all right' or 'It's OK' or 'It's working'.
10	Heute vormittag ist ...	The expression 'heute vormittag' has been brought to the beginning of the sentence for emphasis. When this happens the subject always comes after the verb. Notice also line 10 of Dialogue 3.
16	16 Uhr	The 24-hour clock is used in any sort of formal situation.

(b) Notes on Dialogue 2

Stammtisch	A 'Stammtisch' is a table in a Gasthaus which is reserved for certain regular customers on a particular day each week. Nearly every Gasthaus has

its 'Stammtisch' and there is often a notice on it indicating that it is reserved on a particular day. The 'Stammtisch' customers sometimes meet in order to talk about matters of mutual interest but they may also often play cards and in particular the very popular German card game 'Skat'.

6   Seit wann?   Where the English here would be 'How long?' the German is 'Since when?', so the natural answer is 'Seit gestern' (since yesterday)

(c) Notes on Dialogue 3

TSV 1886   The letters TSV stand for 'Turn- und Sportverein' and the date indicates the year in which the club was founded.

(d) Word list

Here is a list of the most important words in the dialogue. You should learn them by heart. They are given here in the order in which they occur in the dialogues.

N.B. Names of parts of the body are given in the Grammatical Summary.

die Assistentin (-nen)	(female) assistant
die **Prax**is (**Prax**en)	practice (of a doctor)
der Arzt (¨e)	doctor
sehen	to see
heute	today
der **Vor**mittag (-e)	morning
nichts	nothing
der **Nach**mittag (-e)	afternoon
nun	now
die **Kopf**schmerzen (plural)	headache
alles	everything
der Bauch	stomach
der **Durch**fall	diarrhoea
seit	since
gestern	yesterday
ver**schrei**ben	to prescribe
etwas	something
der **Rü**cken (-)	back
stechend	sharp, shooting (of a pain)
der Schmerz (-en)	pain

immer	always
die Nacht (⸚e)	night
dumpf	dull
der **Fuß**ball	football

(e) Some phrases

Heute **vor**mittag	this morning
Heute **nach**mittag	this afternoon
Es tut mir leid	I'm sorry
Gott sei Dank!	Thank goodness!
Das geht	That's all right
Auf **Wie**der**hö**ren	Goodbye (on the telephone)
Was fehlt **Ih**nen?	What's the matter?
... tut weh	... hurts
O weh!	Oh dear!

(f) Further useful vocabulary

These words occur later in the chapter. You will find it useful to learn them too.

der **Zahn**arzt (⸚e)	dentist
das **Fie**ber	fever or high temperature
mehrere	several
die **Stun**de (-n)	hour
der Tag (-e)	day
leicht	slight
stark	strong or severe
blutig	bloody
ge**broch**en	broken
das Buch (⸚er)	book
die **Rei**se (-n)	journey
nett	nice
die **Schwes**ter (-n)	sister

Structural explanations

(a) Structures to learn

(i) How to make an appointment to see the doctor

Ich möchte		I'd like to see the
den Arzt ⎫ sehen		⎰ doctor
den Zahnarzt ⎭		⎱ dentist

Geht es			Is		
heute vormittag			this morning		
heute nachmittag		?	this afternoon		possible?
morgen			tomorrow		
morgen abend			tomorrow evening		

Kommen Sie um	Come at
10 Uhr	ten o'clock
14 Uhr	two o'clock
16 Uhr 30	four thirty

(ii) How to describe symptoms of illness

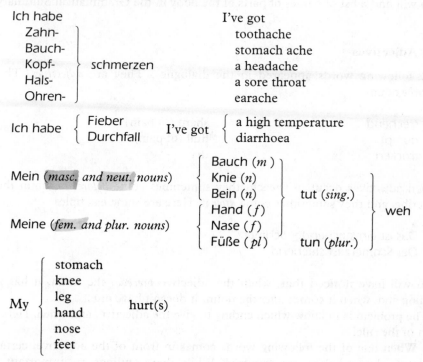

Ich habe		I've got
Zahn-		toothache
Bauch-		stomach ache
Kopf-	schmerzen	a headache
Hals-		a sore throat
Ohren-		earache

Ich habe	Fieber	I've got	a high temperature
	Durchfall		diarrhoea

Mein (*masc. and neut. nouns*) Bauch (*m*), Knie (*n*), Bein (*n*) tut (*sing.*)

Meine (*fem. and plur. nouns*) Hand (*f*), Nase (*f*), Füße (*pl*) tun (*plur.*) weh

My	stomach	hurt(s)
	knee	
	leg	
	hand	
	nose	
	feet	

(iii) How to say how long symptoms have lasted

Seit	gestern	Since yesterday
	mehreren Stunden	For several hours
	drei Tagen	For three days

(iv) How to describe the type of pain

Es tut weh	It hurts or aches
Wo tut es weh?	Where does it hurt?

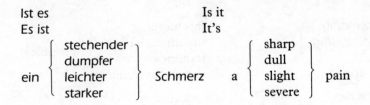

(b) Grammar

(i) Parts of the body

You will find a list of names of parts of the body in the Grammatical Summary.

(ii) Adjectives

The following words appeared in the dialogues. They are *adjectives*. They *describe* nouns.

stechend	sharp (of pain)
dumpf	dull (of pain)
trocken	dry

When adjectives occur in speech, they sometimes come *before* the noun they describe, and they sometimes come *after* it. Here are some examples.

Das ist ein stechend<u>er</u> Schmerz
Der Schmerz ist stechend

You will have noticed that, when the adjective *precedes* the noun, it has an ending and, when it comes *after* the noun, it doesn't have one.

The problem is to know which ending to give the adjective, and when. Here is part of the rule:

When one of the following words comes in front of the adjective, certain endings, shown below, are required. While these endings are important in *written* German, getting them wrong will hardly ever prevent you from being understood. So take heart!

ein	a; an	unser	our
kein	not a	euer	your (*familiar plural*)
mein	my		
dein	your (*familiar*)	Ihr	your (*polite*)
sein	his/its (*m* and *n*)	ihr	their
ihr	her/its (*f*)		

Note the endings of the adjectives after 'ein', 'kein', 'mein', etc.

Sing.

	Masc.	**Fem.**
	a dull pain	a bloody nose
nominative	ein dumpf<u>er</u> Schmerz	eine blutig<u>e</u> Nase
accusative	einen dumpf<u>en</u> Schmerz	eine blutig<u>e</u> Nase

	Neut.
	a broken leg
nominative	ein gebrochen<u>es</u> Bein
accusative	ein gebrochen<u>es</u> Bein

Plur. (all genders)

		Masc.	**Fem.**	**Neut.**
nominative	keine gebrochen<u>en</u>	Arme	Rippen	Beine
accusative	keine gebrochen<u>en</u>	Arme	Rippen	Beine

Exercises

A

Exercise 1

What would you say if:

1 The filling in your wisdom tooth has come out.
2 You have eaten too many cherries.
3 You drank too much wine last night.
4 Your throat feels raw.
5 You have an infection in your ear.
6 You have a fever.
7 Your shoes are too tight.
8 That meat you had yesterday wasn't fresh.
9 You have tripped up and fallen on your knee.
10 Your temperature is 103°.

N.B. In Germany temperatures are given in Centigrade or Celsius. Normal body temperature (98.4° Fahrenheit) is around 36.6° Celcius.

Exercise 2

Now it's your turn to play the part of the patient in a conversation with a doctor. You will be prompted in English on your recording. Speak in the pauses and then listen to the doctor's replies.

After the exercise you can hear an example of the whole dialogue as a check.

Exercise 3

Say the following parts of your body hurt:

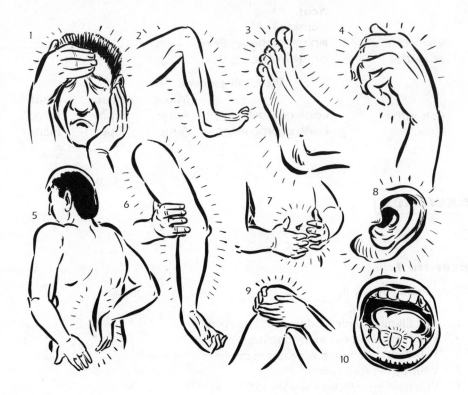

 B

Exercise 4

You are feeling very negative about life. Answer all the following questions in the negative.

1 Ist das ein gutes Buch?
2 Ist das eine schöne Frau?
3 Ist das eine ruhige Straße?
4 Ist das ein ruhiges Zimmer?
5 War das ein schöner Abend?

6 War das eine gute Reise?
7 War das eine ruhige Nacht?
8 War das ein schöner Ausblick?

Exercise 5

You are still feeling very negative. Answer the following questions.

1 Haben Sie eine ruhige Frau?
2 Haben Sie ein gutes Zimmer?
3 Haben Sie einen schönen Ausblick?
4 Haben Sie ein neues Buch?
5 Haben Sie einen neuen Fußball?
6 Haben Sie einen guten Doktor?
7 Haben Sie eine nette Schwester?
8 Haben Sie eine ruhige Straße?

Exercise 6   Beim Arzt: Difficulty in getting an appointment to see the doctor

Don't forget to read the questions below first before listening to this dialogue, and remember: you do not have to understand every word, just listen for the information you need.

1 What is the doctor's name?
2 What is the receptionist called?
3 What does Herr von Luck want?
4 Does he have an appointment already?
5 Does he succeed in getting an appointment?
6 When is the next available appointment?
7 Finally the receptionist recommends that he calls the emergency services. Rearrange the words below to recreate her sentence (bear in mind that she is interrupted by Herr von Luck):

---

müssen ja es glaube Notdienst so wenn ist den dringend anrufen dann ich Sie

---

Was darf es sein?

Shopping

 Dialogues

Dialogue 1

It will soon be Elke's birthday, and Fritz Löb wants to buy her a pullover. However, he is rather unused to buying ladies' clothes.

1 Verkäuferin: Was darf es sein?
  Fritz: (speaking by instinct)
    Ich schaue mich nur um.

Ich möchte einen Pullover

Verkäuferin: Ja, bitte schön.

Fritz: (clears his throat)

Verkäuferin: Ja? Was darf es sein, bitte?

5   Fritz: Ich möchte einen Pullover.

Verkäuferin: Ja. Herren- oder Damenpullover?

Fritz: Einen Damenpullover suche ich.

Verkäuferin: Ja. Welche Größe trägt die Dame?

Fritz: O, ich weiß es nicht genau.

10   Mittelgröße, glaube ich.

Verkäuferin: So wie ich?

Fritz: (embarrassed and trying not to look too closely)
       Ja, so ungefähr.

Verkäuferin: Ja, Größe vierzig.
       An welches Material hatten Sie gedacht?

15   Fritz: Ach ja. Das Material. Natürlich.

Verkäuferin: Wolle? Baumwolle? Oder eine Kunstfaser?

Fritz: Wolle! Ja, aus Wolle.

Verkäuferin: Ich habe hier einen schönen roten Pullover.
       Der ist aus Wolle.

20   Fritz: Nein. Sie hat schon einen roten Pullover.
       Haben Sie diese Art in blau?

Verkäuferin: Hat die Dame blaue Augen?

Fritz: Eigentlich ja.

Verkäuferin: Ich habe hier einen blauen Pullover.

25   Fritz: Ja. Der blaue Pullover ist bestimmt schön.
       Was kostet er?

Verkäuferin: 90 Mark.

Fritz: Ich nehme ihn.

Dialogue 2

Frau Meyer has been needing a pair of new shoes for ages.

1   Verkäufer: Kann ich Ihnen helfen?

Frau Meyer: Ich brauche neue Schuhe.

Verkäufer: Ja, bitte schön.
       (looking at Frau Meyer's shoes)
       Sie tragen die Größe 37, glaube ich.

5   Frau Meyer: Nein. Ich trage immer die Größe 36.

Verkäufer: (sceptically) Ach so.

Frau Meyer: Was kosten die braunen Schuhe im Schaufenster?

Verkäufer: Die sind Größe 37.

Frau Meyer: Haben Sie die braunen Schuhe eine Nummer kleiner?

10   Verkäufer: Ja, die gleichen Schuhe habe ich hier.
       Sie sind aber schwarz.

Frau Meyer: Kann ich sie anprobieren?

Verkäufer: Selbstverständlich können Sie sie anprobieren.

Kann ich sie anprobieren?

Frau Meyer: (taking a few steps)
  Au!!! Das tut weh!
15 Sie sind zu klein.
  Verkäufer: Möchten Sie die braunen Schuhe anprobieren?
  Frau Meyer: Sind die Sohlen aus Leder?
  Verkäufer: Nein. Die braunen Schuhe haben
    Kunststoffsohlen.
20 Frau Meyer: Kunststoffsohlen! Furchtbar!
    Das gefällt mir überhaupt nicht.
    Haben Sie keine Schuhe mit Ledersohlen?
  Verkäufer: Na, freilich.
    Schauen Sie.
25 Diese blauen Schuhe sind sehr elegant.
    Sie sind hundertprozentig aus Leder.
  Frau Meyer: Welche Größe?
  Verkäufer: Größe 37.
  Frau Meyer: Was kosten sie?
30 Verkäufer: Sie kosten 225 Mark.
  Frau Meyer: Was? Das ist mir zu teuer!
    Auf Wiedersehen!
  Verkäufer: Auf Wiedersehen!
  Frau Meyer: (grumbling to herself) Allerhand! Allerhand ist das! 225
35 Mark!!

Information

(a) Notes on Dialogue 1

7   Einen Damenpullover

Note how the positions of the subject and the object in this sentence have been reversed. In German the object quite often comes at the beginning of a sentence, so that it can be emphasised. German is able to do this quite easily because the masculine object of a sentence is 'marked', in this case by the letters '-en', which are added to the word 'ein'.

9   ich weiß es

Note how German has to say 'Ich weiß es' (I know *it*), where English would normally just say 'I know'.

14   An welches Material ...?

Where English says 'think *of*', German says 'denken *an*'.

17   aus Wolle

English says 'made *of* wool'. German says '*aus* Wolle'.

19   Der ist ...

The subject pronoun is normally 'er', 'sie' or 'es'. However, to give the pronoun emphasis the words 'der', 'die' or 'das' are frequently used.

(b) Notes on Dialogue 2

6   Ach so

This expression allows you to express polite interest in what other people are saying, even if you don't feel up to uttering a word yourself. It means 'Oh, really', 'is that what you mean?', 'how interesting!', 'indeed'. It sometimes contains an element of surprise at what is being said. Whichever of these meanings you intend the phrase to have, the one constant underlying significance of the phrase is that you are being told something which you did not know before. Another useful expression is 'Aha', meaning 'I see'.

7   im Schaufenster

The word 'im' is a contraction of 'in dem'.

8 Die sind …	See note to line 19 on Dialogue 1.
10 die gleichen Schuhe	See note to line 7 on Dialogue 1.
21 Das gefällt mir	Don't try to translate this expression literally. Just treat it as meaning 'I like that'. For more information, see p. 269.
21 überhaupt nicht	This phrase and 'gar nicht' are very useful idioms meaning 'not at all'.
23 Freilich	This expression, meaning 'certainly' or 'of course' is used in the south of Germany. In other parts of the country you might hear 'natürlich' or 'sicher' used in the same context.
24 Schauen Sie	The verb 'schauen' (to look) tends to be used more in the south of Germany and in Austria. In the north it would be more normal to use the verb 'sehen', or 'gucken'.
26 Hundertprozentig	Literally: '100%'. This useful word can be used for expressions such as 'absolutely' or 'completely'.

(c) Word list

Here is a list of the most important words in the dialogues. You should learn them by heart. They are given here in the order in which they occur in the dialogues.

die Verkäuferin (-nen)	(female) sales assistant
der Pullover (-)	pullover
der Herrenpullover (-)	gentleman's pullover
die Dame (-n)	lady
suchen	to look for
die Größe (-n)	size
tragen (trägt)	to wear
wissen (weiß)	to know
genau	exactly
die Mittelgröße	medium size
glauben	to believe
ungefähr	approximately
das Material	material
natürlich	of course
die Wolle	wool
die Baumwolle	cotton
die Kunstfaser (-n)	synthetic

rot	red
schon	already
die Art	sort or kind
blau	blue
das **Auge** (-n)	eye
eigentlich	actually
be**stimmt**	really or certainly
kosten	to cost
der Ver**käuf**er (-)	salesman
helfen (hilft)	to help
brauchen	to need
neu	new
der Schuh (-e)	shoe
braun	brown
das **Schau**fenster (-)	window (of a shop)
klein	small
gleich	the same
aber	but
schwarz	black
an__probieren	to try on
selbstver**ständ**lich	of course
können (kann)	to be able to or to be allowed to
die **Sohl**e (-n)	sole
das **Led**er	leather
der **Kunst**stoff	man-made material
furchtbar	terrible
freilich	certainly
schauen	to look
ele**gant**	elegant
hundertpro**zen**tig	entirely
teuer	dear, expensive

(d) Some phrases

Was darf es sein?	Can I help you?
Ich **schau**e mich nur um	I'm just looking round

(e) Further useful vocabulary

These words occur later in the chapter. You will find it helpful to learn them too.

zahlen	to pay
die **Kas**se (-n)	cashdesk, till
die **Far**be (-n)	colour
der Rock (¨e)	skirt
die **Ho**se (-n)	trousers
das **Nacht**hemd (-en)	nightshirt
die **Blu**se (-n)	blouse
die **Wes**te (-n)	waistcoat
das Kleid (-er)	dress

der **Man**tel (¨)	coat
die **Ja**cke (-n)	jacket
der **Ba**deanzug (¨e)	swimsuit
das Hemd (-en)	shirt
das **Blou**son (-s)	blouson
der **An**zug (¨e)	suit
der **Re**genmantel (¨)	raincoat
groß	big
weiß	white
heißen	to be called
schnell	fast
kaufen	to buy
sitzen	to sit
um	around
rund	round
der Tisch (-e)	table
der **Kun**de (-n)	male customer
die **Kun**din (-nen)	female customer
lang	long
kurz	short
grün	green

Structural explanations

(a) Structures to learn

(i) Phrases to use when you go shopping:

Ich schaue mich nur um	I'm just looking
Ich weiß es nicht genau	I don't know exactly
Das ist mir zu teuer	That's too expensive

(ii) Phrases which you may hear when you go shopping:

Kann ich Ihnen helfen?	Can I help you?
Was darf es sein?	What would you like?
Welche Größe?	Which size?
Welche Farbe?	Which colour?
Welches Material?	Which material?
Sonst noch etwas?	Anything else?
Darf es noch etwas sein?	Anything else?
Haben Sie sonst noch einen Wunsch?	Anything else?
Zahlen Sie an der Kasse, bitte	Please pay at the till.

(iii) How to ask if you can try on an article of clothing (women's):

Kann ich	den Rock	anprobieren?	skirt
	die Hose		trousers
	das Nachthemd		nightshirt
	die Bluse		blouse
	die Weste		waistcoat
	das Kleid		dress
	den Mantel		coat
	die Jacke		jacket
	den Badeanzug		swimsuit

(iv) Men, of course, may wish to have the same privileges:

Kann ich	das Hemd	anprobieren?	shirt
	das Blouson		blouson
	die Jacke		jacket
	die Hose		trousers
	den Anzug		suit
	den Regenmantel		raincoat

(v) How to ask for something a little bit different from what you have been shown

The diagram below allows you to make up lots of different sentences, so that you can ask for something different.

Haben Sie	diese Art diese Farbe diese Größe dieses Material	eine Nummer	größer kleiner	?
		in	blau rot weiß	
		aus	Wolle Leder Nylon	

Have you got	something like this	a size	bigger smaller	?
	this colour this size this material	in	blue red white	
		in	wool leather nylon	

(vi) How to ask the price

The diagram below will cover most things you are likely to want to buy:

Was { kostet { der Anzug/er / die Bluse/sie / das Hemd/es }   kosten   die Schuhe/sie } ?

What { does { the suit/it / the blouse/it / the shirt/it }   do   the shoes/they } cost?

(b) Grammar

(i) Verbs

In Chapter 2, we looked at some common *regular* and *irregular* verbs. Here are some more: the regular ones first. Regular verbs, you will remember, keep their stem unchanged and use the standard set of endings. Once again, you will find the most frequently used forms of the verbs given here. The full table is in the Grammatical Summary.

● *The verb* 'suchen' *(to seek/look) for*   ● *The verb* 'glauben' *(to believe)*

ich (I)		e		ich		e
er (he)		t		er		t
sie (she)	SUCH-	t		sie	GLAUB-	t
wir (we)		en		wir		en
Sie (you)		en		Sie		en

- *The verb 'brauchen' (to need)*

ich		e
er		t
sie	BRAUCH-	t
wir		en
Sie		en

Now for the *irregular* verbs!

- *The verb 'tragen' – (to wear)*

Note how the vowel sounds change with the addition of an Umlaut.

ich	trage
er	trägt
sie	trägt
wir	tragen
Sie	tragen

And part of the verb 'MÖGEN' (to like). It enables you to say what you *would like*, as in the sentence: Ich möchte einen Pullover – 'I would like a pullover'.

ich möchte	(I would like)	
er möchte	(he would like)	
sie möchte	(she would like)	} einen Pullover
wir möchten	(we would like)	
Sie möchten	(you would like)	

This part of the verb is slightly irregular, in that the 'er' form and the 'sie' form end in '-e' instead of the more usual '-t'.

(iii) Adjectives

In the previous chapter, we looked at the endings of adjectives when they are preceded by words like 'ein', 'kein', 'mein', 'unser', and so on. In this chapter, we look at the endings of adjectives when they are preceded by words like 'der' (the), 'dieser' (this), and so on.

Der blaue Pullover ist sehr elegant	The blue pullover is very elegant
Die elegante Dame heißt Frau Müller	The elegant lady is called Mrs Müller
Das alte Taxi fährt schnell	The old taxi goes fast
Diese braunen Schuhe sind aus Leder	These brown shoes are made of leather

The above adjectives all form part of the *subject* of their respective sentences, and so, as we saw in Chapter 5, they are said to be in the 'nominative case'. We can summarise this rule thus:

		Masc.	Fem.	Neut.	Plur. (all genders)
Adjectives after 'der', 'dieser'	*nominative*	-e	-e	-e	-en

Consider the following sentences.

Fritz kauft den blauen Pullover	Fritz buys the blue pullover
Elke braucht die weiße Bluse	Elke needs the white blouse
Wir sitzen um den runden Tisch	We are sitting around the round table
Konrad hat das rote Hemd	Konrad has the red shirt
Haben Sie die blauen Schuhe?	Have you got the blue shoes?

In each of these sentences, the adjectives are part of the *direct object* of their respective sentences, and they are consequently in the 'accusative case', as we saw in Chapter 5. The third sentence contains a phrase with a preposition governing the 'accusative case'. We can summarise the rule about adjectives when they occur in the 'accusative case' thus:

		Masc.	Fem.	Neut.	Plur. (all genders)
Adjectives after 'der', 'dieser'	*accusative*	-en	-e	-e	-en

It is the *masculine* form of the adjective which has a different spelling in the accusative case. The difference is the letter 'n'.

You will find a full account of the endings of adjectives in the Grammatical Summary. It is worth pointing out, however, that although it is very *easy* to explain how the adjectives make their endings, it is very *hard* to remember the rules well enough to get the endings right when you are speaking. Take heart from the thought that mistakes will seldom prevent you from communicating your meaning to a German speaker. Come back to the adjective endings again and again, and you will gradually begin to get them right as you practise them.

Exercises

Get ready to go shopping in Germany and be ready to get exactly what you want. Here are some more useful words.

Colours

pastellgrün	pastel green
rosa	pink
mittelbraun	medium brown
gold	gold coloured
beige	beige
hellblau	light blue
dunkelrot	dark red
gelb	yellow
natur	natural colour

Materials

Baumwolle	cotton
Seide	silk
Krepp	crepe
Leinen	linen
Cord	corduroy
Samt	velvet
Gabardine	gabardine
Popeline	poplin
Polyester	polyester
Acryl	acrylic
Viskose	viscose

Most of these are easily washed in a washing machine. They are then marked:

Vollwaschbar

Exercise 1

Study this model conversation carefully.

Verkäuferin: Was darf es sein?
Kunde: (Ich möchte einen Pullover.)
Verkäuferin: Welche Größe brauchen Sie?

Kunde: (Größe 40.)
Verkäuferin: An welches Material hatten Sie gedacht?
Kunde: (Wolle.)
Verkäuferin: Welche Farbe möchten Sie?
Kunde: (Ich möchte hellblau, bitte.)
Verkäuferin: Der ist sehr elegant.
Kunde: (Ja, der gefällt mir.)
   (Was kostet er?)

Here are some clothes that you want to buy. Don't forget to look up the equivalent sizes on p. 299.

1   You fancy a skirt made of poplin. It ought to be dark red. Your size is 14. Don't forget to ask the price.
2   You've been thinking about a crepe blouse for some time. Your size is 16. How about a delicate shade of pink?
3   You've been meaning to treat yourself to a silk shirt for ages. You want a white one, size 12.
4   Those leather jackets in Germany are really good value. A dark brown one would just suit you, size 20.

 ## Exercise 2

Now it's your turn to go shopping. You are shopping in the Mönckebergstraße in Hamburg. You go into Karstadt, a well-known store, where the sales girl offers you a number of things. You like them all. Ask how much they cost. You will be given suggested answers on the recording after the pause.

B

  ## Exercise 3

Check that you know what the following German sentences mean.

1   Ich schaue mich nur um.
2   Ich möchte einen Pullover.
3   Ich weiß es nicht genau.
4   An welches Material hatten Sie gedacht?
5   Der blaue Pullover ist bestimmt schön.
6   Ich brauche neue Schuhe.
7   Ich trage immer Größe 40.
8   Kann ich sie anprobieren?
9   Haben Sie keine Schuhe mit Ledersohlen?
10   Das ist mir zu teuer.

Exercise 4

Translate the following sentences into German.

1　What do they cost?
2　I don't like that at all.
3　Are the soles made of leather?
4　Have you got the same sort of thing a size smaller?
5　How much are the brown shoes in the window?
6　I would like a nightshirt.
7　I'm just looking.
8　The shirt is made of silk.
9　How much are the shoes?
10　The pullover is too expensive.

Exercise 5

Put the following expressions into German.

1　The white skirt.
2　The red trousers.
3　The black shoes.
4　The long dress.
5　The brown jacket.

6　The light blue shirt.
7　The brown suit.
8　The short raincoat.
9　The green blouse.
10　The little black dress.

Exercise 6　Im Kleidungsgeschäft: Problems in buying a present for a girlfriend

Don't forget to read the questions below before listening to this dialogue, and remember: you do not have to understand every word, just listen for the information you need. You will hear a new word: 'das Geschenk' (the present/gift).

1　What does the young man want to buy as a present?
2　What size does the girlfriend take?
3　What is the first colour that the man is offered?
4　They do not have a red one in the right size. What size do they have it in?
5　Does he end up buying one?

8 Haben Sie Kinder?

Families and nationalities

 Dialogues

Dialogue 1

Antonio Raggi is always short of money. He is very aware of this, particularly when Elke wears her smart clothes to work. He has decided to try and get a week-end job in an Italian restaurant. He goes off to see the manager of the Pizzeria Paolo.

<pre>
 1 Antonio: Guten Tag!
   Inhaber: Guten Tag!
   Antonio: Ich komme wegen der Stelle als Kellner.
   Inhaber: Ach ja.
 5   Haben Sie Erfahrung als Kellner?
   Antonio: Nein, leider nicht.
   Inhaber: Hmm. Sprechen Sie Italienisch?
   Antonio: Natürlich.
        Ich bin Italiener.
10 Inhaber: Ah, Sie sind Italiener.
        Von wo kommen Sie?
   Antonio: Ich komme aus Napoli.
   Inhaber: Napoli! Na ja, Napoli!
        Ich komme aus Benevento.
15 Antonio: Na. Wunderbar!
        Meine Tante Concetta kommt aus Benevento.
   Inhaber: Nein!
   Antonio: Doch, doch.
   Inhaber: Fantastico, fantastico!
20   Wann können Sie anfangen?
</pre>

Dialogue 2

Fritz Löb is visiting a lovely church near Landshut. He has come especially to see it. (Elke is just not interested in seeing yet another church.) The parson is showing him round.

1 Pfarrer: Die Kirche ist sehr alt, Herr Löb.
    Fritz: Ja, das sieht man.
    Pfarrer: Über dreihundert Jahre alt.
    Fritz: Tatsächlich?
5 Pfarrer: Ja.
    Schauen Sie.
    Der Altar ist schön, nicht wahr?
    Fritz: Das stimmt, wirklich.
    Er ist wunderschön.
10 Pfarrer: Riemenschneider.
    Fritz: Ach so.
    Tilman Riemenschneider.
    Pfarrer: Ja.
    Sagen Sie, Herr Löb.
15 Was sind Sie von Beruf, wenn ich fragen darf?
    Fritz: Ich bin Hauptschullehrer.
    In München.
    Pfarrer: Ach so.
    Sind Sie verheiratet?
20 Fritz: Ja. Das heißt, wir leben getrennt.
    Pfarrer: Das tut mir leid.
    Fritz: Danke.
    Pfarrer: Haben Sie Kinder?
    Fritz: Nein, ich habe keine Kinder.
25 Pfarrer: Es ist vielleicht besser so.
    Fritz: Ja, es ist besser so.
    Kleine Kinder brauchen einen Vater.
    Pfarrer: Das stimmt.

Information

(a) Notes on Dialogue 1

3	wegen	This word means 'on account of'. It is very useful when you want to explain a reason. It is followed by a noun in the genitive case. See Grammatical Summary page 283.

7	Italienisch	In German, adjectives of nationality are written with a small letter: 'ein italienisches Restaurant'. In this sentence 'Italienisch' is a noun, meaning the Italian language.
8	Natürlich	'Of course'. Other words meaning the same could be: 'selbstverständlich', 'sicher' or 'freilich'.
9	Ich bin Italiener	This means, literally, 'I am an Italian', but notice that in German there is no indefinite article when describing someone's nationality. The same applies to professions – where in English we would say 'I am a teacher', in German it is 'Ich bin Lehrer' (see line 16 of Dialogue 2).
13	Napoli	The German form of the name of the town Naples is 'Neapel'. Antonio is here speaking in Italian.
18	Doch, doch	Remember that this word means 'yes' when it is used emphatically, after somebody else has used a negative.

(b) Notes on Dialogue 2

2	Das sieht man	The German word 'man' can be the subject of any verb. It means 'one'. In English we quite often use 'you' when we mean 'everybody'. We say, for instance 'you mustn't drive fast in a built-up area', when we really mean 'no-one' must do it. We say, for instance, in English 'You can drink alcohol in a pub when you are over 18'. What we really mean is everyone can, or 'one' can. German always uses 'man' in order to show that the idea is general to many people. The form of the verb is the same as the 'er' form or 'sie' form.
4	Tatsächlich	Another word meaning the same thing would be 'wirklich'.

6	Schauen Sie	Remember that in the north of Germany you may hear an alternative version of this expression: 'Sehen Sie'.
10	Riemenschneider	Tilman Riemenschneider was a famous sculptor, who worked principally in wood. He worked during the fifteenth and sixteenth centuries, and there are many fine altars carved by him to be seen in churches, especially in the south of Germany.
14	Sagen Sie	This is very useful phrase, which indicates to the person you are talking to that you are about to ask them a question.
15	wenn ich fragen darf	Do not attempt to analyse this phrase now. Simply use it in order to mean 'if you don't mind my asking'. You will find a brief discussion of word order in subordinate clauses in the Grammatical Summary on page 279.
16	Hauptschullehrer	In Germany all children go to the 'Grundschule' at the age of 6. When they reach 10+ they transfer to the 'Hauptschule' ('main' school), leading usually to apprenticeships, or the 'Realschule' ('intermediate' school), leading to posts in middle management or the civil service. Some children go to a 'Gymnasium', which is the most academic of the schools.
20	wir leben getrennt	This literally means 'we live separated'.
23	Haben Sie Kinder?	Note that where English would need the word 'any', German does not.

(c) Word list

Here is a list of the most important words in the dialogue. You should learn them by heart. They are given here in the order in which they occur in the dialogues.

der **In**haber (-)	owner
kommen	to come

wegen	on account of
die **Stel**le (-n)	job or position
der **Kell**ner (-)	waiter
die E**rfah**rung	experience
leider	unfortunately
sprechen (spricht)	to speak
na**tür**lich	naturally
der Ita**lie**ner (-)	Italian
von	from, of
wunderbar	wonderful
die **Tan**te (-n)	aunt
wann?	when?
können (kann)	to be able
an_fangen (fängt an)	to begin
der **Pfarr**er (-)	vicar, minister etc.
die **Kir**che (-n)	church
sehr	very
alt	old
sehen (sieht)	to see
hundert	a hundred
das Jahr (-e)	year
tat**säch**lich?	really?
der **Al**tar (ᵉe)	altar
wirklich	really
wunderschön	very beautiful
sagen	to say
der Be**ruf** (-e)	job/profession
fragen	to ask
der **Leh**rer (-)	teacher
ver**heir**atet	married
leben	to live
ge**trennt**	separated
das Kind (-er)	child
viel**leicht**	perhaps
besser	better
brauchen	to need
der **Va**ter (ᵉ)	father
klein	small

(d) Some phrases

Das stimmt	That's right
Was sind Sie von Be**ruf**?	What is your job?
Das heißt	That is to say
Das tut mir leid	I'm sorry (to hear that)

(e) Further useful vocabulary

These words occur later in the chapter. You will find it useful to learn them too.

woher?	where from?
ein wenig	a little
verlobt	engaged
ledig	single
geschieden	divorced
verwitwet	widowed
Geschwister (plural)	brothers or sisters
der Sohn (¨e)	son
die Tochter (¨)	daughter
das Baby (-s)	baby
der Bruder (¨)	brother
die Schwester (-n)	sister

Structural explanations

(a) Structures to learn

(i) How to ask somebody their nationality and how to state your own

	Men	Women	
Sind Sie	Deutscher	Deutsche	(German)
Ich bin	Engländer	Engländerin	(English)
	Franzose	Französin	(?) (French)
	Spanier	Spanierin	(Spanish)
	Däne	Dänin	(Danish)

(ii) How to ask where people come from, and how to say where you come from yourself

Woher sind Sie?
Von wo kommen Sie? Ich komme aus

- Deutschland
- England
- Schottland
- Frankreich
- Spanien
- Dänemark

(iii) How to ask whether somebody speaks a particular language

Sprechen Sie

- Deutsch
- Englisch
- Französisch ?
- Spanisch
- Dänisch

Ja
Nein
Ein wenig } a little
Ein bißchen

(iv) How to ask if someone is married, and how to refer to your own status

Sind Sie verheiratet?

Ich bin
- verheiratet
- nicht verheiratet
- verlobt — engaged
- ledig — single
- geschieden — divorced
- verwitwet — widowed

(v) How to ask about a person's family

Haben Sie
Geschwister		brothers or sisters
Kinder	?	children
Söhne		sons
Töchter		daughters

Ja, ich habe
Ja, wir haben
einen Bruder	a brother
eine Schwester	a sister
ein Baby	a baby
ein Kind	a child
einen Sohn	a son
eine Tochter	a daughter

Ich habe
Wir haben
} { zwei drei
Brüder	brothers
Schwestern	sisters
Kinder	children
Söhne	sons
Töchter	daughters

Nein, { ich habe wir haben }
| keinen Bruder |
| keine Schwester |
| kein Baby |
| kein Kind |
| keinen Sohn |
| keine Tochter |

(vi) How to ask about someone's job or profession

Was sind Sie von Beruf?

Ich bin

Men	Women	
Architekt	Architektin	architect
Student	Studentin	student
Arzt	Ärztin	doctor
Lehrer	Lehrerin	teacher
Polizist	Polizistin	policeman/woman
Verkäufer	Verkäuferin	salesman/woman

(b) Grammar

(i) Nouns of nationality

You will find a list of nouns of nationality in the Grammatical Summary.

(ii) Languages

There is also a list of European languages there.

(iii) More about adjectives

Sometimes adjectives occur by themselves (i.e. not after words such as 'ein', 'mein' etc. or 'der', 'dieser', etc.), as in the sentence:

Kleine Kinder brauchen   Young children need a father
  einen Vater

You will find the endings of such 'unaccompanied' adjectives in the Grammatical Summary.

Exercises

A

Exercise 1

Read the following dialogue.

Pfarrer: Sagen Sie, Herr Schmidt.
  Sind Sie verheiratet?
Herr Schmidt: Ja.
Pfarrer: Und haben Sie Kinder?
Herr Schmidt: Ja, ich habe zwei Kinder.
Pfarrer: Aha.

Play out the above scene, imagining that the circumstances are different. If possible, take turns with a partner, each taking a role.

1 Herr Schmidt is divorced and has no children (remember what the parson said in the dialogue!).
2 He is widowed and has three children.
3 He is separated and has one child.
4 He is not married (this will be a shorter conversation).

Exercise 2

Now you are going to practise answering questions about your family. Listen to your recording. You will be asked first if you are married and then how many children you have. Each time, assume that you are married. The English voice will prompt you with how many children you have and whether they are boys or girls. You will be given suggested answers on the recording after the pause.

 B

Exercise 3

State your job as one of the following:

Exercise 4 Vorstellungsgespräch: An interview for a job

Don't forget to read the questions below before listening to this dialogue, and remember: you do not have to understand every word, just listen for the information you need. You will need the word 'mittags' (lunchtime, noon).

1 What is Frau Meyer looking for?
2 What are the hours?
3 What is the pay proposed?
4 What rate is finally agreed?
5 On what day does the job start?
6 At what time?

9 Wie ist das Wetter?

Places and weather

 Dialogues

Dialogue 1

Elke has taken herself to the Alte Pinakothek, a famous art gallery in Munich. She finds it quite refreshing not to have Fritz trailing about with her for once. Poor Fritz! He'd better watch out!

1 Mann: Entschuldigen Sie!
   Elke: Ja?
   Mann: Ich wollte nur sagen … das ist ein sehr elegantes Kleid.
   Elke: Oh, vielen Dank.
5 Das ist sehr nett von Ihnen.
   Mann: Sie haben einen norddeutschen Akzent.
   Elke: Ja. Ich komme aus Mölln.
   Mann: Mölln? Wo ist denn Mölln?
   Elke: In Norddeutschland.
10 Nicht weit von Hamburg.
   Mann: Ach so! In der Nähe von Hamburg.
   Elke: Ja. Zwischen Hamburg und Lübeck.
   Mann: Wie ist die Landschaft dort?
   Elke: Es gibt einen großen See dort, und eine sehr schöne Kirche.
15 Mann: Haben Sie noch Verwandtschaft dort?
   Elke: Ja. Mein Bruder wohnt in Mölln, bei meinen Eltern.
   Mann: Ach, Sie haben einen Bruder.
   Elke: Ja. Er kommt nächste Woche nach München.
   Er ist begeisterter Skiläufer.
20 Mann: Gibt es denn keinen Schnee in Mölln?
   Elke: Nein. Im Winter regnet es sehr viel.
   Aber es gibt nicht viel Schnee.
   Mann: So, so, so.

Das Holstentor in Lübeck

Dialogue 2

Antonio is enjoying the Oktoberfest, a famous beer festival which is held every year in Munich. He is sitting in a 'Bierzelt', where he has been listening to the brass band playing. He has just got talking to a young woman sitting opposite him. She is dressed in a very nice 'Dirndl'.

1 Antonio: Prost!
   Junge Frau: Prost!
   Antonio: Sind Sie Münchenerin?
   Junge Frau: Nein. Ich komme aus Bad Reichenhall.
5 Antonio: Wo ist denn Bad Reichenhall?
   Junge Frau: Nicht weit von Salzburg.
     Und Sie?
   Antonio: Ich komme aus Neapel.
     Aber jetzt bin ich Münchener.
10 Junge Frau: So.
   Antonio: Was gibt es dort zu sehen, in Bad Reichenhall?
   Junge Frau: Es gibt ein schönes Kurhaus und gute Geschäfte.
   Antonio: Und die Landschaft?
     Wie ist dort die Landschaft?

Die Landschaft ist wunderbar

15 Junge Frau: Ach, die Landschaft ist wunderbar!
            Es gibt hohe Berge.
     Antonio: Das ist schön.
     Junge Frau: Ja. Der Predigtstuhl zum Beispiel.
            Das ist ein sehr hoher Berg.
20 Antonio: Wie ist das Wetter dort?
     Junge Frau: Meistens schön.
            Es gibt viel Schnee im Winter.
     Antonio: Und im Sommer?
     Junge Frau: Im Sommer regnet es manchmal.
25   Leider.

Information

(a) Notes on Dialogue 1

Alte Pinakothek   This is a famous art gallery in Munich
                                          containing a very important collection

of oil paintings from all over the world.

| 6 | Akzent | Most Germans speak with a regional accent. It is fairly easy to hear whether somebody comes from northern Germany or Bavaria for instance. The practised ear can identify quite easily the different regions of Germany just by listening to a few sentences. This regional accent does not, however, provide any information about social class. |

| 11 | In der Nähe von | This expression means 'near'. You can think of it as an abbreviated form of 'in the neighbourhood of'. |

| 12 | Hamburg und Lübeck | Hamburg is Germany's most important port. It stands on the river Elbe, with access to the North Sea. Lübeck is about 35 miles away, standing just back from the Baltic Sea. Hamburg is an independent city state in the German Federation. |

| 15 | Verwandtschaft | This is a very general word which stands for any form of blood relationship. |

| 18 | Er kommt | Remember that German, like English, can use the present tense with an expression of future time, to indicate the future. |

(b) Notes on Dialogue 2

| Oktoberfest | This is a festival which attracts many tourists from all over Germany and abroad. It takes place on a large area of ground, specially reserved for this and other festivals. The attractions include a funfair, with lots of roundabouts, shooting booths, and stalls selling food and drink. The centre-piece, however, consists of the large tents ('Bierzelte') where brass bands play and where litre tankards of beer ('Biersteine') are served by waitresses who manage to carry five in each hand. |

Dirndl	This is a traditional costume still frequently worn in the southern part of Bavaria and in Austria. It has a fitted bodice and a full skirt, with an apron over the skirt.
3 Münchenerin	This is the feminine form of 'Münchener' and means somebody who lives in Munich.
4 Bad Reichenhall	This is a well-known spa in the south-eastern tip of Germany, on the frontier with Austria.
12 Kurhaus	This is where guests go to take the waters: the pump room.
18 Der Predigtstuhl	This is a mountain just to the south of Bad Reichenhall which reaches the height of 1617 metres.

(c) Word list

Here is a list of the most important words in the dialogues. You should learn them by heart. They are given here in the order in which they occur in the chapter.

nur	just/only
sagen	to say
sehr	very
ele**gant**	elegant
das Kleid (-er)	dress
nett	nice
norddeutsch	North German
der Ak**zent** (-e)	accent
wo?	where?
weit	far
von	from
zwischen	between
die **Land**schaft (-en)	countryside
dort	there
groß	large
der See (-n)	lake
schön	beautiful
die **Kir**che (-n)	church
noch	still
die Ver**wandt**schaft	relations
der **Bru**der (⸚)	brother
wohnen	to live

die **El**tern (plural only)	parents
die **Wo**che (-n)	week
be**gei**stert	enthusiastic
der **Ski**läufer (-)	skier
der Schnee	snow
der **Win**ter	winter
es **reg**net	it is raining
viel	much
Prost!	Cheers!
aber	but
jetzt	now
sehen	to see
gut	good
das **Ge**schäft (-e)	shop; business
der Berg (-e)	mountain
das **Wet**ter	weather
meistens	usually
der **Som**mer	summer
manchmal	sometimes
leider	unfortunately

(d) Some phrases

Ent**schuldi**gen Sie	Excuse me; I beg your pardon
Das ist sehr nett von **Ih**nen	That is very nice of you
Nicht weit von	Not far from
In der **Näh**e von	Near
Es gibt	There is; there are
Bei meinen **El**tern	With my parents
Was gibt es dort zu **seh**en?	What is there to see there?
Zum **Bei**spiel	For example

(e) Further useful vocabulary

These words occur later in the chapter. You will find it helpful to learn them too.

der Brief (-e)	letter
der Kuß (**Küss**e)	kiss
das **Ge**schenk (-e)	present
die **Fahr**karte (-n)	ticket (for travel)
der **Schlüss**el (-)	key
mit	with
zu	to
der **Blei**stift(-e)	pencil
die **Halt**estelle(-n)	stop (for buses or trams)
süddeutsch	South German

Structural explanations

(a) Structures to learn

(i) How to ask where a place is

Wo ist { Mölln / Bad Reichenhall / Zirndorf } ?   Where is { Mölln / Bad Reichenhall? / Zirndorf }

(ii) How to say that one place is near another place

{ Mölln / Bad Reichenhall / Zirndorf } ist { nicht weit von / in der Nähe von / bei } { Hamburg / Salzburg / Nürnberg }

{ Mölln / Bad Reichenhall / Zirndorf } is { not far from / near / near } { Hamburg / Salzburg / Nuremburg }

(iii) How to ask for information about a place

Wie ist die Landschaft dort?   What is the countryside like there?
Was gibt es dort zu sehen?   What is there to see there?

(iv) How to describe a place

Es gibt { eine sehr schöne Kirche / einen großen See / ein schönes Kurhaus / gute Geschäfte }

a very beautiful church
a large lake
a fine Kurhaus
good shops

(v) How to ask what the weather is like

Wie ist das Wetter?

(vi) How to describe the weather

(Das Wetter ist) meistens schön   The weather is usually nice

{ Im Winter / Im Sommer } regnet es { sehr viel / manchmal }

N.B. The subject of this sentence is 'es'. However, the sentence begins with the phrase: 'Im Winter/Im Sommer' for emphasis, and the subject comes after the verb.

{ In winter / In summer } it rains { a lot / sometimes }

Es gibt { nicht viel / viel } { Schnee }   (im Winter)

$$\text{There is} \quad \left\{ \begin{array}{l} \text{not much} \\ \text{a lot of} \end{array} \right\} \quad \text{snow} \qquad \text{(in winter)}$$

(b) Grammar

(i) Seasons

You will find a list of expressions about the seasons of the year in the Grammatical Summary.

(ii) Months

There is a list of the months there too.

(iii) The indirect object

Do you remember how we defined the direct object of a verb in Chapter 5, with the story of the dog biting the postman? Now we have to turn our attention to another concept called the *indirect object*.

Let us imagine that the postman is determined to make friends with the dog. Consider the sentence: *The postman gives the dog a bone*. We know that *the postman* does the giving, and that phrase is consequently the subject of the sentence. The thing that is given is *a bone*, and that is therefore the direct object of the sentence.

The person, or thing, to whom or for whom things are given, bought, sent, taken, etc. – in other words, the recipients – are *indirect objects*. Here are some examples:

I bought (my wife) some flowers
She sent (the man) a letter
We took (him) some chocolate
He threw (her) a kiss
She gave (the car) a good kick

Note that these sentences still make good sense if the *indirect object*, in brackets, is deleted. This would *not* be the case if the *direct objects* were to be deleted.

In German, the *indirect object* is marked or signalled by special forms of the definite and indefinite articles, the personal pronouns and possessive adjectives. They are said to be in the '*dative case*'.

(iv) Definite articles in the dative case

Er gibt <u>dem Mann</u> den Brief	He gives the man the letter (He gives the letter to the man)
Er gibt <u>der Frau</u> das Geld	He gives the woman the money (He gives the money to the woman)
Er gibt <u>dem Mädchen</u> (das Mädchen) einen Kuß	He gives the girl a kiss (He gives a kiss to the girl)

N.B. The gender of the word 'Mädchen' is neuter in German, despite its meaning.

> Er gibt <u>den Kindern</u> Geschenke   He gives the children presents
>   (He gives presents to the children)

We can summarise the rule for *definite articles* in the *dative case*, thus:

	Masc.	**Fem.**	**Neut.**	**Plur.**	(all genders)
dative	dem	der	dem	den	

(v) Indefinite articles and possessive adjectives in the dative case

> Er gibt <u>seinem Vater</u> den Brief   He gives his father the letter
>   (He gives the letter to his father)
> Er gibt <u>seiner Frau</u> das Geld   He gives his wife the money
>   (He gives the money to his wife)
> Er gibt <u>einem Mädchen</u> seinen   He gives a girl his coat
>   Mantel   (He gives his coat to a girl)
> Er gibt <u>ihren Kindern</u>   He gives her children presents
>   Geschenke   (He gives presents to her children)

We can summarise the rule for *indefinite articles* and *possessive adjectives* in the *dative case*, thus:

		Masc.	**Fem.**	**Neut.**	**Plur.**
dative	(a, an)	einem	einer	einem	–
	(not a)	keinem	keiner	keinem	keinen
	(my)	meinem	meiner	meinem	meinen
	(his/its)	seinem	seiner	seinem	seinen
	(her/its)	ihrem	ihrer	ihrem	ihren
	(our)	unserem	unserer	unserem	unseren
	(your)	Ihrem	Ihrer	Ihrem	Ihren

You will find a full list of possessive adjectives in the dative case in the Grammatical Summary.

(vi) Key letters for the dative case

For definite and indefinite articles, as well as for possessive adjectives, the key letters signalling the dative case are as follows:

	Masc.	**Fem.**	**Neut.**	**Plur.**
dative	m	r	m	n

(vii) Personal pronouns

> Er gibt mir einen Brief   He gives me a letter
> Er gibt ihm einen Mantel   He gives him a coat
> Er gibt ihr das Geld   He gives her the money
> Er gibt uns unsere Fahrkarten   He gives us our tickets
> Er gibt Ihnen den Schlüssel   He gives you the key

We can summarise the rule for *personal pronouns* in the *dative case*, thus:

Nominative	Dative
ich	mir
er	ihm
sie	ihr
wir	uns
Sie	Ihnen (*polite form*)

Remember that the polite form has a capital letter. You will find a complete list of personal pronouns in the dative case in the Grammatical Summary.

(viii) Prepositions with the dative case

Certain *prepositions* accompany the *dative case*. Here are some example sentences from the dialogues in this chapter.

> Das ist sehr nett von Ihnen
> Mein Bruder wohnt bei meinen Eltern
> Zum (zu dem) Beispiel

The commonest of the prepositions which always accompany the dative case are: 'mit' (with), 'von' (from, of) and 'zu' '(to, at).

Er fährt mit einem Freund nach Deutschland	mit einem Freund: with a friend
Er schreibt mit dem Bleistift	mit dem Bleistift: with the pencil
Sie kommt mit mir	mit mir: with me
Er kommt von meinem Haus	von meinem Haus: from my house
Er wohnt nicht weit von dem Berg	nicht weit von dem Berg: not far from the mountain
Ich spreche von ihm	von ihm: of him
Er geht zu meiner Frau	zu meiner Frau: to my wife
Sie geht zur (zu der) Haltestelle	zur Haltestelle: to the bus stop

In the Grammatical Summary you will find a list of *prepositions* which always accompany the *dative case*.

N.B. When a noun occurs in the dative case in the plural, it always ends in '-n'.

Exercises

A

Exercise 1

Say where the following towns are.

Example: Wo ist Fürth?
> Nicht weit von Nürnberg.

1   Wo ist Oldenburg?

2   Wo ist Braunschweig?

3   Wo ist Paderborn?

4   Wo ist Limburg?

5   Wo ist Wiesbaden?

6   Wo ist Heidelberg?

7   Wo ist Cadolzburg?

8   Wo ist Warnemünde?

9   Wo ist Potsdam?

10 Wo ist Weimar?

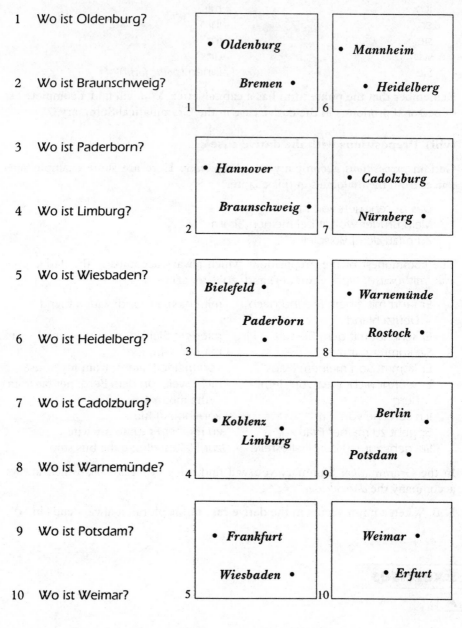

Exercise 2

Say where the following places are.

Example: Wo ist Lübeck?
        Lübeck ist in Norddeutschland.

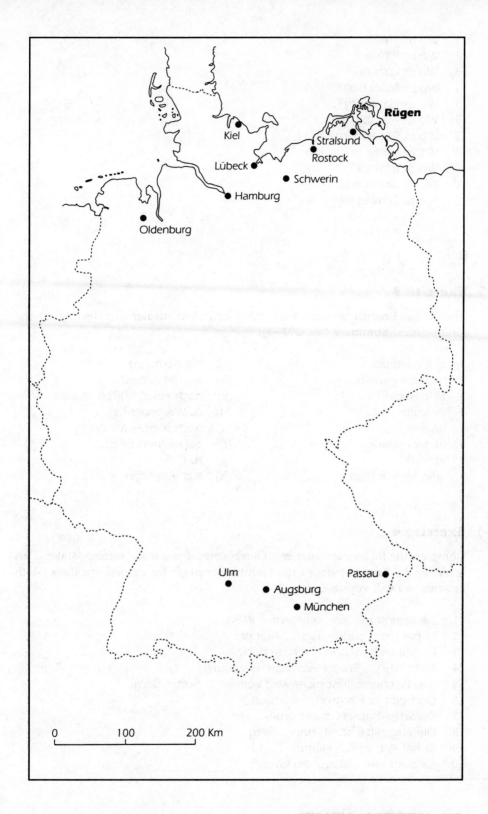

1 Wo ist Kiel?
2 Wo ist Passau?
3 Wo ist Lübeck?
4 Wo ist München?
5 Wo ist Hamburg?
6 Wo ist Augsburg?
7 Wo ist Oldenburg?
8 Wo ist Ulm?
9 Wo ist Rostock?
10 Wo ist Stralsund?
11 Wo ist Schwerin?

B

Exercise 3

Match the English phrases with the German equivalents, referring to the Grammatical Summary (pp. 291–4):

1	at Christmas	(a)	mit dem Zug
2	with my parents	(b)	bei der Arbeit
3	by mistake	(c)	nach einer halben Stunde
4	by train	(d)	zu Weihnachten
5	on foot	(e)	nach meiner Meinung
6	in my opinion	(f)	bei meinen Eltern
7	at work	(g)	zu Fuß
8	after half an hour	(h)	aus Versehen

Exercise 4

Complete the following sentences. Don't worry if you make some mistake. This is one of the hardest parts of the German language for English speakers. With practice you will improve.

1 Sie kommt mit ein... elegant... Kleid.
2 Er hat ein... süddeutsch... Akzent.
3 Es gibt ein... schön... Kirche dort.
4 Mein klein... Bruder wohnt in Hamburg.
5 Bad Reichenhall ist nicht weit von ein... hoh... Berg.
6 Dort gibt es ein groß... Kurhaus.
7 Bei Schaffhausen ist ein groß... See.
8 Die Zugspitze ist ein hoh... Berg.
9 Er hat ein weiß... Hemd.
10 Sie trägt ein... blau... Pullover.

Exercise 5   In der Wirtschaft: Starting a conversation in a pub

Don't forget to read the questions below before listening to this dialogue, and remember: you do not have to understand every word, just listen for the information you need. You will need the word 'die Insel' (island).

1   What sort of beer does the customer order?
2   Where does the customer come from?
3   He says he works in the docks. What is the German word for docks?
    Listen carefully to what he says.
    Ich arbeite auf einer _____ .
4   When the barmaid is asked if she knows Rostock she says no, but she knows
    Mecklenburg-Vorpommern. Which line does she give as her reason?
    (a)   Ich war letztes Jahr dort im Süden auf Urlaub.
    (b)   Ich bin nächstes Jahr dort im Norden auf Urlaub.
    (c)   Ich war letztes Jahr dort im Norden auf Urlaub.
5   Which part did she visit?
6   Can you gather what she says she is going to do right at the end?

⑩ Revision tests

In this chapter you will have an opportunity to consolidate the language you have learned in the previous nine chapters. Each test indicates whereabouts in the earlier part of the book you ought to search if you have forgotten a particular point.

Test 1   How to introduce somebody (Chapter 1)

You live in an old-fashioned family, where all your brothers and your cousins and your aunts live in the same house. You bring a colleague home for a meal and introduce all the members of the family to him one by one. There are some words in this exercise, and so you ought to consult the pronunciation key before you do it.

> First introduce your wife
> Then your father – Vater (*m*)
> Then your mother – Mutter (*f*)
> Then your son – Sohn (*m*)
> Then your daughter – Tochter (*f*)
> Then your uncle – Onkel (*m*)
> Then your aunt – Tante (*f*)

Test 2   Possessive adjectives (Chapter 1)

Like everybody else, you are proud of your own house and inquisitive about other people's houses. Together with your husband (or wife), you take your guest round the house and show off its special features.

> You show the guests your garden – Garten (*m*)
> Your kitchen – Küche (*f*)
> Your bedroom – Schlafzimmer (*n*)
> Your garage – Garage (*f*)

Your dog – Hund (*m*)
Your cat – Katze (*f*)

Test 3   Greetings (Chapter 1)

1   What would you say to somebody you met at 8 o'clock in the morning?
2   What would you say to somebody who had just poured you out a drink?
3   What would you say if the telephone rang while you were talking to somebody?
4   What would you say to your son if he was just going off on holiday?
5   What would you say if your boss asked you out to dinner and you spilt your wine all over the best tablecloth?
6   What would you say as you left a friend who was ill in hospital?
7   What would you say to your husband just before you turned the light out at night?
8   What would you say if you stood on somebody's toe?
9   What would you say if you arrived late at the theatre, and had to reach your seat in the middle of the row after the play had started?
10 What would you say to your girlfriend as you prepared to tackle a juicy steak at a restaurant?

Test 4   Staying in hotels (Chapter 3)

Here is a model letter, written to confirm a hotel booking made by telephone.

An das Hotel Atlantik   Bristol
An der Alster   den 2. April

D - 20099 Hamburg

Sehr geehrte Damen und Herren,
hiermit bestätige ich meine Reservierung für (ein Einzelzimmer mit Dusche) für die Zeit vom (27. Juni) bis zum (30. Juni) einschließlich.

Mit freundlichen Grüßen

Notes:
1   The address of the hotel you are writing to goes in the top left-hand corner of the writing paper. Note that a blank line is inserted before the name of the town, together with its postal code. The name of the street comes before.
2   When writing your own address on writing paper you only write the name of the town. You generally write your address on the back of the envelope.
3   The date is written as shown. The number is always followed by a full stop.

4 When writing to a hotel, the greeting is as shown. The first word after the comma has a small letter (unless it is a noun or a formal pronoun).
5 The standard greeting at the end of a formal letter is 'Mit freundlichen Grüßen'.

Translations of key terms in the model letter:

Sehr geehrte Damen und Herren	Dear Sir /Madam
Hiermit bestätige ich ...	This is to confirm
Einschließlich	Inclusive
Mit freundlichen Grüßen	Yours faithfully /sincerely

Those parts of the letter in brackets can be changed to fit in with your particular requirements. Practise writing the following letters, each of which is intended to confirm a hotel booking made earlier by telephone.

The letter D in the address indicates a town in Germany (D is Deutschland). The letter A in the address indicates Austria.

1 Hotel Sonnenhof
   Wagnerstraße 10
   D – 94481 Grafenau

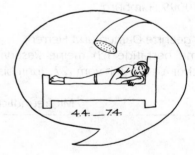

2 Hotel Bergland
   Unterstraße 4

   A – 6416 Obsteig
   Tirol

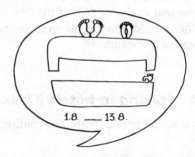

3 Hotel Wachtelhof
  Mittelstraße 1

  A – 5761 Hinterthal

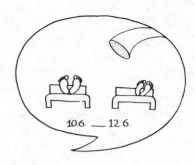

4 Sporthotel Fellhoist
  Teichstraße 12

  D – 23775 Großenbrode

5 Frühstückspension „Olga"
  Hauptstraße 91

  A – 5600 St. Johann
  Salzburger Land

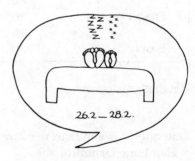

Test 5   Greetings and making hotel bookings (Chapter 3)

You are a tourist enquiring in a hotel about accommodation. You take part in a conversation with the receptionist on your recording. You will be prompted in English when it's your turn to speak. You will be given suggested responses after the pauses.

Test 6　Asking the times of departure and arrival of trains
(Chapter 4)

HAMBURG – FRANKFURT – BASEL		
		IC
		175
Hamburg–Altona	ab	9.32
Hamburg–Dammtor	an	9.38
	ab	9.39
Hamburg Hbf	an	9.44
	ab	9.45
Hamburg–Harburg	an	9.59
	ab	10.00
Hannover	an	11.10
	ab	11.14
Göttingen	an	12.09
	ab	12.10
Fulda	an	13.36
	ab	13.37
Frankfurt (M)	an	14.36
	ab	14.42
Mannheim	an	15.26
	ab	15.34
Karlsruhe	an	16.02
	ab	16.03
Freiburg	an	17.03
	ab	17.04
Basel	an	17.46

Look at these dialogues:

(a)

> Reisender:　Wann fährt der Zug nach
>   Hamburg–Dammtor ab?
> Angestellte:　Er fährt um 9 Uhr 32 ab.
> Reisender:　Wann kommt er in Hamburg–Dammtor an?
> Angestellte:　Er kommt um 9 Uhr 38 an.
> Reisender:　Muß ich umsteigen?
> Angestellte:　Nein, der Zug fährt direkt.

(b)

> Reisender:　Wann fährt der Zug nach Hamburg Hbf (Hauptbahnhof) ab?
> Angestellte:　Er fährt um 9 Uhr 39 ab.
> Reisender:　Wann kommt er in Hamburg Hbf an?
> Angestellte:　Er kommt um 9 Uhr 44 an.

Reisender: Muß ich umsteigen?
Angestellte: Nein, der Zug fährt direkt.

Make up dialogues similar to these. If you are studying with a partner, take it in turns to ask the questions.

This is where you are:

1 Hamburg Hbf
2 Hannover
3 Göttingen
4 Mannheim
5 Fulda
6 Freiburg
7 Frankfurt
8 Hamburg–Harburg
9 Hannover
10 Karlsruhe

This is where you want to go:

Freiburg
Fulda
Basel
Freiburg
Karlsruhe
Basel
Freiburg
Frankfurt
Frankfurt
Basel

Test 7   Verbs with separable affixes (Chapter 4)

Put into German

1 Grandma rings up on Saturday.
2 Ingrid goes out on Tuesday.
3 The children tidy up the shop.
4 Mother clears up the toys.
5 Peter washes up the plates.
6 Inge buys provisions.
7 Helmut washes up on Sunday.
8 The boss gives up his work.
9 Mary (Maria) closes the shop.
10 Grandma goes out on Saturday.

Test 8   Finding your way by bus and tram (Chapter 5)

Can you complete the following dialogue? If you are working with a partner, take it in turns to play the parts.

Dialogue A

Müller: ......
Meier: Ja, bitte?
Müller: ......
Meier: Nach Opladen?
  Nein, dieser Bus fährt nach Ludwigshafen.
Müller: ......
Meier: Sie brauchen die Nummer 14.

Dialogue B

Schmidt: ......
Schüth: Ja. Kann ich Ihnen helfen?
Schmidt: ......
Schüth: Nein, nicht zum Schauspielhaus.
   Sie fährt zum Hofgarten.
Schmidt: ......
Schüth: Sie brauchen die Nummer 1.
   Sie fährt zum Schauspielhaus.
Schmidt: ......

Test 9   The definite article (Chapter 5)

Complete the following sentences:

1   ... Professor heißt Doktor Schmidt.
2   Wo ist ... Tasse?
3   Hier ist ... Buch.
4   ... Kaffee ist heiß.
5   Hier ist ... Frau.
6   ... Auto fährt schnell.
7   ... Mann heißt Herr Müller.
8   ... Einladung kommt heute.
9   ... Zimmer ist groß.
10 ... Stadt ist klein.

Test 10   Describing symptoms of illness (Chapter 6)

Look carefully at the doctor's part of the following dialogue. Then make up the patient's role and speak it aloud. Read aloud the doctor's part (if you are working with a partner, take it in turns to play the role of the doctor and the patient).

Arzt	**Patient**
1 Guten Tag.	
	2 ......
3 Was fehlt Ihnen denn?	
	4 ......
5 Ihr Bein? Ist es ein leichter Schmerz?	
	6 ......
7 Ach so, stechend. Seit wann tut es weh?	
	8 ......
9 So, so. Drei Tage schon. Kein Fußball für Sie.	10 ......

Test 11 Describing symptoms of illness (Chapter 6)

Poor Sepp Steinbauer has fallen off his bicycle while on his way to a football match. He wanted to see 1.FC Nürnberg versus Bayern München. He's been taken to hospital where the staff nurse is trying to find out how badly he's hurt. From his answers it seems he is only just alive. You play the part of Sepp.

Note: Don't try to make up sentences like the nurse's. Just use her questions as clues to the answers. Example:

Schwester: Tut der Kopf weh?
Sepp: Ja, mein Kopf tut weh.
Schwester: Und das Bein?
Sepp: Ja, mein Bein tut weh.

Now begin:

Schwester: Tut der Kopf weh?
Schwester: Und das Bein?
Schwester: Wie geht's Ihrem Knie?
Schwester: Was ist mit dem Rücken?
Schwester: Tut es am Hals weh?
Schwester: Haben Sie Schmerzen am Ellbogen?
Schwester: Ist Ihr Ohr wund?
Schwester: Und die Nase?
Schwester: Die Schulter ist verletzt, glaube ich.
Schwester: O, und der Finger auch.

Test 12 Finding exactly what you want when shopping
(Chapter 7)

You are in Munich in the Kaufhaus Oberpollinger. This time you are a difficult customer to please.

1 Verkäuferin: Hier habe ich ein schönes Hemd.
   (You want something in the same material, but blue.)
2 Verkäuferin: Das ist ein schöner Rock.
   (You want something like this, but a size smaller.)
3 Verkäuferin: Dieser Anzug ist sehr schön.
   (You want the same colour, but in wool.)
4 Verkäuferin: Diese Schuhe sind sehr elegant.
   (You want this colour a size larger.)
5 Verkäuferin: Hier habe ich ein Hemd aus Seide.
   (You want the same material, but in light blue.)
6 Verkäuferin: Das ist ein schöner Regenmantel.
   (You want the same sort of thing in cotton.)
7 Verkäuferin: Der Pullover hier ist nicht teuer.
   (You want the same colour in polyester.)

8 Verkäuferin: Ein sehr elegantes Nachthemd.
(You want the same sort of thing in black.)

9 Verkäuferin: Mm, die Jacke ist aber schön.
(You want the same sort of thing in velvet.)

10 Verkäuferin: Nehmen Sie dieses Hemd?
(You want the same size in white.)

 Test 13 Describing the weather (Chapter 9)

Expressions

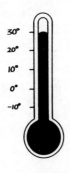

Es ist sehr warm!

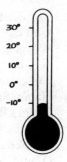

Es ist sehr kalt!

Es gibt viel Schnee.

Es regnet.

Example: Using the symbols, describe the climate in Munich

Sommer

Winter

München

Wie ist das Wetter in München?
A: Es ist sehr heiß im Sommer.
    Und es gibt viel Schnee im Winter.

Sommer   Winter

1   Wie ist das Wetter in Hamburg?

2   Wie ist das Wetter in Bad Reichenhall?

3 Wie ist das Wetter in London?

4 Wie ist das Wetter in Nürnberg?

5 Wie ist das Wetter in Kiel?

 Test 14 An der Hotelrezeption: Taking a room in a hotel

Don't forget to read the questions below before listening to this dialogue, and remember: you do not have to understand every word, just listen for the information you need.

1 In which town is the tourist?
2 How long does she want to stay?

3   What sort of room does she want?
4   What is the price?
5   What does the price include?
6   Which room does she have?
7   What does the receptionist point out to the tourist right at the end?

11 Ein Tisch für zwei

Eating out

Dialogues

Dialogue 1

Fritz is telephoning the restaurant, in order to reserve a table for himself and Elke.

1 Besitzer: Restaurant das Blaue Haus.
          Guten Tag.
    Fritz: Guten Tag.
       Ich möchte einen Tisch für heute abend.
5 Besitzer: Für wie viele Personen?
    Fritz: Für zwei.
    Besitzer: Um wieviel Uhr, bitte?
    Fritz: Um acht Uhr.
    Besitzer: Ja, um acht Uhr.
10   Ich habe einen Tisch um acht Uhr.
    Fritz: Sehr gut.
    Besitzer: Auf welchen Namen, bitte?
    Fritz: Löb. L - O - Umlaut - B.
    Besitzer: Herr Löb.
15   Ist in Ordnung, Herr Löb.
    Fritz: Auf Wiederhören!
    Besitzer: Auf Wiederhören!
    (Fritz and Elke have arrived at the restaurant)
    Fritz: Guten Abend!
    Empfang: Guten Abend!
20 Fritz: Ich habe einen Tisch reserviert.
    Empfang: Für wie viele Personen?
    Fritz: Für zwei Personen.
    Empfang: Auf welchen Namen, bitte?
    Fritz: Löb.

Restaurant das Blaue Haus

Vorspeisen und Salate
- Gulaschsuppe DM 12,-
- Zwiebelsuppe DM 12,-
- Melone mit Schinken DM 15,-
- Käsesalat mit Brot DM 15,-
- Wurstsalat mit Brot DM 15,-

Hauptgerichte
- Gemischtes vom Grill (verschiedene Fleischsorten, Erbsen, Pommes frites) DM 25,-
- Texas Steak (mit Pommes frites oder Bratkartoffeln und Salat) DM 30,-
- Gebratene Kutterscholle (mit Bratkartoffeln und Salat) DM 30,-

Nachspeisen
- Eis (Vanille, Schokolade, Pfefferminz, Zitrone) DM 7,-

25 Empfang: Ach ja.
Herr Löb.
Kommen Sie, bitte.

Dialogue 2

Fritz and Elke are considering the menu.

  1 Fritz: Möchten Sie eine Vorspeise?
      Elke: Ich möchte eine Suppe – eine Zwiebelsuppe.
      Fritz: Und dann?
      Elke: Ein Texas Steak.
  5   Und Sie?
      Was möchten Sie?
      Fritz: Ich glaube, daß ich auch eine Suppe möchte – eine Gulaschsuppe.
      Und dann ... auch ein Texas Steak.
      Kellner: Haben Sie gewählt?
10 Fritz: Einmal Zwiebelsuppe.
      Einmal Gulaschsuppe.
      Kellner: Einmal Zwiebelsuppe.
      Einmal Gulaschsuppe.

Fritz: Und dann – zweimal Texas Steak.
15 Elke: Ohne Pommes frites, bitte.
Kellner: Zweimal Texas Steak.
Einmal mit Pommes frites.
Einmal ohne.
Jawohl.
20 Fritz: Möchten Sie etwas trinken?
Elke: Ja, ich möchte bitte ein Viertel Rotwein.
Fritz: Zwei Viertel Rotwein, bitte.
Kellner: Zwei Viertel Rotwein.
Danke schön.

Information

(a) Notes on Dialogue 1

16 Auf Wiederhören!

Remember that this is a special greeting for finishing a telephone conversation.

(b) Notes on Dialogue 2

1 Vorspeise

This word can mean either 'a starter' or 'hors d'oeuvre'.

2 eine Suppe

Note that German uses '*eine* Suppe' where in English we say '*some* soup'.

7 daß ich auch eine Suppe möchte

You will find a brief discussion of word order in subordinate clauses in the Grammatical Summary on page 279.

10 Einmal

Literally, this word means 'once'. Apart from the number of train tickets it can also indicate how many portions or dishes you want. 'Zweimal' – 'two (portions)', i.e. one for each person.

21 Viertel

This refers to a quarter of a litre. The wine would be served in a small carafe.

(c) Word list

der Besitzer (-)   owner
das Restaurant (-s)   restaurant
der Tisch (-e)   table

heute	today
heute abend	this evening
wie viele?	how many?
die Person (-en)	person
reservieren	to reserve
die Vorspeise (-n)	hors d'oeuvre
die Suppe (-n)	soup
die Zwiebelsuppe (-n)	onion soup
das Steak (-s)	steak
dann	then
glauben	to believe
auch	also, too
die Gulaschsuppe (-n)	goulash soup
ohne	without
die Pommes frites	chips
etwas	something
trinken	to drink
das Viertel (-)	quarter
der Rotwein (-e)	red wine

(d) Some phrases

Um wieviel Uhr?	At what time?
Auf welchen Namen?	What name?
Auf Wiederhören	Goodbye (phone)
Was möchten Sie?	What would you like?

(e) Further useful vocabulary

die Speisekarte (-n)	menu
die Weinkarte (-n)	wine list
das Wasser	water
essen (ißt)	to eat
zahlen	to pay
die Rechnung (-en)	bill
spät	late
wo?	where?
welch-?	which?
wer?	who?
warum?	why?
was?	what?
wohin?	where (to)?
was für?	what sort of?
wie?	how?
schmecken	to taste
heute nachmittag	this afternoon
heute morgen	this morning
morgen	tomorrow
morgen abend	tomorrow evening
morgen nachmittag	tomorrow afternoon

morgen früh	tomorrow morning
gestern	yesterday
gestern **ab**end	yesterday evening
gestern **nach**mittag	yesterday afternoon
gestern **mor**gen	yesterday morning
die **Wo**che (-n)	week
das Jahr (-e)	year
der **Mo**nat (-e)	month
der Tag (-e)	day
die Min**u**te (-n)	minute
die **Stun**de (-n)	hour
vor	ago
dies-	this
nächst-	next
letzt-	last

(f) *Menu vocabulary*

gar**niert**	dressed
ge**back**en	baked
ge**brat**en	fried
ge**füllt**	stuffed
ge**grillt**	grilled
ge**kocht**	boiled
ge**räuch**ert	smoked
in **Essig**	in vinegar
mit **Sahn**e	creamed
nach **Müll**erin Art	meunière
poch**iert**	poached
der **Apfelkuch**en	apple pie
der **Apfelsaft**	apple juice
das be**leg**te Brot	sandwich
das Bier	beer
die **Bock**wurst	thick, boiled sausage
die **Bow**le	cold punch
das **Brat**hähnchen	roast chicken
Bratkart**off**eln	fried potatoes
die **Brat**wurst	fried pork sausage
das **Bröt**chen	bread roll
das ge**koch**te Ei	boiled egg
das **Rühr**ei	scrambled egg
Spiegel**eier**	fried eggs
der **Eis**becher	ice-cream sundae
das **Eis**bein	pork shank in jelly
die **Ent**e	duck
der Fisch	fish
das Fleisch	meat
die For**ell**e	trout
die **Frank**furter	hotdog sausage
das **Früh**stück	breakfast

das Geflügel	poultry
das Gemüse	vegetables
Getränke	beverages
das Gulasch	goulash
das Hackfleisch	minced meat
das Hähnchen	chicken
die Hühnersuppe	chicken soup
der Hummer	lobster
der Kaffee	coffee
das Kalbfleisch	veal
die Kalbshaxe	leg of veal
das Kalbsschnitzel	veal escalope
die Kartoffel	potato
Salzkartoffeln	boiled potatoes
der Käse	cheese
der Kuchen	cake, tart or flan
der Lachs	salmon
die Leber	liver
der Leberkäs	sliced meat loaf
der Leberknödel	liver dumplings
das Matjesfilet	herring fillet
die Milch	milk
das Mineralwasser	mineral water
die Nachspeise	pudding, dessert or sweet
das Obst	fruit
das Omelett	omelette
der Pfannkuchen	pancake
das Pfeffersteak	steak spiced with pepper
die Portion	portion
das Ragout	ragout
der Rehbraten	roast venison
das Rindfleisch	beef
der Rollmops	rollmop herring
der Saft	juice
die Sahne	cream
der Salat	salad
der grüne Salat	green salad
der Kartoffelsalat	potato salad
das Salz	salt
das Sauerkraut	sauerkraut
der Schinken	ham
die Schlagsahne	whipped cream
der Schnaps	schnapps
das Schnitzel	escalope
das Schweinefleisch	pork
das Schweineschnitzel	pork escalope
die Schweinshaxe	leg of pork
der Spargel	asparagus
die Speisekarte	menu
die Suppe	soup
die Tagessuppe	soup of the day

der Tee	tea
eine **Tass**e Tee	a cup of tea
ein **Känn**chen Tee	a pot of tea
die To**maten**suppe	tomato soup
die **Tort**e	gateau
das **Vier**tel	quarter of a litre
der Wein	wine
der **Wein**brand	brandy
das **Wien**er **Schnit**zel	veal escalope with breadcrumbs
die Wurst	sausage
der **Zucke**r	sugar
die **Zwie**bel	onion

Structural explanations

(a) *Structures to learn*

(i) How to ask if there is a table

Haben Sie einen Tisch	Have you got a table
frei	free
für zwei ?	for two ?
für vier	for four

(ii) How to call the waiter or waitress

Herr Ober!	Waiter!

The practice of calling the waitress 'Fräulein' is now losing favour. It's better to catch her eye and say what you want, e.g. 'Ich möchte bestellen' (I'd like to order).

(iii) How to ask for the menu or the wine list

Die Speisekarte, bitte!	The menu, please
Die Weinkarte, bitte!	The wine list, please
Ich möchte	I'd like to see the
die Weinkarte $\Big\}$ sehen	wine list
die Speisekarte	menu

(iv) How to ask someone what they would like to eat or drink

Was möchten Sie?	What would you like?

Ich möchte $\Big\}$
Möchten Sie

einen Cognac
eine Vorspeise   (?)
ein Mineralwasser

I'd like $\Big\}$
Would you like

a Cognac
a starter   (?)
a mineral water

Note the form of 'ein'.

Möchten Sie/Ich möchte
    etwas essen/etwas trinken
	Would you like/I'd like something to
	    eat/something to drink

(v) How to order

Einmal Zweimal Dreimal	} { Texas Steak Gulaschsuppe	One Two Three	} { Texas steak(s) goulash soup(s)

N.B. 'Einmal', 'zweimal', etc., indicate the number of portions required, corresponding to the number of people who require them. In German, the noun remains in the singular after 'zweimal', 'dreimal', etc.

(vi) How to ask for the bill

(Ich möchte) zahlen, bitte
(Ich möchte) die Rechnung, bitte

(vii) How to ask the time

Wieviel Uhr ist es? Wie spät ist es?	What time is it?
Wann ...? Um wieviel Uhr ...? }	When? At what time?

(viii) Expressions of time

● *The hours*

Es ist = It is   Um = At

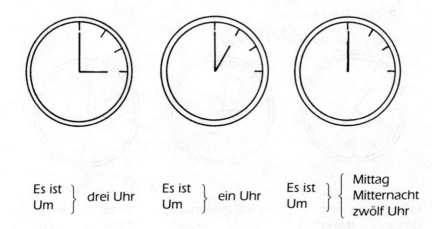

Es ist Um }	drei Uhr	Es ist Um }	ein Uhr	Es ist Um } {	Mittag Mitternacht zwölf Uhr

- *Time past the hour*

Es ist } fünf (Minuten)
Um   }   nach neun

Es ist } fünfundzwanzig (Minuten)
Um   }   nach sechs

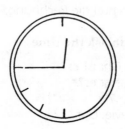

Es ist } Viertel nach
Um   }   sechs

Es ist } halb zehn
Um   }

N.B.! 'Half' *towards* the next hour.

- *Time to the hour*

Es ist } zwanzig
Um   }   (Minuten)
          vor elf

Es ist } Viertel vor
Um   }   zwölf

Es ist } zehn vor
Um   }   zwölf

(b) Grammar

(i) Simple questions

1	Möchten Sie eine Vorspeise? Möchten Sie etwas trinken?	The verb comes first
2	Was möchten Sie? Was möchten Sie trinken?	The sentence begins with a question word

(ii) Further question words, or interrogatives

Wo?	– Where?	Wo möchten Sie essen? Where would you like to eat?
Welcher? (m)	– Which?	Welcher Wein ist billiger? Which wine is cheaper?
Welche? (f)	– Which?	Welche Vorspeise ist besser? Which hors d'oeuvre is better?
Welches? (n)	– Which?	Welches Mineralwasser schmeckt gut mit Whisky? Which mineral water tastes good with whisky?
Wer?	– Who?	Wer ist im Restaurant? Who is in the restaurant?

N.B. 'false friend': don't confuse 'wer?' with 'wo?'

Warum?	– Why?	Warum trinken Sie Pils? Why are you drinking Pils?
Was?	– What?	Was trinken Sie? What are you drinking?
Wohin?	– Where (to)?	Wohin gehen Sie? Where are you going (to)?
Was für?	– What sort of?	Was für Bier trinken Sie? What sort of beer are you drinking?
Wie?	– How?	Wie kochen Sie Jägerschnitzel? How do you cook Jägerschnitzel?

(iii) How to say which day

heute	today
heute abend	this evening/tonight
heute nachmittag	this afternoon
heute morgen	this morning
morgen	tomorrow
morgen abend	tomorrow evening/night
morgen nachmittag	tomorrow afternoon
morgen früh	tomorrow morning

gestern	yesterday
gestern abend	yesterday evening/night
gestern nachmittag	yesterday afternoon
gestern morgen	yesterday morning

(iv) How to express relative time

diese nächste letzte	} Woche (f)	this next last	} week

dieses nächstes letztes	} Jahr (n)	this next last	} year

diesen nächsten letzten	} Monat (m)	this next last	} month

in drei	{ Tagen Wochen Monaten Jahren	in three	{ days weeks months years

vor drei	{ Tagen Wochen Monaten Jahren	three	{ days weeks months years } ago

in fünf	{ Minuten Stunden	in five	{ minutes hours

Exercises

A

Exercise 1

With reference to the menu on page 129, work out how you would order under the following conditions. (If you are working with a partner, take turns to play the part of the waiter.)

1 You are by yourself and want a quick meal; one meat dish will do. You want to spend as little as possible. Nothing to drink.
2 You are dining with an important friend and you can afford the best. Curiously, you both have exactly the same taste in food. You decide to have the lot: hors d'oeuvres, fish, meat, dessert, and, of course, your favourite Rhine wine.

RESTAURANT ZUM RITTER
SPEISEKARTE

VORSPEISEN

Krabbencocktail	8,00
Aal in Aspik	9,00
Austern (12)	14,00

SUPPEN

Hühnerbrühe mit Nudeln	6,00
Gulaschsuppe	6,50
Zwiebelsuppe	7,00

EIERSPEISEN

Rührei	6,50
Spiegeleier mit Schinken	7,00
Omelett – verschiedener Art	7,25

FISCHGERICHTE

Rollmops	9,50
Forelle, blau, mit grünem Salat, Salzkartoffeln	14,00
Seezungenfilet mit grünen Bohnen, Salzkartoffeln	16,50

FLEISCHGERICHTE

Eisbein mit Sauerkraut	9,20
'Texas' Steak mit Pommes frites und gemischtem Salat	15,80
Jägerschnitzel mit Pommes frites	16,00
Wiener Schnitzel mit Spiegelei, Salat, Röstkartoffeln	16,30
Zigeunerschnitzel mit Zwiebeln, Reis und grünem Salat	17,00

FÜR DEN KLEINEN APPETIT

Rührei mit Schinken	6,20
Paar Frankfurter mit Pommes frites	6,80

KÄSE

Emmentaler mit Butter, Brot	8,20
Käseplatte, Butter, Brot	10,60

NACHSPEISEN

Gemischtes Kompott	5,00
Eisbecher	5,00
Pfannkuchen	5,70
Ananas flambiert mit Kirschwasser	8,20

GETRÄNKE	Glas	Flasche		Glas	Flasche
Pils	4,50		Sekt		24,50
Export	4,75		Cognac	4,50	
Moselwein	6,00	16,00	Weinbrand	4,00	
Rheinwein	6,00	16,00	Apfelsaft	4,00	
Rotwein	6,00	16,00	Mineralwasser	3,50	

Tasse Kaffee oder Tee   4,10
Kännchen   6,50

UNSERE PREISE SIND ENDPREISE

---

3   You are taking the children out for their first meal in a restaurant. Peter can't stand eggs and Paula has an aversion to sausages. You have a weakness for trout yourself. You do like wine, but you want to set the children a good example.

4 You want to have a light lunch with a colleague. Ham and eggs for you and scrambled egg for her sound appealing. Afterwards, you could share a selection of different cheeses, perhaps, and a cup of coffee.

 ## Exercise 2

You decide to take two friends to a new restaurant in the old Bauhof. Listen to your recording and practise some of the things you will need to say. You will be prompted in English and left a pause to give the German expression, before hearing a model answer.

 B

 ## Exercise 3

Ask your guests if they want to have the same dish that you have chosen.

Example: Ich möchte eine Vorspeise.
Möchten Sie auch eine Vorspeise?
Ich möchte ein Mineralwasser.
Möchten Sie auch ein Mineralwasser?

1 Ich möchte eine Vorspeise.
2 Ich möchte ein Mineralwasser.
3 Ich möchte einen Cognac.
4 Ich möchte eine Gulaschsuppe.
5 Ich möchte eine Forelle.
6 Ich möchte Salzkartoffeln.
7 Ich möchte Eisbein.
8 Ich möchte ein Wiener Schnitzel.
9 Ich möchte eine Käseplatte.
10 Ich möchte ein gemischtes Kompott.

 ## Exercise 4

Ask and say what time it is.

Example: 08:00 Wieviel Uhr ist es?
Es ist acht Uhr.
10:30 Wieviel Uhr ist es?
Es ist halb elf.

1	13:00	6	21:30
2	12:00	7	11:10
3	09:05	8	06:20
4	18:15	9	18:30
5	16:25	10	14:45

Exercise 5 In einem Restaurant: Ordering a meal

Don't forget to read the questions below before listening to this dialogue, and remember: you do not have to understand every word, just listen for the information you need.

Here is the menu (Speisekarte) from which the couple in the dialogue choose. Before you start, look up any words you do not know, then use the menu to help you answer the first four of the questions below.

HOTEL WALDMANN
Speisekarte

Vorspeisen

Zwiebelsuppe	DM 6,–
Tomatensuppe	DM 6,–
Hühnersuppe	DM 6,–
Käsesalat	DM 5,–

Hauptgerichte

Texas Steak	DM 24,–
Wiener Schnitzel	DM 18,50
Jägerschnitzel	DM 18,50
Kalbsleber	DM 17,–
Lachs	DM 26, –

+ Pommes frites, Bratkartoffeln oder Salzkartoffeln
    + Gemischtes Gemüse oder Salat

Nachtisch

Eis	DM 7,–
Apfelstrudel	DM 9,–

---

1 What do the customers order first?
2 What main dish do they order?
3 What do they both order to go with the main dish?
4 What pudding do they order?
5 What kind of coffee do they have?
6 What does the bill come to?
7 How big a tip does the waiter receive?

12 **Kann ich hier parken?**

Asking permission

 Dialogues

Dialogue 1

Parking is always a problem in every town, and Munich is no exception.

  1 Antonio: Entschuldigen Sie!
              (louder) Entschuldigen Sie!

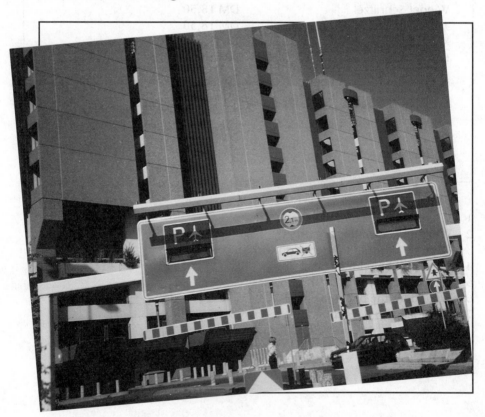

Fahren Sie zum Parkhaus

Polizist: Ja?

Antonio: Kann ich hier parken?

5 Polizist: Nein. Es tut mir leid.

Hier dürfen Sie nicht parken.

Antonio: (pointing) Und dort drüben?

Kann ich dort drüben parken?

Polizist: Nein.

10 Dort dürfen Sie auch nicht parken.

Antonio: Herr Gott nochmal!!

Wo kann ich denn hier parken?

Polizist: Im Parkhaus.

Fahren Sie zum Parkhaus.

15 Antonio: Zum Parkhaus! Zum Parkhaus!

Also zum Parkhaus.

Dialogue 2

Fritz Löb's car won't start, so he goes to see Frau Meyer, who lives in the same block, to see if she can help. Perhaps that dreadful old bicycle of hers is still in working order.

(Fritz rings the front door bell)

1 Frau Meyer: Ja, bitte?

Ach, Sie sind es, Herr Löb.

Fritz: Grüß Gott, Frau Meyer!

Entschuldigen Sie die Störung.

5 Frau Meyer: Was kann ich für Sie tun?

Fritz: Frau Meyer, mein Auto startet nicht.

Die Batterie ist kaputt, glaube ich.

Frau Meyer: O, das tut mir leid.

Fritz: Darf ich bitte Ihr Fahrrad borgen?

10 Frau Meyer: Mein Fahrrad?

Selbstverständlich.

Es ist unten im Keller.

Fritz: Herzlichen Dank.

O, darf ich auch die Pumpe borgen?

15 Frau Meyer: Aber natürlich.

Sie dürfen die Pumpe auch borgen.

Fritz: Recht vielen Dank.

Frau Meyer: Gern geschehen.

Fahren Sie vorsichtig.

20 Fritz: Ja, ja.

Information

(a) Notes on Dialogue 1

10 auch

The word 'auch' has a number of meanings: 'also', 'too', and, in this sentence, 'either', since it is in a sentence containing a negative. Note in particular the position this word has in the sentence and how it is emphasised by the speaker on the recording.

11 Herr Gott nochmal!

This is an expression of real irritation. It is quite colloquial but can be used in any society where it would be permissible to show one's irritation.

(b) Notes on Dialogue 2

4 die Störung

'The disturbance'. Note that German uses a noun, where English uses the expression 'for disturbing you'.

7 kaputt

This is a very useful word which can be used in a large number of situations. Many things, such as a car battery in this instance, can be 'kaputt' where we would normally use an expression in English which was more tailor-made e.g. 'flat'.

12 im Keller

Nearly all German houses have a cellar. In a large house divided into flats or in a block of flats the cellar is divided into compartments, each belonging to one of the families living in the house. Cellars normally contain central-heating boilers and are also used as general storage rooms, especially for bottles of wine.

18 Gern geschehen

This is a very useful phrase with which to respond when somebody thanks you for something. It corresponds to English expressions such as 'that's quite all right', 'you're welcome' or 'don't mention it'.

(c) Word list

können (kann)	to be able; to be allowed
parken	to park
dürfen (darf)	to be allowed
auch	also
das **Park**haus (⸚er)	multi-storey car park
tun	to do
das **Au**to (-s)	car
starten	to start
die Batte**rie** (-n)	battery
ka**putt**	broken
glauben	to believe
das **Fahr**rad (⸚er)	bicycle
borgen	to borrow
selbstver**ständ**lich	of course
unten	downstairs
der **Kel**ler (-)	cellar
die **Pum**pe (-n)	pump
na**tür**lich	of course
vorsichtig	careful; carefully

(d) Some phrases

Dort **drü**ben	Over there
Herzlichen Dank	Thank you very much
Recht **vie**len Dank	Thank you very much
Das geht nicht	That won't do
Das ist un**mög**lich	That is impossible
Auf **kein**en Fall	Under no circumstances

(e) Further useful vocabulary

der **Re**genmantel (⸚)	raincoat
die **Zei**tung (-en)	newspaper
sicher	certainly
schwimmen	swim
die **Zahn**bürste (-n)	toothbrush
die **Zahn**pasta	toothpaste
der **Rasier**apparat (-e)	electric razor
die **Ho**se (-n)	trousers
der **Fern**sehapp**arat**	television set
der **Zu**cker	sugar
das Buch (⸚er)	book
der **Kamm** (⸚e)	comb

Structural explanations

(a) Structures to learn

(i) How to ask permission using the verb 'können'

- *How to ask permission to borrow things*

Kann ich { Ihr Fahrrad / Ihren Regenmantel / Ihre Zeitung } borgen?

- *How to ask permission to do other things*

Kann ich { Ihr Fahrrad / Ihren Regenmantel / Ihre Zeitung } { nehmen? / sehen }

(ii) How to ask permission using the verb 'dürfen'

If you want to be particularly polite, possibly because you are talking to someone of higher status than yourself, you can ask permission by using another verb: 'dürfen'.

It may be that you want to refuse somebody permission to do something, and express the meaning 'you are not allowed to do something'. In this case too, you use the verb dürfen.

Dort dürfen Sie nicht parken
Darf ich Ihr Fahrrad borgen?
Darf ich die Pumpe borgen?

Here are some sentences which show you how this verb can be used:

Darf ich { Ihr Fahrrad / Ihren Regenmantel / Ihre Zeitung } borgen?

(iii) How to give permission

Here are some phrases you can use if you want to give permission to somebody:

Selbstverständlich / Aber natürlich / Sicher / Bitte } of course

(iv) How to refuse permission

Here are some expressions you can use if you want to refuse somebody permission. They range from being quite neutral in tone at the top to being very strong at the bottom.

Nein, es tut mir leid
Nein, das geht nicht
Nein, das ist unmöglich
Nein, auf keinen Fall

(b) Grammar

(i) Verbs

Here are the most frequently used forms of the two verbs we have been looking at in this chapter.

- *The verb 'können' (to be able to)*   *The verb 'dürfen' (to be allowed to)*

ich	kann	I can	ich	darf	I may i.e. am allowed to
er	kann	he can	er	darf	he may
sie	kann	she can	sie	darf	she may
wir	können	we can	wir	dürfen	we may
Sie	können	you can	Sie	dürfen	you may

Both verbs are *irregular* in that their stems change, and their endings do not conform to the standard pattern. You will find these verbs in the Grammatical Summary.

(ii) Meanings of 'können'

The verb können has two meanings. One meaning is associated with asking permission, as we have seen earlier. The primary meaning, however, is connected with *ability*. Thus:

Kann er schwimmen?   Can he (is he able to, does he know how to) swim?
Ich kann schwimmen   I can (am able to) swim

(iii) Sentence patterns

The two verbs 'können' and 'dürfen' can be used in a number of different sentence patterns. Here are some examples:

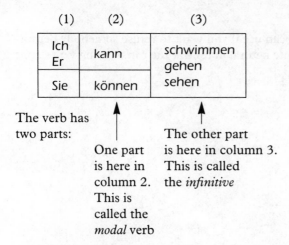

The verb has two parts:

One part is here in column 2. This is called the *modal* verb

The other part is here in column 3. This is called the *infinitive*

A *modal* verb defines the mode, or manner in which something is done. It refers to the necessity, possibility or impossibility of e.g. swimming, going, seeing, etc.

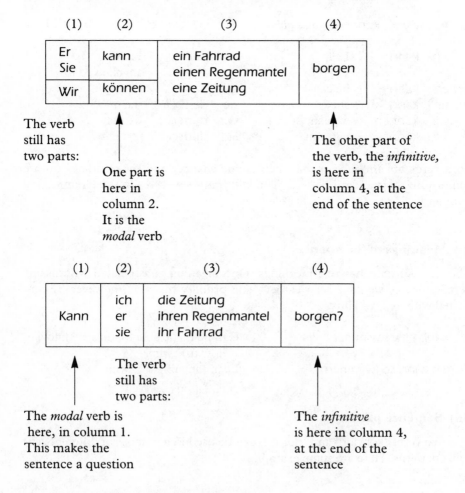

The verb still has two parts:

One part is here in column 2. It is the *modal* verb

The other part of the verb, the *infinitive*, is here in column 4, at the end of the sentence

The verb still has two parts:

The *modal* verb is here, in column 1. This makes the sentence a question

The *infinitive* is here in column 4, at the end of the sentence

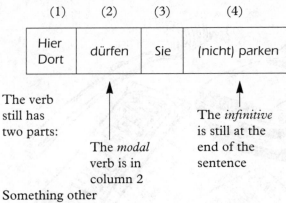

	(1)	(2)	(3)	(4)
	Hier Dort	dürfen	Sie	(nicht) parken

The verb
still has
two parts:

The *modal*
verb is in
column 2

The *infinitive*
is still at the
end of the
sentence

Something other
than the subject
can come at the
beginning for emphasis

Exercises

Exercise 1

Imagine that you are living with a German family and want to borrow some of their things. This is what you would say:

Example: Kann ich Ihr Fahrrad borgen bitte?

Now, how would you ask to borrow the items shown overleaf? Of course, you might not get them.

Exercise 2

Now it's your turn to practise giving or refusing permission. Here are some things which somebody might – with a stretch of the imagination, of course – ask you if they can borrow. When you check the answers, bear in mind that we have printed the answers we think you may have given. We have no means of telling, of course, how generous you are.

1   Kann ich Ihr Fahrrad borgen, bitte?
2   Kann ich Ihre Hose borgen, bitte?
3   Kann ich Ihre Zeitung borgen, bitte?
4   Kann ich Ihren Rasierapparat borgen, bitte?
5   Kann ich Ihre Zahnpasta borgen, bitte?
6   Kann ich Ihr Auto borgen, bitte?
7   Kann ich Ihren Mann borgen, bitte?
8   Kann ich Ihre Frau borgen, bitte?
9   Kann ich Ihren Regenmantel borgen, bitten?
10   Kann ich Ihren Fernsehapparat borgen, bitte?

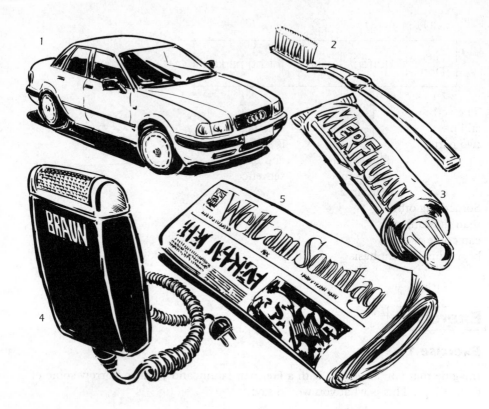

Exercise 3

Look at the answers which are given below and try and work out what the questions must have been.

1 *Question*: ....?
  Answer: Nein, hier dürfen Sie nicht parken.
2 *Question*: ......?
  Answer: Aber natürlich. Mein Fahrrad ist dort drüben.
3 *Question*: ......?
  Answer: Nein, es tut mir leid. Ich habe keinen Zucker.
4 *Question*: ......?
  Answer: Aber sicher. Sie können das Auto nehmen.
5 *Question*: ......?
  Answer: Nein, es tut mir leid. Ich habe nur eine Zahnbürste.

Exercise 4

Imagine that you are staying with a German family called Fiebiger. You have come rather unprepared and you want to borrow a number of things. Listen to the prompts on your recording and supply the questions.

Exercise 5 Im Theater: Coming late to the theatre

Don't forget to read the questions below before listening to this dialogue, and remember: you do not have to understand every word, just listen for the information you need.

1 Which row and seat number does the late arrival have on his ticket?
2 It turns out that the performance has already started: 'Die Vorführung hat schon angefangen'. What happens?
3 He explains he was late because something was delayed: '... hatte Verspätung'. What was it?
4 The lady says she can only let him in during the interval ('Pause'). Fill in the missing words in her sentence.
    Ich _____ Sie erst _____ _____ _____ reinlassen.
5 The man demands to see the manager. Which is the word for manager?
    (a) das Internat   (b) den Intendanten   (c) den Internierten
6 Does he get to see the manager?

⟨13⟩ Was sind Sie von Beruf?

Jobs and professions

 Dialogues

Dialogue 1

Fritz is bringing back Frau Meyer's bicycle which he borrowed when his car wouldn't start.
(He rings the front door bell)

1　Frau Meyer:　Ja, bitte?
　　Ach, Sie sind es, Herr Löb.
　　Fritz:　Grüß Gott, Frau Meyer!
　　Entschuldigen Sie die Störung.
5　　Hier ist Ihr Rad.
　　Frau Meyer:　Vielen Dank.
　　War alles in Ordnung?
　　Fritz:　Ja, alles war in Ordnung.
　　Danke schön.
10　Frau Meyer:　Sie sind Hauptschullehrer, nicht wahr?
　　Fritz:　Ja, das stimmt.
　　Frau Meyer:　Gefällt Ihnen die Arbeit?
　　Fritz:　O ja, sehr.
　　Frau Meyer:　Wann beginnen Sie am Morgen?
15　Fritz:　Wir beginnen um acht Uhr.
　　Frau Meyer:　Ach so.
　　Und wann kommen Sie normalerweise nach Hause?
　　Fritz:　Ich komme gewöhnlich gegen zwei Uhr nach Hause.
　　Frau Meyer:　Wie viele Tage arbeiten Sie in der Woche?
20　Fritz:　Nur fünf.
　　Gott sei Dank.
　　Frau Meyer:　Als ich Schülerin war, hatten wir auch samstags Schule.
　　Fritz:　Ja ja, wir haben es besser.
　　Nun. Vielen Dank noch einmal für das Rad.

In der Schule

25 Frau Meyer: Gern geschehen, Herr Löb.
        Auf Wiedersehen.

Dialogue 2

You will remember that Elke met a man when she was in the Alte Pinakothek.
He has invited her to have a cup of coffee in the museum restaurant.

1 Mann: Was sind Sie von Beruf, wenn ich fragen darf?
  Elke: Ich bin Verkäuferin.
  Mann: Hier in München?
  Elke: Ja, bei Mode Zilling.
5   In der Leopoldstraße.
  Mann: Gefällt Ihnen die Arbeit?
  Elke: O, ja und nein.
     Ich verdiene sehr gut.
  Mann: Wann beginnen Sie mit der Arbeit?
10 Elke: Um acht Uhr.
  Mann: Und haben Sie eine Mittagspause?
  Elke: Ja. Von zwölf bis eins.

Mann: Zwischen zwölf und eins habe ich auch Mittagspause.
Elke: (ironically) Schauen Sie mal!
15 Mann: Wann kommen Sie abends nach Hause?
Elke: Ich habe um fünf Uhr Feierabend.
Mann: Ich auch.
Könnte ich Sie an Ihrem Geschäft abholen?
Ich habe ein Auto.
20 Wir könnten vielleicht aufs Land fahren.
Elke: Vielen Dank.
Aber ich habe mein eigenes Auto.
Mann: Ach so.
Elke: Und heute kommt mein Freund um fünf Uhr.
25 Wir wollen auf dem Viktualienmarkt einkaufen gehen.
Mann: Schade.
Ein anderes Mal vielleicht.
Elke: Vielleicht.

Information

(a) Notes on Dialogue 1

10	nicht wahr?	Another example of this very useful expression for converting a statement into a question. The phrase 'nicht wahr' can be added to any statement in order to turn it into an interrogative.
12	Gefällt Ihnen	'Do you like?' Do not attempt to translate this expression literally. For more information, see p. 269.
17	normalerweise	These phrases are interchangeable and
18	gewöhnlich	and allow you to refer to what is *usual* or *normal*.
22	Als ich Schülerin war	There is a brief note about word order in subordinate clauses on p. 279.
22	hatten	This is the past tense of the verb 'haben' and means 'had'.
22	samstags	Note that by adding an 's' to the end of the word you make the phrase 'on Saturdays'.

(b) Notes on Dialogue 2

12	eins	In colloquial German you can say 'eins' or 'ein Uhr' for 'one o'clock'.

16	Feierabend	This is a very frequent and colloquial expression meaning to finish one's work for the day.
18	Könnte	This form of the verb 'können' simply means 'could'.
25	Viktualienmarkt	Name of a famous food market in Munich.

(c) Word list

das Rad (short for '**Fahr**rad')(⁼er)	bicycle
alles	everything
der **Leh**rer (-)	teacher
die **Ar**beit (-en)	work
sehr	very much
be**ginn**en	to begin
der **Mor**gen (-)	morning
der Tag (-e)	day
arbeiten	to work
die **Wo**che (-n)	week
der **Schü**ler (-)	school pupil (male)
die **Schü**lerin (-nen)	school pupil (female)
die **Schu**le (-n)	school
besser	better
noch **ein**mal	once again
der Be**ruf** (-e)	job; profession
fragen	to ask
die Ver**käu**ferin (-nen)	saleswoman
ver**dien**en	to earn
die **Mit**tagspause (-n)	midday break
zwischen	between
abends	in the evening
das Ge**schäft** (-e)	shop; business
ab_ holen	to call for
viel**leicht**	perhaps
fahren	to drive
eigen	own
der Freund (-e)	(boy) friend
wollen	to want to
einkaufen **geh**en	to go shopping
Schade	What a pity

(d) Some phrases

In **Ord**nung	All right
Das stimmt	That's right
nach **Hau**se	home (going home)
Gegen zwei Uhr	About two o'clock
Gott sei Dank!	Thank God!

Gern geschehen	You're welcome
Aufs Land	Into the country
Ein anderes Mal	Another time

(e) Further useful vocabulary

die **Buch**handlung (-en)	bookshop
das Büro (-s)	office
die Fabrik (-en)	factory
das Hotel (-s)	hotel
die Konditorei (-en)	café or cake shop
das **Kauf**haus (⁻er)	department store
übermorgen	the day after tomorrow
vorgestern	the day before yesterday
jed-	every

Structural explanations

(a) Structures to learn

(i) How to ask somebody what he or she does for a living

Was sind Sie von Beruf?	What do you do?
Sie sind (Lehrer), nicht wahr?	You are (a teacher), aren't you?
Herr Löb ist Lehrer	Mr Löb is a teacher

(ii) How to say what you do (for a living)

The names of jobs held by women frequently end with the letters '-in'.

	Man	**Woman**		
	Arzt	Ärztin		doctor
	Bäcker	Bäckerin		baker
	Busfahrer	Busfahrerin		bus driver
	Kellner	Kellnerin		waiter/waitress
	Lehrer	Lehrerin		teacher
	Leiter	Leiterin		manager(ess)
Ich bin	Polizist	Polizistin	I am a	police officer
	Schüler	Schülerin		schoolboy/girl
	Sekretär	Sekretärin		secretary
	Student	Studentin		student
	Techniker	Technikerin		technician
	Telefonist	Telefonistin		telephonist
	Verkäufer	Verkäuferin		salesperson

There are some exceptions to the above, normally ending in '-e'.

	Man	**Woman**		
	Angestellter	Angestellte		employee
	Beamter	Beamte		civil servant
Ich bin	Empfangschef	Empfangsdame	I am a(n)	(hotel) receptionist
	Friseur	Friseuse		hairdresser
	Hausmann	Hausfrau		house husband/housewife

An 'Angestellte(r)' is a salaried employee, or white-collar worker. A 'Beamte(r)' is a civil servant, holding a tenured position.

(iii) How to ask somebody where they work and how to say where you work

Wo arbeiten Sie?

Ich bin bei (name of firm or company)

Ich bin bei
- Siemens
- Grundig
- Ford
- Mode Zilling
- Mercedes

Ich arbeite in

einer Buchhandlung	die Buchhandlung: bookshop
einem Büro	das Büro: office
einer Schule	die Schule: school
einer Fabrik	die Fabrik: factory
einem Hotel	das Hotel: hotel
einer Konditorei	die Konditorei: café or cake shop
einem Kaufhaus	das Kaufhaus: department store
einem Geschäft	das Geschäft: shop

(iv) How to ask about somebody's hours of work

1 Wann beginnen Sie
- am Morgen?
- mit der Arbeit?

When do you begin
- in the morning?
- work?

Ich beginne
Wir beginnen
} um acht Uhr

I begin
We begin
} at eight o'clock

2 Wann kommen Sie (abends) nach Hause?
When do you come home (in the evening)?

Um sechs Uhr
Ich habe um fünf Uhr Feierabend

At six o'clock
I finish at five o'clock

3   Wie viele $\left\{\begin{array}{l}\text{Tage}\\\text{Stunden}\end{array}\right\}$ arbeiten Sie in der Woche?

How many $\left\{\begin{array}{l}\text{days}\\\text{hours}\end{array}\right\}$ do you work a week?

Nur fünf Tage	Only five days
Ich arbeite fünfunddreißig Stunden	I work 35 hours (a week)

4   Haben Sie eine Mittagspause ?   Do you have a midday break?

$\left.\begin{array}{l}\text{Wann}\\\text{Wie lange}\end{array}\right\}$ haben Sie Mittagspause?

$\left.\begin{array}{l}\text{When}\\\text{How long}\end{array}\right\}$ is your midday break?

Von zwölf bis eins	From twelve to one

(b) Grammar

(i) Expressions of time (frequency)

$\left.\begin{array}{l}\text{meistens}\\\text{in der Regel}\\\text{normalerweise}\\\text{gewöhnlich}\end{array}\right\}$ = usually, as a rule

(ii) Approximate and exact time

gegen drei Uhr	about or towards three o'clock
gerade drei Uhr	exactly (or just) three o'clock

(iii) Today, tomorrow, etc.

heute	today
morgen	tomorrow
übermorgen	the day after tomorrow
gestern	yesterday
vorgestern	the day before yesterday

(iv) Time of day

morgens	in the morning
vormittags	in the morning
nachmittags	in the afternoon
abends	in the evening
nachts	in the night

(v) Time of day

heute früh	early this morning
heute morgen	this morning
heute nachmittag	this afternoon
heute abend	this evening
morgen früh	early tomorrow morning
gestern abend	yesterday evening

(vi) The use of the accusative

jeden Abend	every evening
jeden Freitag	every Friday
diesen Abend	this evening
nächsten Freitag	next Friday

(vii) Use of prepositions

heute in acht Tagen	a week today
heute in vierzehn Tagen	a fortnight today
heute vor acht Tagen	a week ago today

(viii) Regularity

montags	on Mondays
dienstags	on Tuesdays
mittwochs	on Wednesdays
donnerstags	on Thursdays
freitags	on Fridays
samstags	on Saturdays
sonntags	on Sundays

N.B. A small letter is used because it is the notion of regularity which is meant, rather than the name of the day.

(ix) The use of '**gefallen**' to express liking

Gefällt Ihnen (*singular*)   Do you like
- der Pullover — the pullover
- das Wetter   ? — the weather   ?
- der Schnee — the snow

Gefallen Ihnen (*plural*)   Do you like
- die Schuhe — the shoes
- die Geschäfte   ? — the shops   ?
- die Berge — the mountains

				the pullover
Der Pullover				the pullover
Das Wetter	gefällt mir	I like		the weather
Der Schnee	*(singular)*			the snow

				the shoes
Die Schuhe				the shoes
Die Geschäfte	gefallen mir	I like		the shops
Die Berge	*(plural)*			the mountains

Exercises

A

Exercise 1

Look at the pictures opposite and answer the questions.

1 Was ist Herr Moezer von Beruf?
2 Was ist Frau Hacker von Beruf?
3 Was ist Frau Siegling von Beruf?
4 Was ist Herr Mader von Beruf?
5 Was ist Frau Meyer von Beruf?
6 Was ist Frau Bauer von Beruf?
7 Was ist Frau Augustin von Beruf?
8 Was ist Herr Flohr von Beruf?
9 Was ist Herr Kahle von Beruf?
10 Was ist Herr Löb von Beruf?

Exercise 2

Now you are going to practise talking about professions and hours of work. Listen to the example conversation on your recording and then follow the prompts to take part in the conversations. You can repeat the exercise as many times as you like until you can answer confidently.

Exercise 3

Give questions which will produce the following answers.

1 Die Farbe gefällt mir.
2 Die Landschaft gefällt mir.
3 Das Auto gefällt mir.
4 Die Schuhe gefallen mir.
5 Der Wind gefällt mir nicht.
6 Das Material gefällt mir.
7 Das Wetter gefällt mir.
8 Der Schnee gefällt mir.
9 Die Geschäfte gefallen mir.
10 Der Regen gefällt mir nicht.

Herr Kahle

Herr Mader

Frau Augustin

Herr Löb

Herr Moezer

Frau Siegling

Frau Hacker

Frau Bauer

Herr Flohr

Frau Meyer

Exercise 4 Im Café: Making contact with a stranger

Don't forget to read the questions below first before listening to this dialogue, and remember: you do not have to understand every word, just listen for the information you need.

1 How does the young man try to get into conversation with the girl?
2 What had the weather been like at the weekend?
3 How does the young woman come to be in the café?
4 What is her profession?
5 She works for a wholesaler ('Großhandel') but what do they sell?
6 Which branch of the business does she work in?
7 Which skills does she have?
8 Where did she acquire them?
9 Where does she go when she leaves the café?

14 Wo wohnen Sie?

Accommodation

Dialogues

Dialogue 1

Antonio Raggi has come to love the folklore which is so much part of the life in Munich. On this particular day, just before Christmas, he has travelled into the centre of the city on the underground in order to visit the Christkindlmarkt. This is held every year in the days leading up to Christmas and is situated on the Marienplatz just in front of the town hall. One important aspect of the Christkindlmarkt is the many stalls where you can drink 'Glühwein'. Antonio has met Fritz Löb there and has got into conversation with him.

1 Antonio: Prost!
   Fritz: Prost!
   Antonio: Der Glühwein ist schön warm, nicht wahr?
   Fritz: Ja, schön warm.
5 Antonio: Wohnen Sie hier in München?
   Fritz: Ja, ich wohne in der Nietzschestraße.
   Antonio: Wohnen Sie in einem Mietshaus?
   Fritz: Ja, ich habe eine Einzimmerwohnung in einem großen Mietshaus.
10 Antonio: Haben Sie nur ein Zimmer?
   Fritz: Na, ich habe ein Badezimmer und eine Küche.
   Antonio: Und sonst?
   Fritz: Sonst habe ich ein Wohn- und Schlafzimmer.
   Antonio: Ist die Wohnung schön?
15 Fritz: Ja, sie ist klein, aber ganz schön.
   Ich habe viele Bilder dort.
   Antonio: Bilder?
   Fritz: Ja.
   Ich sammle Bilder.
20 Antonio: Hmm. Interessant.

Der Marienplate in München

Dialogue 2

Antonio and Fritz continue talking together.

1 Antonio: Mein Onkel hat auch viele Bilder.
   Fritz: Wo wohnt er?
   Antonio: In Napoli.
   Fritz: Ach, in Neapel.
5 Antonio: Er hat ein Einzelhaus.
   Fritz: Das ist schön.
   Antonio: Er hat sechs Schlafzimmer und zwei Gästezimmer.
   Fritz: Du liebe Zeit!
   Antonio: Stellen Sie sich mal vor!
10   Sechs Schlafzimmer!
   Fritz: Hat er auch einen Garten?
   Antonio: Und ob!
   Er hat Bäume und Sträucher überall.
   Fritz: Sehr schön.
15 Antonio: Aber ich . . .
   Ich habe eine Sozialwohnung in der Kaufmannsstraße.

Fritz: Wie viele Zimmer haben Sie?
Antonio: Ich habe ein Eßzimmer und ein Schlafzimmer.
Fritz: Haben Sie ein Badezimmer und eine Küche?
20 Antonio: Selbstverständlich!
Und ich habe einen Balkon.
Das ist schön.

Information

(a) Notes on Dialogue 1

Christkindlmarkt	The Christkindl market in Munich consists of rows of brightly lit stalls where you can buy sweets, Christmas tree decorations and small items to give as presents. The air is full of the smell of frying sausages and sweetmeats which are being prepared on the spot. Many people take refuge from the very cold air by drinking Glühwein, a sort of mulled wine.
8 Ich habe	In English we often use the verb 'have got'. For example, we say 'I've got a flat in King Street' or 'How many rooms have you got?' German does not have the word 'got'. Consequently, there is no equivalent for this word in a sentence such as 'Ich habe eine Einzimmerwohnung'.
8 Einzimmerwohnung	As this dialogue shows, accommodation is described differently in German. A three-room flat would have three rooms for sleeping/living plus a kitchen and bathroom. So in contrast with English, it is not the bedrooms that are counted.
12 sonst	The expression 'Und sonst?' is very useful because it has the function of inviting somebody to enlarge on what he or she has been saying.

(b) Notes on Dialogue 2

1	auch	Note the position of the word 'auch' which means 'too' or 'also'.
8	Du liebe Zeit!	This is a very useful expression which can be used in many situations in order to express mild astonishment. It can be used equally by men and women in any sort of society, without giving offence.
9	Stellen Sie sich mal vor!	This expression is a bit of a tongue-twister and may need some practice before you can get your tongue round it adequately. It is, however, a very useful expression which can be used on many occasions in order to express surprise tinged with mild disbelief.
12	Und ob!	Like the above two expressions, this has a very wide currency and can be used very frequently in order to give emphasis to something which has been said just previously.

(c) Word list

Prost!	Cheers!
der **Glüh**wein	mulled wine
warm	warm
wohnen	to live
das **Miets**haus (⁻er)	house divided up into flats
die Ein**zim**merwohnung (-en)	one-room flat
groß	big
nur	only
das **Zimm**er (-)	room
klein	small
aber	but
ganz	quite
viel-	many
das Bild (-er)	picture
das **Bad**ezimmer (-)	bathroom
die **Küch**e (-n)	kitchen
das **Wohn**zimmer (-)	living room
das **Schlaf**zimmer (-)	bedroom
die **Woh**nung (-en)	flat
sammeln	to collect

interes**sant**	interesting
der **On**kel (-)	uncle
über**all**	everywhere
das **Ein**zelhaus (¨er)	detached house
das **Gäst**ezimmer (-)	guest room
der **Gar**ten (¨)	garden
der Baum (¨e)	tree
der Strauch (¨er)	shrub
überall	everywhere
die Sozi**al**wohnung (-en)	council flat
das **Eß**zimmer (-)	dining room
der Bal**kon** (-e)	balcony

(d) Further useful vocabulary

das Haus (¨er)	house
das **Ein**familienhaus (¨er)	one-family house
die **Ei**gentums**woh**nung (-en)	owner-occupied flat
das **WC** (-s)	toilet
die Ga**rage** (-n)	garage
das **Schwimm**bad (¨er)	swimming pool
der **Ten**nisplatz (¨e)	tennis court
die Te**rras**se (-n)	terrace
die **Blu**me (-n)	flower
der **En**kel (-)	grandson
der **Flü**gel (-)	wing
der **Schlüs**sel (-)	key
der **Ku**chen (-)	cake
der **Reif**en (-)	tyre
der **Kof**fer (-)	suitcase
der **Kell**ner (-)	waiter
die Hand (¨e)	hand
die Wand (¨e)	wall
die Stadt (¨e)	town
das Boot (-e)	boat
das Ding (-e)	thing
der Arm (-e)	arm
der Ort (-e)	place
der **Ap**fel (¨)	apple
der **Haf**en (¨)	harbour
der **Vo**gel (¨)	bird
die Saat (-en)	seed
die Uhr (-en)	clock
die Tür (-en)	door
die Zahl (-en)	number
der Wald (¨er)	wood
das Dorf (¨er)	village
der Flur (-e)	entrance hall, vestibule
die **Die**le (-n)	entrance hall, vestibule

Structural explanations

(a) Structures to learn

(i) How to ask where someone lives

Wo wohnen Sie?	Where do you live?
Wo wohnt er?	Where does he live?
Wohnen Sie hier in München?	Do you live here in Munich?

(ii) How to ask what sort of a house somebody lives in

Wohnen Sie in einem { Haus / Einfamilienhaus / Mietshaus } ?

Do you live in a { house / one-family house / house divided up into flats } ?

Other types of accommodation:

ein Zweifamilienhaus	a two-family house
eine Wohnung	a flat
eine Sozialwohnung	a council flat
ein Einzelhaus	a detached house
ein Reihenhaus	a terraced house
eine Mietwohnung	a rented flat
eine Eigentumswohnung	an owner-occupied flat

N.B. Approximately half the population in Germany lives in rented accommodation. In the cities there are large numbers of blocks of flats while in the country districts it's more likely that rented flats are in large houses where the owner also lives.

(iii) How to describe where one lives

Wie viele Zimmer haben Sie?	How many rooms have you got?

Ich habe	I've got
eine Küche	a kitchen
ein Badezimmer	a bathroom
ein Wohnzimmer	a living room
ein Eßzimmer	a dining room
ein Schlafzimmer	a bedroom
ein WC	a toilet
ein Gästezimmer	a guest room

| eine Einzimmerwohnung | a one-room flat |
| eine Zweizimmerwohnung | a two-room flat |

(iv) How to ask about other amenities

Haben Sie	Have you got
einen Balkon	a balcony
einen Garten ?	a garden ?
eine Garage	a garage
ein Schwimmbad	a swimming pool

Ich habe	I've got
einen Garten	a garden
einen Balkon	a balcony
einen Tennisplatz	a tennis court
eine Garage	a garage
eine Terrasse	a terrace
viele Bäume	many trees
viele Blumen	many flowers
viele Sträucher	many shrubs

(b) Grammar

Plurals of nouns

In English, we usually indicate that there are *more than one* of a thing by adding the letters 's' or 'es' to a word.

| boy | – | boys | window | – | windows |
| girl | – | girls | box | – | boxes |

The plural of German nouns is formed in a number of different ways. There is no foolproof way of predicting how a particular German noun will make its plural and therefore the best thing to do is to learn the plural form of each noun as it occurs. Below are given some of the most frequently occurring plural formations with a number of nouns in common use in each category.

Some nouns do not change in the plural indicated thus: (-).

Some nouns make their plural by adding an 'e'. This is shown like this: (-e).

der Onkel (-)	uncle	das Boot (-e)	boat
der Enkel (-)	grandson	das Ding (-e)	thing
der Flügel (-)	wing	der Arm (-e)	arm
der Schlüssel (-)	key	der Ort (-e)	place
der Kuchen (-)	cake	der Schuh (-e)	shoe
der Reifen (-)	tyre		
der Koffer (-)	case		
der Kellner (-)	waiter		

Other plurals are made by adding an Umlaut over the vowel and an 'e'. This is shown thus: (ːe).

die Hand (ːe)   hand
die Wand (ːe)   wall
die Stadt (ːe)   town

Some nouns make their plural by just adding an Umlaut. This is shown thus: (ː).

der Apfel (ː)   apple
der Garten (ː)   garden
der Hafen (ː)   harbour
der Vogel (ː)   bird

Many nouns make their plural by adding 'en'. This is indicated thus: (-en).

die Saat (-en)   seed
die Uhr (-en)   clock
die Tür (-en)   door
die Zahl (-en)   number

Some nouns make their plural by adding an Umlaut and 'er'. It is indicated like this: (ːer).

der Mann (ːer)   man
der Wald (ːer)   wood
das Dorf (ːer)   village
das Buch (ːer)   book
das Haus (ːer)   house

If you don't know a plural, here is a rule of thumb which is often helpful.

1   Masculine nouns ending in '-el', '-en' and '-er' don't change in the plural.
2   Many feminine nouns make their plural by adding '-(e)n'.
3   Many neuter nouns make their plural by adding '-er', and an Umlaut if feasible, i.e. on 'a', 'o', 'u'.
4   Many masculine nouns make their plural by adding '-e'. Many of these add an Umlaut if possible.

Exercises

A

Exercise 1

Imagine that the house on the opposite page belongs to you. Here is a conversation you might have with an acquaintance:

Acquaintance: Haben Sie ein Wohnzimmer?
You: Ja, ich habe ein Wohnzimmer.

Answer the following questions in the same way:

1   Haben Sie ein Wohnzimmer?
2   Haben Sie ein Eßzimmer?
3   Haben Sie eine Küche?
4   Haben Sie ein Badezimmer?
5   Haben Sie ein Schlafzimmer?
6   Haben Sie eine Toilette?

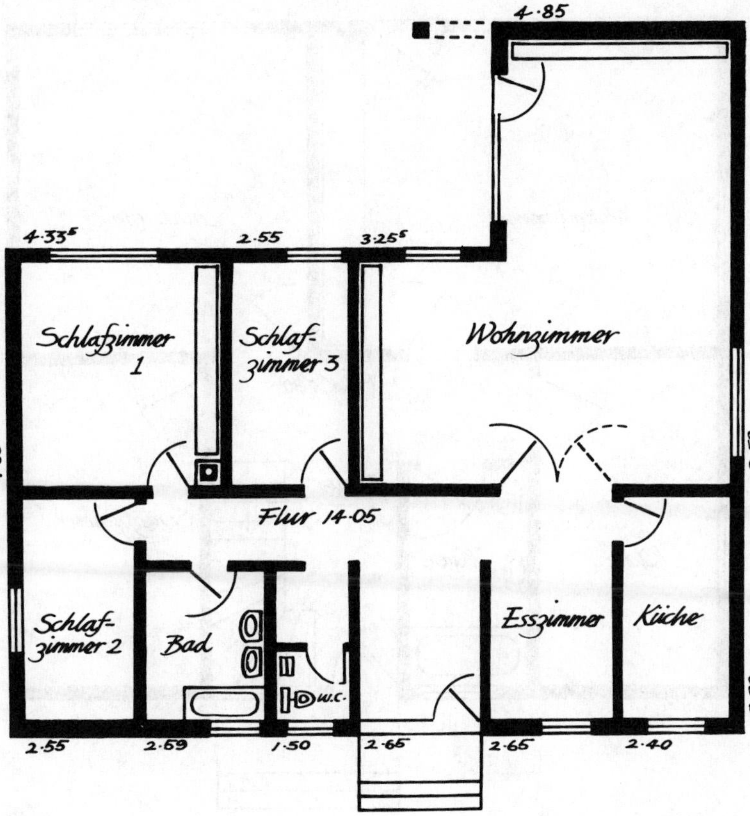
4·85
4·33⁵
2·55
3·25⁵
Schlafzimmer 1
Schlafzimmer 3
Wohnzimmer
4·80
9·58
Flur 14·05
Schlafzimmer 2
Bad
W.C.
Esszimmer
Küche
4·80
2·55
2·59
1·50
2·65
2·65
2·40

Exercise 2

Imagine that the house overleaf belongs to you. Here is a conversation which you might have with a friend:

Friend: Haben Sie ein Wohnzimmer?
You: Ja, ich habe ein Wohnzimmer.
Friend: Haben Sie eine Garage?
You: Nein, eine Garage habe ich nicht.

Answer the following questions in the same way:

1 Haben Sie ein Wohnzimmer?
2 Haben Sie eine Garage?
3 Haben Sie ein Eßzimmer?
4 Haben Sie eine Terrasse?
5 Haben Sie eine Küche?

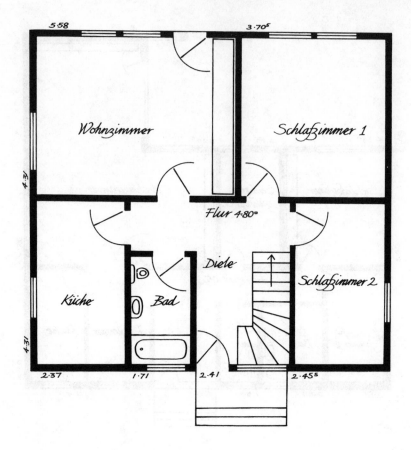

6   Haben Sie einen Balkon?
7   Haben Sie ein Badezimmer?
8   Haben Sie einen Garten?

 Exercise 3

The temptation to keep up with the Joneses sometimes simply cannot be resisted. The case of Helmut Schwarz is a case in point. He thought that he had built the most splendid house in the village but when a retired dentist from the city came and built an even larger house just beside his, he found that he had to keep up with the Winklers. Listen to the beginning of a conversation between the two of them on your recording. You continue by playing the part of Helmut.

Exercise 4

Listen to the recorded dialogues again or read the script in the book. Then answer the following questions.

1 Wohnt Fritz in München?
2 Hat er eine Zweizimmerwohnung?
3 Hat er ein Badezimmer?
4 Hat er eine Küche?
5 Hat er viele Bilder?
6 Wo wohnt Antonios Onkel?
7 Hat er eine Sozialwohnung?
8 Wie viele Schlafzimmer hat er?
9 Wie viele Gästezimmer hat er?
10 Hat Antonio ein Einzelhaus?
11 Hat er ein Eßzimmer?
12 Hat er ein Badezimmer?
13 Hat er eine Küche?
14 Hat er einen Garten?

Exercise 5 Wieder im Café: The two people from Chapter 13 meet again

Don't forget to read the questions below first before listening to this dialogue, and remember: you do not have to understand every word, just listen for the information you need.

1 How does the young woman usually come to town?
2 How long does the journey take?
3 Can you describe her flat?
4 On which floor is her flat?
5 How does she reach her floor?
6 How long has she lived there?
7 What is his suggestion for another meeting?

[15] Interessen

Hobbies and interests

 ## Dialogues

Dialogue 1

Fritz has taken the plunge and invited Elke to come home to his flat after work to have some coffee and cakes.

    1 Fritz: Kommen Sie bitte herein.
       Elke: Danke.
       Fritz: Das ist meine Einzimmerwohnung.
       Elke: Sie ist sehr schön.
    5 Fritz: Sie ist leider etwas zu klein.
       Elke: Sie haben viele Bilder.
               Aber sie sind alle von Kirchen.
       Fritz: Ja, ich interessiere mich für Kirchen.
       Elke: Ja, das sehe ich.
   10 Fritz: Wissen Sie ...
               Ich fotografiere sehr gern.
               Ich fotografiere gern Kirchen.
       Elke: (meaningfully)
               Ja, das sehe ich.
       Fritz: Möchten Sie eine Tasse Kaffee?
   15 Elke: O ja, bitte schön.
       Fritz: Schauen Sie ...
               die Kirche hier ist schön, nicht wahr?
       Elke: (without enthusiasm)
               Hmm.
       Fritz: Sie ist romanisch.
   20 Elke: Tatsächlich?
       Fritz: Ja. Ich interessiere mich sehr für romanische Kirchen.
               Ich fotografiere sie sehr gern.
       Elke: (yawning)

Ich interessiere mich für Kirchen

Ja, das sehe ich.
Fritz: O, entschuldigen Sie.
25 Ihr Kaffee.
Nehmen Sie Zucker?
Elke: Nein, danke.

Dialogue 2

Antonio is talking to a fellow student at the Meisterschule für Mode.

1 Student: Du! Antonio!
Antonio: Was ist los?
Student: Gar nichts.
Ich wollte dir nur etwas sagen.
5 Antonio: Na und ...?
Student: Du weißt ... .
Ich interessiere mich für Italienisch.
Antonio: Ja, das weiß ich.
Student: Und ich esse sehr gern italienisches Essen.

10 Antonio: Ja, das weiß ich auch.
    Student: Also … .
    Gestern war ich in einem italienischen Restaurant.
    Antonio: Wo denn?
    Student: In der St Markus Straße.
15 Restaurant Giovanni heißt es.
    Antonio: Das kenne ich nicht.
    Ist es gut?
    Student: Na, ich esse sehr gern Pizza.
    Und die Pizza war wirklich gut.
20 Antonio: Warst du allein?
    Student: Nein, die Birgit war dabei.
    Sie ißt lieber Cannelloni.
    Antonio: Hm. Waren die Cannelloni auch gut?
    Student: Nicht schlecht.
25 Antonio: Da muß ich auch hin.
    Ich esse furchtbar gern Pizza.

Information

(a) Notes on Dialogue 1

1	Kommen Sie	The English translation gives the typically English, rather tentative form where the German tends to be more direct.
8	für	Where in English we say 'I'm interested *in* something', German uses the word 'für'.
10	Wissen Sie	This is a very useful expression for indicating that you want to say something. It has the effect of telling other people 'Stop talking for a minute and listen to what I'm going to say'.

(b) Notes on Dialogue 2

| 1 | Du! Antonio! | This is a fairly emphatic, but very typical, way of addressing somebody in the familiar form. Although social etiquette in Germany is becoming more liberal and flexible, especially amongst young people (such as these two students), it is best not to use the familiar 'du' form unless you are |

specifically asked to, or someone uses it consistently to you. Inappropriate use can cause offence.

5 Na und ...?

This is another very useful phrase but you should take care to use it only with people you are on fairly good terms with. It can be slightly challenging and provocative. It has a touch of 'So what?' about it.

11 Also

One of the most useful words in German because it has the function of allowing you to say something, while you are still making up your mind what you want to say. It means 'so', and has nothing to do with the English word 'also'.

21 die Birgit

The word 'die' is not necessary but it is very colloquial to say 'die Birgit' or 'der Peter'. It tends to be rather more frequently used in the south of Germany than in the north. It will make you sound very competent to use it occasionally but don't feel obliged to use it every time you say somebody's name.

(c) *Word list*

die Ein**zim**merwohnung (-en)	one-roomed flat
etwas	somewhat
leider	unfortunately
das Bild (-er)	picture
alle	all
sich interess**ier**en für	to be interested in
fotograf**ier**en	to photograph
die **Tass**e (-n)	cup
der **Kaff**ee (singular only)	coffee
tats**äch**lich	indeed
der **Zuck**er (singular only)	sugar
essen (ißt)	to eat
das **Ess**en (-)	food
heißen	to be called
kennen	to know (a person or a place)
wirklich	really
all**ein**	alone
da**bei**	there
schlecht	bad
furchtbar	terribly

(d) Some phrases

Kommen Sie **bit**te her**ein**	Please come in
Ich ... gern	I like ...ing
Das **seh**e ich	I can see that
Was ist los?	What's the matter?
Gar nichts	Nothing at all
Das weiß ich	I know

(e) Further useful vocabulary

die Mu**sik**	music
die Fotogra**fie**	photography
der **Fuß**ball	football
die **Leich**tath**let**ik (singular only)	athletics
das Land (¨er)	country
die **Brief**marke (-n)	stamp
die **Mün**ze (-n)	coin
tanzen	to dance
wandern	to go walking
malen	to paint
lesen	to read
basteln	to make things as a hobby
singen	to sing
kochen	to cook
spielen	to play
die **Kar**te (-n)	card
das Klav**ier**	piano
reiten	to ride (horses)
hören	to hear, listen to
tief	deep
schlafen (schläft)	to sleep

Structural explanations

(a) Structures to learn

(i) How to ask about somebody's interests

Interessieren Sie sich für { Musik / Bilder / Bücher } ?

Musik: music
Bilder: pictures
Bücher: books

(ii) How to say what you are interested in

Ich interessiere mich für
    Fotografie
    Fußball
    Leichtathletik
    andere Länder

Fotografie: photography
Fußball: football
Leichtathletik: athletics
andere Länder: other countries

(iii) How to say that you collect things

Ich sammle	Briefmarken	Briefmarken: stamps
	Münzen	Münzen: coins
	Kupferstiche	Kupferstiche: etchings
	alte Bücher	alte Bücher: old books

(iv) How to say what you enjoy doing

Ich	tanze	gern	tanzen: to dance
	wandere		wandern: to go hiking or walking
	male		malen: to paint
	lese		lesen: to read
	bastle		basteln: to make things as a hobby
	singe		singen: to sing
	koche		kochen: to cook

Ich	spiele gern	Karten	Karten spielen: to play cards
		Bridge	Bridge spielen: to play bridge
		Klarinette	Klarinette spielen: to play the clarinet
		Klavier	Klavier spielen: to play the piano
	fahre gern	Ski	Ski fahren: to go skiing
		Rad	radfahren: to go cycling
	koche gern	Spaghetti	Spaghetti kochen: to cook spaghetti
		Pizza	Pizza kochen: to cook pizza

(v) Intensifiers

gern	nicht gern
sehr gern	gar nicht gern
wirklich sehr gern	überhaupt nicht gern
außerordentlich gern	
furchtbar gern	

These expressions allow you to convey your liking with increasing enthusiasm.

These expressions allow you to express your dislike with increasing strength.

Ich koche	gern	I like cooking
	sehr gern	I like cooking very much
	wirklich sehr gern	I really like cooking a lot
	außerordentlich gern	I like cooking tremendously
	furchtbar gern	I adore cooking

Ich koche	nicht gern	I don't like cooking
	gar nicht gern	I don't like cooking at all
	überhaupt nicht gern	I can't stand cooking

(b) Grammar

(i) Using 'gern'

In German, you use the word 'gern' in order to express the idea of *liking to do something*. Observe the position of the word 'gern' in the sentence, when there is a simple verb.

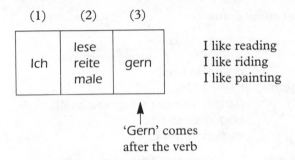

(1)	(2)	(3)	
Ich	lese reite male	gern	I like reading I like riding I like painting

'Gern' comes
after the verb

Observe the following sentences, and see where the word 'gern' occurs.

(1)	(2)	(3)	(4)	
Ich	höre gehe fahre	gern	Musik schwimmen Auto	I like listening to music I like going swimming I like driving a car

Here you see
that the word
'gern' 'belongs
to' the verb

(ii) Preference

If you compare two activities, both of which you enjoy doing, it is possible that you prefer one to the other. The idea of preference is expressed in German as follows:

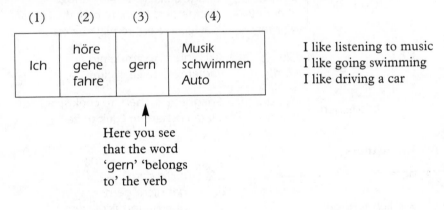

Ich	höre gehe fahre esse	lieber	Musik schwimmen Auto Pizza	I prefer listening to music I prefer going swimming I prefer driving a car I prefer (eating) pizza

This word
provides the
notion of
preference

(iii) Comparing adjectives

If it is things, rather than activities, that you wish to compare, then you will need to know the *comparative form of adjectives*. Then you will be able to say that things are *bigger* and *better*.

Let us look first at some simple adjectives, and see how they make their comparative form.

schön	– schöner (more beautiful)
tief	– tiefer (deeper)
leicht	– leichter (easier)
angenehm	– angenehmer (more pleasant)

Note how there is only one way of expressing this comparison in German although we have two ways in English.

Let us put these comparative adjectives into sentences:

Elke ist schöner als Petra	Elke is more beautiful than Petra
Der Atlantik ist tiefer als die Nordsee	The Atlantic is deeper than the North Sea
Deutsch ist leichter als Französisch	German is easier than French
Schlafen ist angenehmer als Arbeit	Sleeping is more pleasant than work

We can summarise the rule about making the comparative form of the adjective thus:

Add '-er'

(iv) Superlatives

Perhaps you will want to say that something is *biggest* or *best*. Then you will need to know the *superlative form of adjectives*. Here is how the same adjectives make their superlative form.

schön	– der, die, das schönste
tief	– der, die, das tiefste
leicht	– der, die, das leichteste
angenehm	– der, die, das angenehmste

Let us put these superlative adjectives into sentences.

Elke ist die schönste Frau	Elke is the most beautiful woman
Der Stille Ozean ist das tiefste Meer	The Pacific is the deepest sea
Deutsch ist die leichteste Sprache	German is the easiest language
Schlafen ist die angenehmste Tätigkeit	Sleeping is the most pleasant activity

We can summarise the rule about making the superlative form of the adjective thus:

'Add -(e)st'

(v) Irregularities

Unfortunately, there are a number of irregular ways of forming comparative and superlative adjectives. You will find the rules set out in the Grammatical Summary.

Exercises

A

Exercise 1

Here are five questions about what you like. Express your liking for each of them with an increasing degree of enthusiasm.

1 Tanzen Sie gern?
2 Wandern Sie gern?
3 Malen Sie gern?
4 Lesen Sie gern?
5 Singen Sie gern?

Exercise 2

Here are three questions about your likes and dislikes. Answer each of them with an increasing degree of distaste.

1 Kochen Sie gern?
2 Basteln Sie gern?
3 Tanzen Sie gern?

Exercise 3

Imagine that you are one of those people who only likes doing those things which can be done comfortably at home, sitting in the warm. Answer the following questions appropriately.

1 Tanzen Sie gern?
2 Wandern Sie gern?
3 Malen Sie gern?
4 Spielen Sie gern Karten?
5 Fahren Sie gern Ski?
6 Lesen Sie gern?

7 Singen Sie gern?
8 Reiten Sie gern?

B

Exercise 4

There are two tennis players playing in Germany at the moment. One is Boris Becker and the other is Michael Stich. Here are some statements about Becker. See if you can trump them by making comparative statements about Stich.

1 Becker ist groß.
2 Er ist schnell.
3 Er ist gesund.
4 Er ist stark.
5 Er ist jung.
6 Er ist klug.
7 Er spielt hart.
8 Er spielt gut.

(*See Grammatical Summary, Section D.*)

Exercise 5 Über Musik: Talking about your hobby

Don't forget to read the questions below before listening to this dialogue, and remember: you do not have to understand every word, just listen for the information you need. Don't worry if your spelling of the German names is slightly inaccurate. It is catching them and being able to repeat them which is important.

1 What is the man's hobby?
2 What does he like to perform?
3 Does he perform as a soloist?
4 What is he rehearsing at the moment?
5 Where and when is the performance?

16 Wir müssen gehen

'Want' and 'must'

 ## Dialogues

Dialogue 1

Elke is passionately fond of opera. She has succeeded in obtaining tickets to go to the Richard Wagner festival in Bayreuth.

<pre>
 1 Elke: Fritz! Wissen Sie was?
    Fritz: Nein.
    Elke: Herr Zilling hat Karten für Parsifal, und er kann nicht gehen.
    Fritz: Das ist Pech.
 5 Elke: Für ihn, aber nicht für uns.
    Fritz: Wieso?
    Elke: Wollen wir die Karten nehmen?
    Fritz: Was kosten sie?
    Elke: Die Karte hundertsechzig Mark.
10 Fritz: Das ist aber teuer.
    Elke: Es ist doch Bayreuth, wissen Sie?
    Fritz: Ja.
            Muß ich meinen Smoking anziehen?
    Elke: Das ist ja normal.
15   Ich will mein neues Kleid anziehen.
    Fritz: Schön!
    Elke: Ich will auch meinen Seidenmantel tragen.
    Fritz: Ha!
    Elke: Und natürlich meine Perlenkette.
20 Fritz: Wann müssen wir uns entscheiden?
    Elke: O, sofort.
            Wir wollen doch gehen, oder?
    Fritz: (hastily) O ja, selbstverständlich.
            Wann müssen wir die Karten abholen?
</pre>

Die Oper in Bayreuth

Dialogue 2

Frau Meyer has gone to see her doctor because she has been feeling a bit giddy recently.

1   Doktor Storm: Nun, Frau Meyer, was fehlt Ihnen denn?
     Frau Meyer: Es ist mein Kopf, Herr Doktor.
      Mir ist immer wieder schwindlig.
     Doktor Storm: Wie alt sind Sie, Frau Meyer?
5   Frau Meyer: Ich bin fünfundsiebzig Jahre alt.
     Doktor Storm: Und wo wohnen Sie?
     Frau Meyer: In der Nietzschestraße.
     Doktor Storm: Wo ist Ihre Wohnung?
      Im Parterre?
10 Frau Meyer: Nein, Herr Doktor.
      Im dritten Stock.
     Doktor Storm: Und Sie gehen jeden Tag einkaufen?
     Frau Meyer: Ja, und ich hole die kleine Sandra von der Schule.
     Doktor Storm: Ja, ja. Nun, Frau Meyer, Sie müssen etwas weniger
15 herumlaufen.
      Wann stehen Sie morgens auf?

Frau Meyer: Um sechs Uhr.

Doktor Storm: Sie müssen etwas länger im Bett bleiben, und Sie müssen sich jeden Nachmittag eine Stunde hinlegen.

20 Frau Meyer: Muß ich daheim bleiben, Herr Doktor?

Doktor Storm: Nein, Sie brauchen nicht daheim bleiben, aber Sie müssen diese Tabletten nehmen.

Frau Meyer: Muß ich sie abends nehmen? Ich werde nicht einschlafen.

25 Doktor Storm: Nein, Sie brauchen sie nicht abends nehmen.

Frau Meyer: Gott sei Dank!

Information

(a) Notes on Dialogue 1

	Bayreuth	Bayreuth is a town in the north of Bavaria where Richard Wagner established a theatre for the performance of his operas. Each summer there is a festival of his operas there.
3	Parsifal	*Parsifal* is the title of one of Richard Wagner's operas.
8	Wollen wir	Although the verb 'wollen' means literally 'to want to', when it is used in this way 'wollen wir ...?' has the function of making a suggestion. It is consequently best translated in this case as 'Shall we ...?'
9	Die Karte	In order to show the cost of each individual item, German often places the name of the item first thus: 'Die Karte hundertsechzig Mark' – 'Each ticket 160 marks'; 'das Glas zehn Mark zwanzig' – 'DM 10.20 per glass'.
13	Smoking	'Smoking' is the German term for a dinner jacket and matching trousers. It is here translated as 'evening dress'.
22	doch	The word 'doch' in this sentence is rendered in English by 'do', which changes the straightforward statement into a request for confirmation: 'We *do* want to go, (don't we?)'.

| 22 | oder? | The word 'oder?' has the same function as 'nicht wahr?' It can be rendered in English as: 'don't we?' 'haven't I?' 'shan't we?' etc. |

(b) Notes on Dialogue 2

2	Herr Doktor	Remember that when people speak to a doctor and refer to him by his title, they use the word 'Herr' as well as the title.
3	immer wieder	This phrase indicates that something happens over and over again and can therefore be translated as 'always' or 'again and again'.
11	Im	German uses the word 'in' where English uses the word 'on'. 'Im dritten Stock' – 'on the third floor'.

(c) Word list

die **Kar**te (-n)	ticket
gehen	to go
wie**so**?	why?
teuer	expensive
an_ziehen	to put on
nor**mal**	usual
der **Sei**denmantel (¨)	silk coat
tragen (trägt)	to wear
die **Per**lenket**t**e (-n)	pearl necklace
sich ent**schei**den	to decide
so**fort**	at once
ab_holen	to fetch; pick up
der Kopf (¨e)	head
schwindlig	giddy
das Jahr (-e)	year
die **Woh**nung (-en)	flat
der Stock (Stockwerke)	floor (of a building)
jed-	every
ein_kaufen	to go shopping
holen	to fetch
die **Schu**le (-n)	school
weniger	less
he**rum**_laufen (läuft herum)	to run about
auf_stehen	to get up
lang	long, a long time
das Bett (-en)	bed
bleiben	to remain, stay

die **Stun**de (-n)	hour
sich **hin**__legen	to lie down
da**heim**	at home
die Tab**lett**e (-n)	tablet; pill
ein__schlafen (schläft ein)	to go to sleep

(d) Some phrases

Das ist Pech	That's bad luck
Was fehlt **Ihn**en?	What's the matter (with you)?
Im Par**terre**	On the ground floor
Gott sei Dank!	Thank heavens!

(e) Further useful vocabulary

kochen	to cook
rauchen	to smoke
lesen	to read
das Brot	bread
schreiben	write
die **Zahn**bürste (-n)	toothbrush
die **Bad**ehose (-n)	swimming trunks
der **Reise**paß (-pässe)	passport
die **Ein**trittskarte (-n)	(entry) ticket
das Geld	money
die **Land**karte (-n)	map
der **Ten**nis**schläger** (-)	tennis racket
der **Stie**fel (-)	boot
der **Regen**schirm(-e)	umbrella
müde	tired

Structural explanations

(a) Structures to learn

(i) How to say what you want to do

| Ich will | } | { kochen
rauchen
gehen
lesen | I want to
We want to | } | { cook
smoke
go
read |
| Wir wollen | | | | | |

In order to express what you want to do, you use part of the verb 'wollen' and the infinitive of some other verb.

Look at some of the sentences from the dialogues:

Ich will	{	mein neues Kleid	}	anziehen
		meinen Seidenmantel		
Wir wollen		die Karten		nehmen

I want to	{	put on my new dress	
		put on my silk coat	
We want to		take the tickets	

If you look at these sentences carefully, you will see that the infinitive is placed at the end of the sentence.

(ii) How to express what you have to do

Ich muß	}	{	kochen	I must	}	{	cook
Wir müssen			rauchen	We must			smoke
			gehen				go
			lesen				read

When there are other elements in the sentence besides the modal verb, 'müssen' or 'wollen', and an infinitive, then the infinitive is placed at the end of the sentence. Here are some sentences from the dialogue:

Sie müssen	{	etwas weniger	herumlaufen
		etwas länger im Bett	bleiben
		sich	hinlegen
		diese Tabletten	nehmen

Exactly the same applies if you want to ask a question using a modal verb and an infinitive. Have a look at these sentences taken from the dialogue:

Wann müssen wir	{	uns	entscheiden?
		die Karten	abholen?

Or have a look at these sentences:

Muß ich	{	sie abends	nehmen?
		daheim	bleiben?
		meinen Smoking	anziehen?

(iii) How to say that you don't have to do something

In these sentences, taken from the dialogue, the verb which expresses absence of obligation is the verb 'brauchen' used in the negative.

Sie brauchen	{	nicht daheim	bleiben
		sie nicht abends	nehmen

You don't need to stay at home
You don't need to take them in the evening

(b) Grammar

Modal verbs

The three verbs you have been using in this chapter are:

> 'wollen': to want to
> 'müssen': to 'must'/to have to
> 'brauchen nicht': – to 'not have to'/not need to

In order to see how these verbs can be used in sentences, see Chapter 12. Their parts are listed in the Grammatical Summary.

1 The verb 'wollen' indicates a wish, willingness or intention.

Wollen Sie Brot?	Do you want some bread?
Wollen Sie mit(kommen)?	Do you want to come (with me)?
Ich will ihn nicht stören	I don't want to disturb him
Ich will das nicht tun	I don't want to do it

2 The verb 'müssen' denotes some kind of compulsion.

Ich muß nach Hause (gehen)	I must go home
Ich muß lachen	I must laugh, I can't help laughing
Ich muß einen Brief schreiben	I must/have to write a letter

3 The verb 'brauchen' is not normally considered to be amongst the set of modal verbs. Absence of obligation can be expressed by using the verb 'müssen' in the negative form. However, it is probably easier to learn how to express this function of language by using a separate verb. That is why the verb 'brauchen' has been introduced here. Here are some further examples of sentences showing its use.

Sie brauchen keinen Brief schreiben	You don't have to write a letter
Sie brauchen jetzt nicht gehen	You don't have to go now
Sie brauchen nicht zu mir kommen	You don't have to come to me

Exercises

A

Exercise 1

Which of these things would you have to take with you ('mitnehmen') under the following circumstances? For instance, if it was raining, you would need to take your raincoat and you would say 'Ich muß meinen Regenmantel mitnehmen'.

1 What would you need to take if you were going shopping?
2 Suppose you wanted to go hiking.

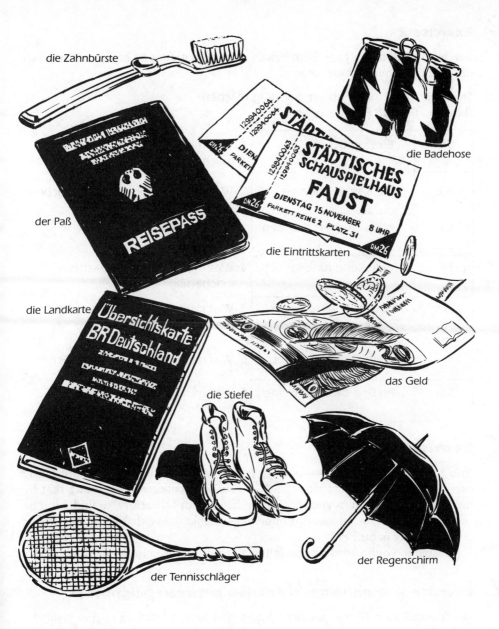

die Zahnbürste

der Paß

REISEPASS

die Landkarte

Übersichtskarte
BR Deutschland

die Badehose

STÄDTISCHES
SCHAUSPIELHAUS
FAUST
DIENSTAG 15 NOVEMBER 8 UHR
PARKETT REIHE 2 PLATZ 31

die Eintrittskarten

das Geld

die Stiefel

der Tennisschläger

der Regenschirm

3   You want to play tennis.
4   How about driving through Germany?
5   You're just off to the theatre.
6   You want to go swimming.
7   You're going abroad for your holiday
8   A weekend away?
9   It's raining.

Exercise 2

Below you will find a page from Fritz's diary. What does he have to do on each day? The first one is done for you.

Question: Was muß Fritz am Sonntag machen?
Answer: Er muß Elke besuchen.

So	Elke besuchen	1 Was muß Fritz am Sonntag machen?
Mo	die Karten abholen	2 Was muß Fritz am Montag machen?
Di	nach Nürnberg fahren	3 Was muß Fritz am Dienstag machen?
Mi	eine Kette für Elke kaufen	4 Was muß Fritz am Mittwoch machen?
Do	einen Tennisschläger kaufen	5 Was muß Fritz am Donnerstag machen?
Fr	nach Stuttgart fahren	6 Was muß Fritz am Freitag machen?
Sa	im Bett bleiben (müde!)	7 Was muß Fritz am Samstag machen?

 Exercise 3

You have arranged to go on holiday with a friend. This friend is notoriously careless at getting things ready and so you have collected everything that he might need and put it in your car. When he rings up, therefore, to find out if he should bring certain things with him, you are able to say that you have already got everything organised.

Listen to your recording and follow the pattern given in the model.

 Exercise 4   Hundedreck: Friction between neighbours

Don't forget to read the questions below first before listening to this dialogue, and remember: you do not have to understand every word, just listen for the information you need.

Note the expressions 'Hundedreck' (dog dirt) and 'wegräumen' (to clear away).

1   Why is the man annoyed?
2   What does he think has caused the problem?
3   Does the woman do as he demands and clear away the dirt?
4   What objection does she raise?
5   What does he threaten to do?

17 Können Sie singen?

Suggestions and proposals

Dialogues

Dialogue 1

The irrepressible Antonio Raggi has spotted a rather nice-looking girl sitting outside a 'Gasthaus' on the Leopoldstraße. Sensing the possibility of an upturn in his love-life, he sits down at the same table.

```
 1  Antonio:   Ist dieser Platz frei?
    Mädchen:   Ja.
    Antonio:   Schönes Wetter, nicht wahr?
    Mädchen:   Ja. Sehr schön.
 5  Antonio:   Ich heiße Antonio.
    Mädchen:   Hmm.
    ...
    Antonio:   Wie heißen Sie?
       Wenn ich fragen darf?
    Mädchen:   Claudia.
10  Antonio:   Claudia. Ein schöner Name.
    Mädchen:   Danke.
    ...
    Antonio:   Sagen Sie, Claudia.
       Können Sie Tennis spielen?
    Mädchen:   Ja.
15  Antonio:   Schön! Wollen wir Tennis spielen?
    Mädchen:   Wann?
    Antonio:   Morgen, vielleicht?
    Mädchen:   Ja, gern.
    Antonio:   Spielen sie oft?
20  Mädchen:   Ziemlich oft.
       Vier- oder fünfmal in der Woche.
    Antonio:   Wo spielen Sie?
```

Schönes Wetter, nicht wahr?

Mädchen:	Im Carlton Club.
Antonio:	Ach?

25   Spielen Sie gut?

Mädchen:	Ach, ganz gut.
	Und Sie?
Antonio:	Nicht sehr gut.
	(To himself) Das gibt's doch nicht!!

Dialogue 2

Fritz has decided that his relationship with Elke ought to take a more positive turn, so he goes to visit her at her flat. He is encouraged when she uses the familiar 'du' form.

1   Fritz: Hallo, Elke!

Elke:	Du, Fritz!
	Komm doch herein!
Fritz:	Danke.

5   Wie geht's dir?

Elke:	Prima!

Fritz: Du, Elke ... .
Wollen wir am Wochenende wegfahren?
Elke: O, ja! Wohin?
10 Fritz: Ich kenne eine sehr hübsche Kirche.
In der Nähe von Rosenheim.
Elke: O nein, Fritz!
Schon wieder eine Kirche!!!
Fritz: Was ist denn los?
15 Elke: Jedes Mal eine Kirche!
Fritz: Kirchen interessieren mich.
Das weißt du.
Elke: Aber du hast jede Woche eine andere Kirche.
Fritz: Es tut mir leid.
20 Elke: Wollen wir nach Kufstein fahren?
Dort können wir Ski fahren.
Fritz: Aber ich kann nicht Ski fahren.
Elke: Aber ich kann sehr gut Ski fahren.
Fritz: Na gut.

Auf dem Idiotenhügel

25   Fahren wir nach Kufstein.
Elke: Ja, du kannst es lernen.
        (to herself) (Auf dem Idiotenhügel!)

Information

(a) Notes on Dialogue 1

8	Wenn	Despite appearances to the contrary, this word very often means 'if'. Here it means 'if I may ask', or as we would say 'if you don't mind my asking'.
13	spielen	Note that this word comes at the end of the sentence. See Chapter 16.
16	Wann	Note this word carefully because it is very similar to the word in line 8. This word, however, is always used in a question: 'When?'
18	gern	This short word is a very economical way of expressing the idea 'I'd like to'.
25	gut	This word can serve both as an adjective and as an adverb. We would here have to translate it as 'well'.

(b) Notes on Dialogue 2

8	wegfahren	Note the position of this word in the sentence. See Chapter 16.
9	Wohin	Germans are very punctilious about indicating the distinction between location and direction. In English we would simply say 'Where?' In German, however, it is essential to indicate the meaning which we still have in our archaic form 'Whither?' It is probably best to think of the meaning of the word 'wohin?' as 'where to?'
16	interessieren mich	Note how German says: (things, e.g. churches) interest me.
27	Idiotenhügel	Although we would say 'nursery slope' in English, the term in German for the slopes where many people can

learn to ski is very condescending. It is best translated as 'idiots' slope'.

(c) Word list

dies-	this
der Platz (¨e)	place; seat
frei	free; vacant
heißen	to be called
spielen	to play
wollen	to wish; want to
morgen	tomorrow
viel**leicht**	perhaps
oft	often
ziemlich	fairly
die **Wo**che (-n)	week
gut	well (as an adverb)
ganz	quite
Prima!	splendid!
das **Woch**enende (-n)	weekend
weg_fahren	to go away
wo**hin**?	where to?
kennen	to know (a person or a place)
hübsch	pretty
interes**sier**en	to interest
wissen	to know (a fact)
ander-	other
Ski fahren	to go ski-ing
lernen	to learn

(d) Some phrases

Wie **hei**ßen Sie?	What is your name?
Komm doch her**ein**	Come in, won't you? (familiar form)
Wie geht's dir?	How are you? (familiar form)
Schon **wie**der!	Again!
Was ist denn los?	What's the matter?
Jedes Mal	Every time
Sehr gut	Very well
Ziemlich gut	Fairly well
Nicht sehr gut	Not very well
Nur **etw**as	Only a little bit
Im **groß**en und **gan**zen	On the whole

(e) Further useful vocabulary

die **Kar**te (-n)	card(s)
spielen	to play
schwimmen	to swim
tanzen	to dance
essen	to eat
der Spa**zier**gang (¨e)	walk

machen	to make, to do
reiten	to ride
malen	to paint
singen	to sing
ausgezeichnet	very well indeed
an	to, by
auf	on, onto
in	in, into
das **Klas**senzimmer (-)	classroom
warten	to wait
das **Ra**dio (-s)	radio
stehen	to stand
der Tisch (-e)	table
stellen	to put
die Milch	milk
der **Kühl**schrank (-̈e)	refrigerator
hängen	to hang
die Wand (-̈e)	wall
halten (hält)	to hold
die **Zei**tung (-en)	newspaper
die Tür (-en)	door

Structural explanations

(a) Structures to learn

(i) How to make a suggestion or proposal

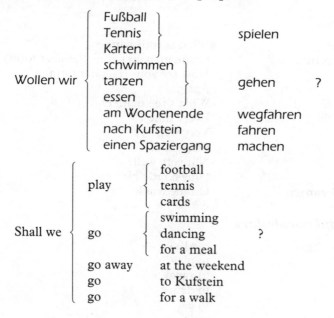

(ii) How to ask what you can do

Können Sie / Kannst du
schwimmen
Ski fahren
reiten ?
malen
singen
tanzen
Tennis / Fußball } spielen

Can you
swim
ski
ride
paint ?
sing
dance
play { tennis / football

(iii) How to say what you can do

Ich kann
schwimmen
Ski fahren
reiten
malen
singen
tanzen
Tennis / Fußball } spielen

I can
swim
ski
ride
paint
sing
dance
play { tennis / football

(iv) How to ask how well someone can do something

Schwimmen sie gut?
Reiten Sie gut?
Singen Sie gut?
Tanzen Sie gut?

BUT:

> Fahren Sie gut Ski?
> Spielen Sie gut Tennis?
> Spielen Sie gut Fußball?

(v) Some replies you can give

ausgezeichnet	very well indeed
sehr gut	very well
ziemlich gut	fairly well
nicht sehr gut	not very well
nur etwas	only a little bit

(b) Grammar

(i) 'Wollen' and 'können'

Here are the most frequently used forms of these two verbs.

● *The verb* 'wollen' *(to want to)*

ich will	I want to
du willst	you want to
er will	he wants to
sie will	she wants to
wir wollen	we want to
Sie wollen	you want to

● *The verb* 'können' *(to be able to)*

ich kann	I can
du kannst	you can
er kann	he can
sie kann	she can
wir können	we can
Sie können	you can

Both these verbs are *irregular* in that their stems change, and their endings do not conform to the standard pattern. However, they are amongst the most important verbs in the whole language and there is no alternative to learning them. You will find them in the Grammatical Summary.

The most frequent sentence patterns in which these verbs operate are as follows:

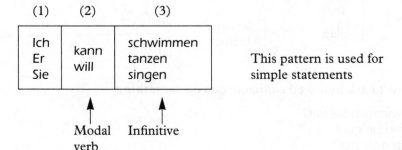

This pattern is used for simple statements

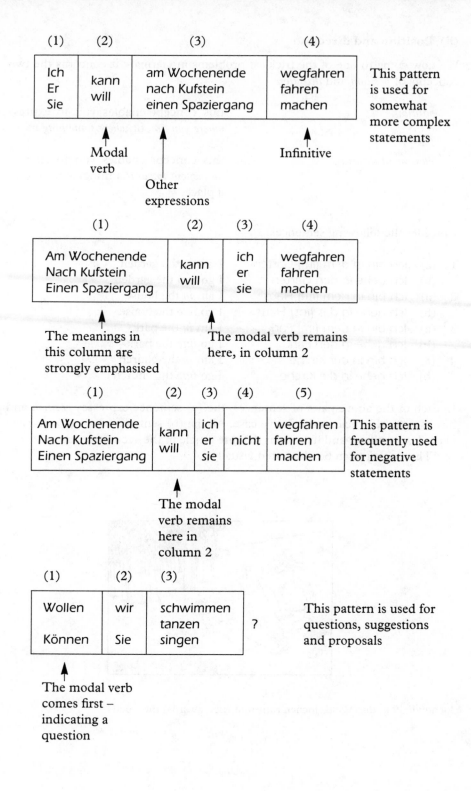

	(1)	(2)	(3)	(4)	
	Ich Er Sie	kann will	am Wochenende nach Kufstein einen Spaziergang	wegfahren fahren machen	This pattern is used for somewhat more complex statements

↑ Modal verb   ↑ Other expressions   ↑ Infinitive

(1)	(2)	(3)	(4)
Am Wochenende Nach Kufstein Einen Spaziergang	kann will	ich er sie	wegfahren fahren machen

↑ The meanings in this column are strongly emphasised   ↑ The modal verb remains here, in column 2

(1)	(2)	(3)	(4)	(5)	
Am Wochenende Nach Kufstein Einen Spaziergang	kann will	ich er sie	nicht	wegfahren fahren machen	This pattern is frequently used for negative statements

↑ The modal verb remains here in column 2

(1)	(2)	(3)		
Wollen Können	wir Sie	schwimmen tanzen singen	?	This pattern is used for questions, suggestions and proposals

↑ The modal verb comes first – indicating a question

(ii) Position and direction

We now come to one of the trickiest problems in German; it concerns the two concepts of *position* and *direction*.

position:	this concept enables you to express *where you are*, or *where something is*.
movement towards:	this concept enables you to express *movement towards* a thing, a person, or a place.

Consider the following sentences:

1	(a)	Ich bin in dem (im) Garten	I am *in* the garden
	(b)	Ich gehe in den Garten	I go *into* the garden
2	(a)	Ich bin in dem (im) Haus	I am *in* the house
	(b)	Ich gehe in das (ins) Haus	I go *into* the house
3	(a)	Ich bin in dem (im) Park	I am *in* the park
	(b)	Ich gehe in den Park	I go *into* the park
4	(a)	Ich bin in der Kirche	I am *in* the church
	(b)	Ich gehe in die Kirche	I go *into* the church

In each of the above pairs of sentences, the (a) sentence expresses *position* and has its definite article in the dative case. All the (b) sentences express *movement towards* something, and have their definite article in the accusative case.

This concept can be illustrated visually:

Jochen läuft in den Wald: Jochen runs into (i.e. towards) the wood

Jochen läuft in dem (im) Wald: Jochen is running in (i.e. within/inside) the wood

The pictures show how important this concept is in German. The only difference between the two sentences is the definite article, once in the *accusative* indicating *movement toward* the wood, and once in the *dative* indicating Jochen's *position* inside the wood. Consequently, the only way German speakers have of understanding correctly what is meant is by correct use of the two cases.

Certain verbs, such as 'wohnen' (to live), 'sein' (to be) and 'sitzen' (to be sitting) always indicate *position*. Other verbs, such as 'fahren' (to go, to drive), and 'gehen' (to go, to walk) always indicate *movement*. When you use one of these verbs, therefore, it is especially important to use the correct case.

The following three prepositions are the most frequently used for indicating either *movement toward* or *position*:

an	to, by
auf	on, onto
in	in, into

The rule can be summarised thus:

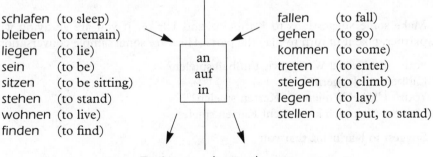

schlafen	(to sleep)		fallen	(to fall)
bleiben	(to remain)		gehen	(to go)
liegen	(to lie)		kommen	(to come)
sein	(to be)	an	treten	(to enter)
sitzen	(to be sitting)	auf	steigen	(to climb)
stehen	(to stand)	in	legen	(to lay)
wohnen	(to live)		stellen	(to put, to stand)
finden	(to find)			

Dative case   Accusative case

You will find a list of those prepositions which can be used with either the *accusative* or the *dative* case in the Grammatical Summary.

Do not forget, however, that there are also prepositions which can *only* be used with the *accusative*, just as there are those which can *only* be used with the *dative*. You will find these in the Grammatical Summary. They were dealt with in Chapters 5 and 9.

Exercises

A

Exercise 1

This is Karlheinz. He enjoys play-ing football and cards. He likes ski-ing and going for walks.

This is Ulrike. She likes dancing, swimming and riding and playing tennis.

Make some suggestions to Karlheinz and Ulrike. If you are studying with a partner, take it in turn to play the parts. Here are some sample conversations:

You: Karlheinz! Wollen wir Fußball spielen?
Karlheinz: Ja, gern.
You: Ulrike! Wollen wir Karten spielen?
Ulrike: Nein, ich kann nicht Karten spielen.

Suggest to Karlheinz that you

1 play football,
2 go riding,
3 play cards,
4 play tennis,
5 go for a walk.

Then propose to Ulrike that you

6   go dancing,
7   go ski-ing,
8   go swimming,
9   play football,
10 play cards.

Exercise 2

You are one of those people who are either extremely good at an activity, or absolutely awful. As it happens, your strengths lie in swimming, riding, tennis and cards; and your weaknesses in ski-ing, dancing, football, singing and painting. Answer the questions on the recording depending on whether you are good at the activity or not.

B

Exercise 3

Complete the following sentences:

1   Der Junge geht in d– Schule.
2   Der Lehrer arbeitet in d– Schule.
3   Die Klasse kommt in d– Klassenzimmer.
4   Die Mädchen warten in d– Klassenzimmer.
5   Das Radio steht auf d– Tisch.
6   Ich stelle die Milch in d– Kühlschrank.
7   Das Bild hängt an d– Wand.
8   Ich halte meine Zeitung unter d– Arm.
9   Ich gehe an d– Tür.
10 Ich stelle die Tasse auf d– Tisch.

Exercise 4   Junges Eheglück: An unenthusiastic husband

Where will the love-birds go for their holiday ('Urlaub')? Crete? The island of Sylt? Or somewhere more exotic ...? Don't forget to read the questions below before listening to this dialogue, and remember: you do not have to understand every word, just listen for the information you need.

1   What does the wife want to talk about?
2   What is her first suggestion?
3   What is her husband's reaction?
4   What is her second suggestion?
5   What is his reaction?
6   What two complaints does he have about London?
7   What proposal does he make?

18 **Ich möchte reisen**

Dreams and wishes

 Dialogues

Dialogue 1

Elke and Fritz have been enjoying the ski-ing at Kufstein (she possibly somewhat more than he). Now they are lying side by side on camp beds in the sun at
the top of the ski slope. Elke is looking through some travel brochures.

```
 1   Elke:   Fritz?
     Fritz:  Ja?
     Elke:   Es ist schön hier, nicht?
     Fritz:  Ja. Sehr schön.
 5   Elke:   Du bist wirklich lieb, weißt du?
     Fritz:  Ja?
     ...
     Elke:   Fritz?
     Fritz:  Ja?
     Elke:   Weißt du was?
10   Fritz:  Nein.
     Elke:   Ich möchte nach Amerika fahren.
     Fritz:  Tatsächlich?
     Elke:   Ja. Ich möchte Hollywood sehen.
     Fritz:  Hollywood?
15   Elke:   Ja. Und ich möchte New York besuchen.
     Fritz:  Ach, New York ist doch nicht schön.
     Elke:   Doch, doch!
             Und ich möchte mit einer Straßenbahn in San Francisco
             fahren.
20   Fritz:  Warum möchtest du mit einer Straßenbahn fahren?
     Elke:   Ach, du verstehst nicht.
             In San Francisco ist das so romantisch.
     Fritz:  Aber teuer.
     Elke:   Das ist typisch „Mann"!!
```

Es ist schön hier, nicht?

25   Du denkst nur ans Geld.
       Ich möchte reisen.
       Ich möchte die Welt sehen.

Dialogue 2

Frau Meyer is telephoning her best friend in order to impart the great news.

1   Frau Meyer: Leni? Weißt du was?
        Die Inge kriegt ein Kind!
    Leni: Nein. Das ist ja wunderbar!
        Wo ist sie denn?
5   Frau Meyer: In Liverpool.
    Leni: Ach ja, richtig.
        In England.
    Frau Meyer: Ich fahre natürlich nach Liverpool.
    Leni: Ja, natürlich.
10   Frau Meyer: Ich muß meinen Mantel reinigen lassen.
    Leni: Ja, selbstverständlich.
    Frau Meyer: Und ich muß mir ein neues Kleid machen lassen.
    Leni: Ja, freilich.
    Frau Meyer: Dann brauche ich einen Fotoapparat.

15   Ich muß meinen alten Fotoapparat reparieren lassen.
    Leni: Sicher.
    Frau Meyer: Dann muß ich auch etwas Geld wechseln.
    Leni: Ja, klar.
    Frau Meyer: Was für Geld haben sie dort in England?
20   Dollar, nicht?
    Leni: Nein. Sie haben Pfund und 'Pence'.
    Frau Meyer: Ach so. Ja.
    Dann muß ich mir die Haare waschen lassen.
    Leni: Moment, Irmgard.
25   Wann erwartet Inge ihr Kind?
    Frau Meyer: Nächstes Jahr.
    Im März.
    Leni: Hör' mal, Irmgard!
    Du hast doch noch viel Zeit.

Information

(a) Notes on Dialogue 1

11 fahren

Note the difference in the word order between German and English. In German the infinitive comes at the end of the sentence. See also lines 13, 15, 19, 20 and 28.

25 ans Geld

The meaning of 'an' in this sentence is 'of'. 'Denken an' - 'to think of'

(b) Notes on Dialogue 2

2 kriegt

There are two verbs in German which mean 'to get' or 'to receive'. They are 'kriegen' and 'bekommen'. Of the two, 'kriegen' is slightly more colloquial. In this particular sentence the word 'kriegen' is probably best rendered by 'to have', since in English we say 'to have a child'.

Once again the present tense is used here with future meaning.

6 richtig

In German there are several expressions for agreeing with what somebody else has just said. Leni uses a number of them.

richtig (line 6)
natürlich (line 9)
selbstverständlich (line 11)
freilich (line 13)
sicher (line 16)
klar (line 18)

17 etwas

This word when used together with a noun means 'some': 'etwas Geld' – 'some money', 'etwas Milch' – 'some milk', 'etwas Butter' – 'some butter'.

19 Was für ... ?

This useful phrase means 'What sort of ... ?'

(c) Word list

wirklich	really
lieb	sweet, nice
tatsächlich	really; indeed
besuchen	to visit
die Straßenbahn (-en)	tram
warum?	why?
verstehen	to understand
romantisch	romantic
teuer	dear; expensive
typisch	typical
denken	to think
reisen	to travel
die Welt	world
kriegen	to get
das Kind (-er)	child
wunderbar	wonderful
richtig	right; correct
reinigen	to clean
freilich	of course
brauchen	to need
der Fotoapparat (-e)	camera
reparieren	to repair
sicher	certainly
wechseln	to change
klar	obviously
die Haare (used in plural)	hair
waschen (wäscht)	to wash
erwarten	to expect
das Jahr (-e)	year
die Zeit	time

(d) Further useful vocabulary

sprechen	to speak
zahlen	to pay
telefonieren	to make a telephone call
schlafen	to sleep
schmutzig	dirty
die Armbanduhr (-en)	wristwatch
kaputt	broken
der Hut (⸚e)	hat
dreckig	dirty
das Hemd (-en)	shirt
die Brille (-n)	glasses, spectacles

Structural explanations

(a) Structures to learn

(i) How to say you would like to do something and how to ask somebody what they would like to do

Ich möchte	nach Amerika	fahren	
	New York	besuchen	
	Hollywood	sehen	
	die Welt	sehen	
	Herrn Schmidt	sprechen	(?)
Möchten Sie	–	reisen	
	–	zahlen	
	–	telefonieren	
	–	schlafen	
	–	gehen	

I should like	to go	to America
	to visit	New York
	to see	Hollywood
	to see	the world
	to speak	to Mr Smith (?)
	to travel	
Would you like	to pay	
	to make a telephone call	
	to sleep	
	to go	

(ii) How to say that you would like to have something done

Ich muß Ich möchte }	{ meinen Mantel meinen Fotoapparat ein neues Kleid mir die Haare	reinigen reparieren machen waschen } lassen

I must I should like to }	have { my coat my camera a new dress my hair	cleaned repaired made washed

(iii) How to ask when things will be ready

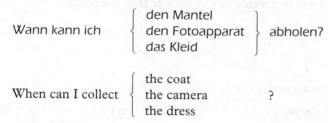

Wann ist {	der Mantel der Fotoapparat das Kleid }	fertig?

When will {	the coat the camera the dress }	be ready?

(iv) How to ask when you can collect things

Wann kann ich {	den Mantel den Fotoapparat das Kleid }	abholen?

When can I collect {	the coat the camera the dress	?

Exercises

A

Exercise 1

You had an accident on the way home and fell off your bicycle. All your clothes are dirty and all your breakables are broken. You have to set about restoring the damage. You go to the various shops. What do you say?

1 Diese Jacke ist schmutzig. Ich möchte sie ......
2 Diese Armbanduhr ist kaputt. Ich möchte sie ......
3 Mein Hut ist dreckig. Ich möchte ihn ......

4 Mein Fotoapparat ist kaputt. Ich möchte ihn ......
5 Dieses Hemd ist schmutzig. Ich möchte es ......
6 Diese Hose ist dreckig. Ich möchte sie ......
7 Meine Brille ist kaputt. Ich möchte sie ......

Exercise 2

Now you will get a chance to practise saying what you want to do. Listen to the English prompts on your recording and say the correct German phrase using 'Ich möchte ...'. You will be given a model answer after the pause.

B

Exercise 3

Unscramble the following sentences:

1 Ich möchte mir die Haare	(a)	Hamburg fahren.
2 Er will seinen	(b)	wechseln.
3 Elke will New York	(c)	Kleid machen lassen.
4 Ich möchte die	(d)	Herrn Schmidt sprechen.
5 Er möchte nach	(e)	reinigen lassen.
6 Wir müssen das Geld	(f)	waschen lassen.
7 Wir möchten	(g)	zahlen.
8 Sie muß sich ein neues	(h)	Apparat reparieren lassen.
9 Kann ich bitte	(i)	Welt sehen.
10 Sie will ihren Mantel	(j)	besuchen.

Exercise 4   Träume: Pushing your luck

Don't forget to read the question opposite before listening to this dialogue, and remember: you do not have to understand every word, just listen for the information you need.

Can you pick out what the young wife wants and put her requests in the correct sequence?

Gestern und vorgestern

Talking about the past

 Dialogues

Dialogue 1

Fritz is furious that Elke has kept him waiting – yet again.

```
1   Fritz:   Mensch!
             Wo warst du denn?
    Elke:    Was ist denn los?
             Mein Bus hatte Verspätung.
5   Fritz:   Er hatte gestern Verspätung.
             Und heute hat er schon wieder Verspätung.
    Elke:    Gestern hatte mein Bus nicht Verspätung.
    Fritz:   Doch, doch!
             Er hatte dreißig Minuten Verspätung.
10  Elke:    Das stimmt nicht.
    Fritz:   Doch! Das stimmt.
             Ich war um sieben Uhr vor dem Kino.
             Und du warst erst um sieben Uhr dreißig da.
    Elke:    Ich war pünktlich da.
15           Du warst einfach zu früh am Kino.
    Fritz:   Und warum warst du vorgestern nicht pünktlich?
    Elke:    Ich war im Geschäft.
    Fritz:   Was? Bis acht Uhr?
             Das glaube ich nicht!
20  Elke:    Ich hatte sehr viel zu tun.
    Fritz:   Und der Chef war auch da, nicht wahr?
    Elke:    Natürlich.
             Er hatte auch viel zu tun.
    Fritz:   Aha. Jetzt verstehe ich...
```

Dialogue 2

Antonio is walking along the street when he sees Frau Meyer apparently searching for something.

1   Antonio: Kann ich Ihnen helfen?
    Frau Meyer: Ach, ich habe meine Armbanduhr verloren.
    Antonio: Hier, auf der Straße?
    Frau Meyer: Ja, das glaube ich.
5   Ich bin in die Stadt gefahren.
    Und ich habe dort Kaffee getrunken.
    Antonio: Haben Sie die Uhr vielleicht in der Stadt verloren?
    Frau Meyer: Nein.
    Ich habe sie im Bus noch gesehen.
10 Antonio: Haben Sie an der Haltestelle gesucht?
    Frau Meyer: Ja, natürlich.
    Dort habe ich Frau Moezer getroffen.
    Ich bin mit ihr zur Post gegangen.
    Antonio: Haben Sie die Uhr vielleicht in der Post verloren?
15 Frau Meyer: Nein, das glaube ich nicht.
    Antonio: Sind Sie direkt von der Post hierher gekommen?
    Frau Meyer: Nein. Ich habe zuerst Äpfel gekauft.
    Bei Schötz.
    Antonio: Ach so. Bei Schötz.
20 Wie lange sind Sie bei Schötz geblieben?
    Frau Meyer: Ach, nicht lange.
    Fünf Minuten vielleicht.
    Antonio: Haben Sie in Ihrer Tasche gesucht?
    Frau Meyer: Was?
25 Antonio: Haben Sie in Ihrer Tasche gesucht?
    Frau Meyer: Da ist sie!

Information

(a) Notes on Dialogue 1

1   Mensch!   This is a much-used expression in German, which you will hear very frequently if you go there. It conveys a certain feeling of indignation on the part of the speaker, and you should be wary of using it unless you feel you know the person you are speaking to well enough.

4	Verspätung	Note that where in English we say something or someone *is late*, in German one says something *has lateness*.
10	Das stimmt nicht	This phrase should be treated as an idiom, and not translated.
12	um sieben Uhr	In German, expressions of time come before expressions of place.
13	erst	In expressions of time, this word means 'not until'.

(b) Notes on Dialogue 2

2	verloren	Note that this part of the verb (the past participle) comes at the end of the sentence.
4	das glaube ich	Get used to the order of the words in this expression, and use it as an idiom when you want to say 'I think so'.
6	getrunken	English very often uses the verb 'to have' with food or drink. German, however, always specifies whether one is eating or drinking.
7	vielleicht	This word means 'perhaps'.

(c) Word list

der Bus (-se)	bus
schon **wie**der	again
die Minute (-n)	minute
vor	in front of
das **Ki**no (-s)	cinema
pünktlich	on time
einfach	simply
früh	early
vorgestern	the day before yesterday
das **Geschäft** (-e)	shop; business
bis	until
glauben	to believe
sehr viel	very much

tun	to do
der Chef (-s)	boss
ver**steh**en	to understand
helfen (hilft)	to help
die **Arm**banduhr (-en)	wristwatch
ver**lier**en	to lose
die **Straße** (-n)	street
die Stadt (¨e)	town
trinken	to drink
die **Hal**testelle (-n)	bus or tram stop
suchen	to seek, look for
treffen (trifft)	to meet
die Post (Postämter)	post office
di**rekt**	straight, directly
zu**erst**	first of all
der **Ap**fel (¨)	apple
kaufen	to buy
wie **lang**e?	how long?
bleiben	to stay; remain
nicht **lang**e	not long
viel**leicht**	perhaps
die **Ta**sche (-n)	pocket; bag

(d) Some phrases

Was ist denn los?	What's the matter?
Das stimmt nicht	That's not true, correct
Das **glau**be ich nicht	I don't believe it

(e) Further useful vocabulary

die **Kett**e (-n)	necklace
gegen	against
der Film (-e)	film

Structural explanations

Grammar

(i) Past tenses

When referring to the past, two tenses are used in German. The first past tense is known as the *Imperfect* or *Simple Past*, and the other is known as the *Perfect* tense or *Compound Past*.

(ii) The Simple Past (also known as the Imperfect tense)

When referring to the past in German, this tense is used mainly with the verbs 'haben' and 'sein' and with a number of verbs of speaking, e.g. 'sagen' (to say).
   Here are some examples taken from Dialogue 1:

Wo warst du denn?
Ich war um sieben Uhr vor dem Kino
Du warst erst um sieben Uhr dreißig da
Ich war pünklich da
Ich war im Geschäft

Mein Bus hatte Verspätung
Er hatte gestern Verspätung
Ich hatte sehr viel zu tun
Er hatte auch viel zu tun

● *Here are the forms of the Simple Past tense of 'sein'(to be).*

ich war	I was
du warst	you were (*familiar*)
er war	he was
sie war	she was
es war	it was
wir waren	we were
ihr wart	you were (*familiar*)
Sie waren	you were (*formal or polite*)
sie waren	they were

● *Here are the forms of the Simple Past tense of 'haben' (to have).*

ich hatte	I had
du hattest	you had (*familiar*)
er hatte	he had
sie hatte	she had
es hatte	it had
wir hatten	we had
ihr hattet	you had (*familiar*)
Sie hatten	you had (*formal or polite*)
sie hatten	they had

Remember when you want to say: 'I was', or 'we were', or 'I had', or 'they had', these are the forms to use.
   You should use the same tense if you want to say 'I said'. The Simple Past tense of the verb 'to say' is given in the Grammatical Summary.

(iii) The Compound Past (also known as the Perfect tense)

In this course, you are going to learn the Compound Past of verbs *other than* 'haben', 'sein' and 'sagen'. As the word *compound* indicates, this tense is made by using parts of two verbs.

Consider the following sentences taken from Dialogue 2 and try to discover how this tense is constructed.

Ich <u>habe</u> meine Armbanduhr <u>verloren</u>   (verlieren: to lose)
Ich <u>habe</u> dort Kaffee <u>getrunken</u>   (trinken: to drink)
Ich <u>habe</u> sie im Bus <u>gesehen</u>   (sehen: to see)
Ich <u>habe</u> zuerst Äpfel <u>gekauft</u>   (kaufen: to buy)

Here is an analysis of these sentences.

(1)	(2)	(3)	(4)
Ich Ich Ich Ich	Form of the verb haben	meine Armbanduhr Kaffee sie Äpfel	verloren getrunken gesehen gekauft

In column 2 comes a present tense form of the verb 'haben'. This is called the *auxiliary* verb

In column 4, at the *end* of the sentence, comes a form of the verb which carries the meaning. This form of the verb is called the *past participle*

Here are some more sentences from Dialogue 2. Look and see how they are constructed.

<u>Haben</u> Sie die Uhr in der Stadt <u>verloren</u>?
<u>Haben</u> Sie an der Haltestelle <u>gesucht</u>?
<u>Haben</u> Sie die Uhr in der Post <u>verloren</u>?
<u>Haben</u> Sie in Ihrer Tasche <u>gesucht</u>?

Here is an analysis of these sentences.

(1)	(2)	(3)	(4)
Form of the verb haben	Sie Sie Sie Sie	die Uhr in der Stadt an der Haltestelle die Uhr in der Post in Ihrer Tasche	verloren? gesucht? verloren? gesucht?

The *auxiliary* verb is at the beginning of the sentence in column 1. This indicates that the sentences are questions

The *past participle* comes in column 4, at the end of the sentence

(iv) Compound Past tense with 'sein'

All the verbs we have looked at so far make their *Compound Past* tense by using the verb 'haben'. Unfortunately, this is not always the case. A small group of very important verbs make the *Compound Past* by using the verb 'sein'.

Consider the following sentences taken from Dialogue 2.

Ich bin in die Stadt gefahren   (fahren: to go/drive)
Ich bin mit ihr zur Post gegangen   (gehen: to go)

Here is an analysis of the sentences.

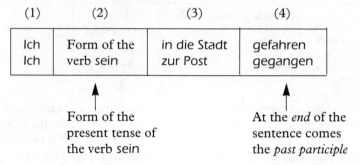

(1)	(2)	(3)	(4)
Ich	Form of the	in die Stadt	gefahren
Ich	verb sein	zur Post	gegangen

Form of the present tense of the verb sein

At the *end* of the sentence comes the *past participle*

Here are some more sentences from Dialogue 2. Look and see how they are constructed.

Sind Sie direkt von der Post hierher gekommen?
    (kommen: to come)
Wie lange sind Sie bei Schötz geblieben?
    (bleiben: to stay/remain)

Here is an analysis of these sentences.

(1)	(2)	(3)	(4)	(5)
–	Form of	Sie	von der Post	gekommen?
Wie lange	the verb sein	Sie	bei Schötz	geblieben?

The *auxiliary* verb sein is here

The *past participle* is at the *end* of the sentence

(v) Summary

We can summarise the rule about making the Compound Past tense thus:

1. The *Compound Past* is made with part of the present tense of the verb 'haben' or 'sein'. This is called the *auxiliary verb*.
2. The other part of this tense is called the *past participle*.
3. The *past participle* comes at the end of the sentence, whether it is a question or a statement.

Two vital questions remain:

1 How does each individual verb make its past participle?
2 Which verbs make their Compound Past tense with 'haben', and which with 'sein'?

These questions may be answered by consulting the list of verbs in the Grammatical Summary.

Exercises

A

Exercise 1

Imagine that this is your diary. Say what you did on each day of the week. Here is an example:

Montag – Ich bin nach Solingen gefahren.

Mo	*nach Solingen fahren*
Di	*Armbanduhr kaufen*
Mi	*Kette für Inge suchen*
Do	*mit Elke ins Kino gehen*
Fr	*Wein mit Peter trinken*
Sa	*Bayern-München gegen Hamburg sehen*
So	*in die Kirche gehen*

Exercise 2

Look at your diary for Tuesday, the 2nd of May. You are going to need it to answer the questions of a rather aggressive policeman on your recording. What *were* you doing that day?

Dienstag 2. Mai

09·00	im Büro
10·00	in der Post
11·00	am Marktplatz
12·00	im Gasthaus Bauer
13·00	bei Müller
14·00	im Café
15·00	im Zug
16·00	
17·00	
18·00	

Exercise 3

Put the following sentences into the Perfect tense.

1 Ich trinke Bier.
2 Ich gehe in die Stadt.
3 Er fährt nach Bremen.
4 Wir kommen um 8 Uhr.
5 Sie bleiben zu lange.
6 Sie kauft ein Hemd.
7 Wir suchen eine Wohnung.
8 Sie verliert ihre Armbanduhr.
9 Ich sehe einen guten Film.
10 Sie treffen Herrn Schüth.

Exercise 4   Probleme einer Geschäftsfrau: Rough weather ahead

This time listen to the dialogue without reading the questions first. Remember: you do not have to understand every word. Then try to answer the questions, playing through the dialogue again to fill in any gaps.

1 From where has the wife just returned?
2 What did she do when she arrived at the airport?
3 What is Monsieur Dupont's position?
4 How old is he?
5 What is Monsieur Saunier's position?
6 And Monsieur Blamont's?
7 When did she start work on Tuesday?
8 What did she do for lunch?
9 What hours did she work in the afternoon?
10 What happened later in the evening?
11 How did she return to her hotel?
12 What time did she arrive at the office this morning?
13 Did the contract get signed?

Revision tests

In this chapter you will have an opportunity to consolidate the language you have learned in the previous nine chapters. Each test indicates whereabouts in the later part of the book you ought to search if you have forgotten a particular point.

 Test 1 Ordering a meal (Chapter 11)

You're taking a friend out to dinner to celebrate his/her birthday.

Waiter: Guten Abend!
You: Greet him.
  Ask for a table for two.
Waiter: Kommen Sie, bitte.
You: Ask for the menu.
Waiter: Die Speisekarte, bitte schön.
You: Ask your friend if he/she would like an hors d'oeuvre.
Friend: Ja, bitte.
You: Ask your friend if he/she would like oysters.
Friend: Austern. O ja!
You: Order the oysters for both of you.
Waiter: Zweimal Austern.
You: Ask your friend if he/she would like a Zigeunerschnitzel.
Friend: Nein, danke, ich möchte ein Jägerschnitzel.
You: Order one Jägerschnitzel and a Wiener Schnitzel.
Waiter: Jawohl.
You: Ask your friend if he/she would like something to drink.
Friend: O ja. Ich möchte einen Rotwein. Und Sie?
You: Say you'd like red wine too.
  Order two red wines.
Waiter: Ja.

If you are learning with a friend, take it in turns to play the parts.

Test 2 Finding a table in a restaurant (Chapter 11)

Sort out these phrases spoken by a head waiter and a customer at his restaurant in order to make an intelligible conversation. If you are working with a partner, take a part each. The customer begins.

Customer	*Head waiter*
Für zwei	Für wie viele Personen?
Ich möchte einen Tisch	Guten Abend
Guten Abend	Kommen Sie, bitte

Test 3 Reserving a table by phone (Chapter 11)

Now try to sort this one out. The customer begins.

Customer	*Head waiter*
Um acht Uhr	Auf welchen Namen?
Für zwei	Für wann?
Guten Tag!	Ist in Ordnung
Ich möchte einen Tisch	Für wie viele Personen?

Auf Wiederhören!   Um wieviel Uhr?
Schmidt   Guten Tag!
Für heute abend

Test 4 Ordering food in a restaurant (Chapter 11)

Order the following dishes:

One apple pie	Three herring fillets
Two roast chickens	Two ice cream sundaes
One boiled egg	One pepper steak
Two portions of duck	Two apple juices
Three portions of liver	One portion of sauerkraut
One meat loaf	Three portions of pork

Test 5 Asking to borrow things (Chapter 12)

What would you say if you had very accommodating neighbours?

1   You want to borrow a table for a party.
2   Could you have a friend's dress, just for the evening?
3   There's one extra for dinner; you need another chair (der Stuhl).
4   Your pullover has a stain.
5   You didn't have time to wash your shirt.
6   You ought really to have a blouse to go with that skirt.
7   There's a button off your jacket.
8   You have just torn your trousers.
9   It's raining and you have left your raincoat at the office.
10 The children need another nightshirt for dressing up in.

Test 6   A Riddle (Chapter 13)

How can you mention all the days of the working week, without saying Monday, Tuesday, Wednesday, etc.?

Test 7   Using the dative to express liking (Chapter 13)

Answer the following questions. The ticks and crosses will give you a clue as to the answer you should give.

1   Gefällt Ihnen das Wetter?   √
2   Gefällt Ihnen der Sonnenschein (sunshine)?   √
3   Gefällt Ihnen der Regen (rain)?   X

4 Gefällt Ihnen der Schnee? √
5 Gefällt Ihnen der Wind? ✗
6 Gefällt Ihnen die Landschaft? √
7 Gefällt Ihnen das Meer (sea)? √
8 Gefällt Ihnen der Nebel (fog)? ✗
9 Gefällt Ihnen der Strand (beach)? ✗
10 Gefallen Ihnen die Berge? √

Test 8　Types of accommodation (Chapter 14)

Translate into German

1 I live in a house.
2 I live in an owner-occupied flat.
3 I live in a one-family house.
4 I like in a terraced house.
5 I live in a house divided up into flats.
6 I live in a detached house.
7 I live in a two-family house.
8 I live in a flat.
9 I live in a council flat.
10 I live in a rented flat.

Test 9

Imagine that you are the sort of person who is only good at activities which can be done in the open air and which involve being very energetic. Listen to your recording and answer the questions. You will be given a model answer after the pause.

Test 10　Describing hobbies and interests (Chapter 15)

What would you say to somebody who asked you 'Haben Sie ein Hobby?'

1 Assuming that you were interested in music.
2 If you were interested in pictures.
3 If your passion was collecting books.
4 Assuming you were a keen photographer.
5 If you were a football fan.
6 If you liked watching athletics.

Test 11　Saying what you must/have to do (Chapter 16)

Overleaf is a page from Fritz's diary. Can you answer the questions?

So	Elke besuchen
Mo	die Karten abholen
Di	nach Nürnberg fahren
Mi	eine Kette für Elke kaufen
Do	einen Tennisschläger kaufen
Fr	nach Stuttgart fahren
Sa	im Bett bleiben

1 Was muß Fritz am Donnerstag machen?
2 Was muß er am Dienstag machen?
3 Was muß er am Sonntag machen?
4 Was muß er am Mittwoch machen?
5 Was muß er am Montag machen?
6 Was muß er am Freitag machen?
7 Was muß er am Samstag machen?

Test 12 'Können' and 'wollen' (Chapter 17)

Translate into German

1 Can you play tennis?
2 Shall we go for a walk?
3 Can you dance?
4 He can swim.
5 They want to play football.
6 We can play cards.
7 Shall we go to London?
8 Can she sing?
9 He doesn't want to drink.
10 You can't swim.

 ## Test 13 Bürokratie: Rules are rules!

Don't forget to read the questions below before listening to this dialogue, and remember: you do not have to understand every word, just listen for the information you need.

1 What is the woman's problem with her visitor's pass?
2 Who is her appointment with?
3 What does she offer to try to solve her problem?
4 What is the solution?

Pronunciation key

The best way to achieve good pronunciation is to practise with the recording. You should listen to each word as it is spoken on the recording concentrating on the particular sound to be practised. This is indicated by *italics*. You should pay particular attention to the vowel sounds because, in comparison with English pronunciation, a greater proportion of them in German are pure, that is to say they consist of one vowel sound only. There are, however, some diphthongs in German, and these are indicated separately. When a word, or part of a word, begins with a vowel, it is uttered with a slight explosion of breath at the back of the throat, similar to a very slight cough. This is called a 'glottal stop'. On the whole the consonants of German are the same as in English, and the learning problem here is to become used to the fact that certain letters of the alphabet indicate different sounds in German from English.

Vowels

/a/		is pronounced like /b*u*nker/	Example: D*a*nke (thank you)
/a/	–	long is pronounced like /f*a*ther/	Example: T*a*g (day)
/e/		is pronounced like /p*e*t/	Example: w*e*lcher (which)
/e/	–	long is pronounced like /f*ey*/	Example: T*ee* (tea)
/i/		is pronounced like /b*i*t/	Example: b*i*tte (please)
/ie/	–	long is pronounced like /h*e*re/	Example: h*ie*r (here)
/o/		is pronounced like /c*o*ffer/	Example: K*o*ffer (suitcase)
/o/	–	long is pronounced like /gr*ow*n/	Example: w*o*hnen (to live)
/u/		is pronounced like /p*u*ll/	Example: *u*nd (and)
/u/	–	long is pronounced like /b*oo*t/	Example: G*u*ten Tag (Good Day)

Modified vowels

The vowel sounds shown above are changed slightly by the addition of an *Umlaut* (-).

/ä/	is pronounced like /pe*ck*/	Example: Äpfel (apples)
/ä/ –	long is pronounced like /l*ate*/	Example: spät (late)
/ö/ –	is pronounced like /c*ur*/	Example: Streichhölzer (matches)
/ö/ –	long is pronounced like /t*ur*n/	Example: schön (beautiful)
/ü/	This sound does not exist in English, and the way to make it is to purse your lips as if to whistle, and then without moving them say a short /i/	Example: hübsch (pretty)
/ü/ –	long Purse the lips the same way, as if to whistle, and without moving them say /ee/	Example: Bücher (books)
/ei/	is pronounced like /m*i*ne/	Example: nein (no)
/au/	is pronounced like /h*owl*/	Example: Frau (Mrs)
/eu/	is pronounced like /c*oy*/	Example: heute (today)
/äu/	is pronounced like /c*oy*/	Example: Fräulein (Miss)

When a vowel comes before two consonants, it is usually 'short', e.g. Äpfel, bitte. When a vowel comes before a single consonant, or the letter 'h', it is usually 'long', e.g. wohnen, hier.

Consonants

These are the main differences from English:

/j/	is pronounced like /*y*acht/	Example: ja (yes)
/r/	This sound is made at the back of the mouth when it comes at the beginning or middle of a word.	Example: Frau (Mrs)
/v/	is pronounced like /*f*an/	Example: von (from)
/w/	is pronounced like /*v*ase/	Example: wieder (again)
/z/	is pronounced like /ca*ts*/	Example: Zimmer (room)

Note that English has this sound, but does not put it at the beginning of a word as German does.

/ch/	when it follows the vowels a, o, u, or au is pronounced like /lo*ch*/	
		Example: Bach (stream)
/ch/	when it comes anywhere else is pronounced like /*h*uge/	
		Example: ich (I)
/sch/	is pronounced like /*sh*ip/	Example: schön (beautiful)
/sp/	is pronounced like /shp/	Example: spät (late)
/st/	is pronounced like /sht/	Example: Stein (stone)
/s/	when it comes before vowels has a buzzing sound like /*z*oo/	
		Example: Sie (you)

/s/	in other positions is pronounced like /hou*s*e/

Example: ist (is)
Rathaus (town hall)

/b/	when it occurs at the end of a word or a syllable is pronounced like /p/

Example: grob (vulgar)

/d/	when it comes at the end of word or a syllable is pronounced like /t/

Example: Hand (hand)

/g/	when it comes after /i/ (-ig) is pronounced like /ch/ as in '*h*uge'

Example: hungrig (hungry)

The pronunciation key given here is only an approximation. Treat it as a rough guide. If you are able to implement it, it will make you understandable amongst speakers of German, but to obtain a really good accent you should practise with the recording.

Stress

The best way to learn how the syllables of German words are stressed is to listen carefully to the recorded dialogues.

As an additional help, the *word lists*, show the stressed syllables in bold type. The letters of the German alphabet are virtually the same as in English. There are four exceptions. These are asterisked.

Aa	Hh	Öö *	Üü *	The two dots over the vowels /a/o/u/
Ää *	Ii	Pp	Vv	are called an UMLAUT.
Bb	Jj	Qq	Ww	
Cc	Kk	Rr	Xx	The symbol between /s/ and /t/ is
Dd	Ll	Ss	Yy	called sz (eszett).
Ee	Mm	ß *	Zz	
Ff	Nn	Tt		
Gg	Oo	Uu		

Answers to exercises

Chapter 1   Guten Tag!

Exercise 1   1 Gute Nacht!   2 Viel Glück!   3 Prost/Zum Wohl!
4 Guten Morgen!   5 Gute Reise!   6 Gute Besserung!   7 Guten Abend!
8 Viel Spaß/Viel Vergnügen!   9 Guten Tag/Grüß Gott!

Exercise 2   1 Guten Abend, Herr Doktor!   2 Darf ich meine Frau
vorstellen?   3 Angenehm.   4 Kommen Sie herein.   5 Bitte, nehmen Sie
Platz.   6 Danke schön für die Einladung.   7 Eine Tasse Kaffee?   8 Bitte
sehr!   9 Nein, danke.   10 Entschuldigen Sie!

Exercise 4   1(b) Frau Bauer   2 Herr and Frau Schmidt   3 To come in

Chapter 2   Wie komme ich ... ?

Exercise 1   1 Wie komme ich zum Krankenhaus?   2 Wie komme ich zur
Sparkasse?   3 Wie komme ich zum Bahnhof?   4 Wie komme ich zum
Sportplatz?   5 Wie komme ich zum Hallenbad?   6 Wie komme ich zum
Freibad?   7 Wie komme ich zur Grundschule?   8 Wie komme ich zum
Altenheim?   9 Wie komme ich zur Kapuzinerkirche?   10 Wie komme ich
zum Campingplatz?   11 Wie komme ich zum Kindergarten?   12 Wie
komme ich zur Reithalle?   13 Wie komme ich zum Minigolfplatz?   14 Wie
komme ich zum Waldrestaurant?   15 Wie komme ich zum Marktplatz?   16
Wie komme ich zur Post?   17 Wie komme ich zum Rathaus?   18 Wie
komme ich zum Parkplatz?

Exercise 2   1 Wie komme ich zur Audi-Werkstatt?   2 Wie komme ich zur
Volkswagen-Werkstatt?   3 Wie komme ich zur Opel-Werkstatt?   4 Wie
komme ich zur Ford-Werkstatt?   5 Hard luck, you'd better go on to Munich.

Exercise 4   1 A: Wie weit ist es nach Dessau, bitte?   B: Einundzwanzig
Kilometer ungefähr.   2 A: Wie weit ist es nach Halle, bitte?
B: Zweiundfünfzig Kilometer ungefähr.   3 A: Wie weit ist es nach Jena,

bitte? B: Hundertein Kilometer ungefähr. 4 A: Wie weit ist es nach Linz, bitte? B: Dreiundzwanzig Kilometer ungefähr. 5 A: Wie weit ist es nach Kitzbühel, bitte? B: Neununddreißig Kilometer ungefähr. 6 A: Wie weit ist es nach Kufstein, bitte? B: Neun Kilometer ungefähr. 7 A: Wie weit ist es nach Zürich, bitte? B: Sechsundfünfzig Kilometer ungefähr. 8 A: Wie weit ist es nach Tübingen, bitte? B: Einundsiebzig Kilometer ungefähr. 9 A: Wie weit ist es nach Ansbach, bitte? B: Sechsundfünfzig Kilometer ungefähr. 10 A: Wie weit ist es nach Fulda, bitte? B: Fünfundvierzig Kilometer ungefähr.

Exercise 5 1 (b) Zirndorf 2 15 kilometres

Chapter 3   Ein Doppelzimmer bitte

Exercise 1 1 Guest: Haben Sie ein Zimmer frei? Hotel: Jawohl. Was für ein Zimmer? Guest: Ein Einzelzimmer. Hotel: Für wie lange? Guest: Für eine Nacht. 2 Guest: Haben Sie ein Zimmer frei? Hotel: Jawohl. Was für ein Zimmer? Guest: Ein Einzelzimmer mit Dusche. Hotel: Für wie lange? Guest: Für eine Nacht. 3 Guest: Haben Sie ein Zimmer frei? Hotel: Jawohl. Was für ein Zimmer? Guest: Ein Doppelzimmer mit Bad. Hotel: Für wie lange? Guest: Für zwei Nächte. 4 Guest: Haben Sie ein Zimmer frei? Hotel: Jawohl. Was für ein Zimmer? Guest: Ein Einzelzimmer mit Dusche. Hotel: Für wie lange? Guest: Für eine Woche. 5 Guest: Haben Sie ein Zimmer frei? Hotel: Jawohl. Was für ein Zimmer? Guest: Ein Zweibettzimmer. Hotel: Für wie lange? Guest: Für zwei Nächte. 6 Guest: Haben Sie ein Zimmer frei? Hotel: Jawohl. Was für ein Zimmer? Guest: Ein Doppelzimmer mit Dusche. Hotel: Für wie lange? Guest: Für eine Woche. 7 Guest: Haben Sie ein Zimmer frei? Hotel: Jawohl. Was für ein Zimmer? Guest: Ein Einzelzimmer mit Bad. Hotel: Für wie lange? Guest: Für drei Nächte. 8 Guest: Haben Sie ein Zimmer frei? Hotel: Jawohl. Was für ein Zimmer? Guest: Ein Doppelzimmer. Hotel: Für wie lange? Guest: Für vier Nächte. 9 Guest: Haben Sie ein Zimmer frei? Hotel: Jawohl. Was für ein Zimmer? Guest: Ein Einzelzimmer. Hotel: Für wie lange? Guest: Für drei Nächte. 10 Guest: Haben Sie ein Zimmer frei? Hotel: Jawohl. Was für ein Zimmer? Guest: Ein Einzelzimmer mit Dusche. Hotel: Für wie lange? Guest: Für zwei Nächte.

Exercise 2 1 Guten Tag! 2 Guten Tag, der Herr! 3 Haben Sie ein Zimmer frei? 4 Ja, ein Zimmer habe ich. 5 Haben Sie ein Einzelzimmer frei? 6 Für wie lange, bitte? 7 Für eine Nacht. 8 Für eine Nacht. Das geht in Ordnung. 9 Ich nehme das Zimmer. 10 Tragen Sie sich bitte ein!

Exercise 4 1 Haben Sie ein Einzelzimmer? 2 Wie lange bleiben Sie? 3 Ich nehme das Zimmer. 4 Entschuldigen Sie, bitte. 5 Wie komme ich nach Stauting? 6 Fahren Sie hier geradeaus. 7 Er biegt hier nach links ab. 8 Nehmen Sie dann die erste Straße links. 9 Gehen Sie die Marktstraße hoch. 10 Haben Sie einen Tisch für zwei? 11 Ich habe einen Tisch um 8 Uhr. 12 Sie bleiben eine Nacht. 13 Sie kommen zur Adriastraße.

Exercise 5   1 Der zweite Mai neunzehnhundertachtundsiebzig.   2 Der sechzehnte Juni neunzehnhundertzweiundachtzig.   3 Der einunddreißigste Dezember neunzehnhundertneunundneunzig.   4 Der elfte August neunzehnhundertzweiundachtzig.   5 Der siebenundzwanzigste März neunzehnhundertdreiundachtzig.   6 Der siebzehnte Mai neunzehnhundertfünfundachtzig.

Exercise 6   1 A single room   2 One night only   3 She asks him to register

Chapter 4   Hin und zurück

Exercise 2   1 Reisender: Zweimal zweiter Klasse nach Hamburg, bitte. Angestellte: Hin und zurück?   Reisender: Nein, einfach.   2 Reisende: Einmal zweiter Klasse nach Bremen, bitte.   Angestellte: Hin und zurück? Reisende: Ja, hin und zurück, bitte.   3 Reisender: Einmal erster Klasse nach Hamm, bitte.   Angestellte: Hin und zurück?   Reisender: Nein, einfach. 4 Reisender: Einmal erster Klasse nach Münster, bitte.   Angestellte: Hin und zurück?   Reisender: Ja, hin und zurück, bitte.   5 Reisender: Dreimal zweiter Klasse nach Dortmund, bitte.   Angestellte: Hin und zurück? Reisender: Nein, einfach.   6 Reisender: Zweimal zweiter Klasse nach Düsseldorf, bitte.   Angestellte: Hin und zurück?   Reisender: Nein, einfach. 7 Reisender: Zweimal zweiter Klasse nach Bonn, bitte.   Angestellte: Hin und zurück?   Reisender: Ja, hin und zurück, bitte.   8 Reisender: Einmal erster Klasse nach Koblenz, bitte.   Angestellte: Hin und zurück?   Reisender: Ja, hin und zurück, bitte.   9 Reisender: Zweimal zweiter Klasse nach Köln, bitte.   Angestellte: Hin und zurück?   Reisender: Nein, einfach. 10 Reisender: Dreimal erster Klasse nach München, bitte.   Angestellte: Hin und zurück?   Reisender: Ja, hin und zurück, bitte.

Exercise 3   1 Der Zug kommt in München an.   2 Peter steigt in Dortmund um.   3 Der Bus fährt um 8 Uhr ab.   4 Herr Müller wäscht ab.   5 Frau Müller trocknet ab.   6 Die Kinder räumen nicht auf.   7 Ulrike ruft an. 8 Peter gibt auf.   9 Oma kauft ein.   10 Hans schließt das Haus ab.

Exercise 4   1 Wann fährt der Zug nach Bonn ab?   2 Wir schließen den Laden ab.   3 Oma geht am Dienstag aus.   4 Peter ruft am Mittwoch an. 5 Ich komme um 8 Uhr an.   6 Mutter wäscht die Teller ab.   7 Die Kinder trocknen die Teller ab.   8 Er kauft Lebensmittel ein.   9 Der Chef gibt seine Arbeit auf.   10 Ich räume die Spielsachen auf.

Exercise 5   1 Bremen   2 A return ticket   3 52 marks   4 10.30   5 11.43 6 No, it goes direct to Bremen

Chapter 5   Taxi, bitte!

Exercise 1   Fährt dieser Bus nach Egersdorf?   Fährt dieser Bus nach Steinach?   Fährt dieser Bus zum Stadttheater?   Fährt dieser Bus zum Rathaus?   Fährt dieser Bus zum Flughafen?   Fährt dieser Bus zur

Stadtmitte? Fährt dieser Bus zur Goethestraße? Fährt diese Straßenbahn nach Egersdorf? Fährt diese Straßenbahn nach Steinach? Fährt diese Straßenbahn zum Stadttheater? Fährt diese Straßenbahn zum Rathaus? Fährt diese Straßenbahn zum Flughafen? Fährt diese Straßenbahn zur Stadtmitte? Fährt diese Straßenbahn zur Goethestraße? Fährt die Nummer 15 nach Egersdorf? Fährt die Nummer 15 nach Steinach? Fährt die Nummer 15 zum Stadttheater? Fährt die Nummer 15 zum Rathaus? Fährt die Nummer 15 zum Flughafen? Fährt die Nummer 15 zur Stadtmitte? Fährt die Nummer 15 zur Goethestraße?

Exercise 3 1 Er hat kein Auto. 2 Sie möchte keinen Kaffee. 3 Er ist kein Professor. 4 Sie hat keine Einladung. 5 Wir haben keinen Hund. 6 Das ist nicht der Bahnhof. 7 Der Garten ist nicht groß. 8 Der Vater ist nicht alt. 9 Frau Meier ist nicht jung. 10 Raggi ist nicht in Hamburg.

Exercise 4 1 (b) Kußberger 2 (a) Robert-Koch-Straße 210 3 To the station 4 (c) Sabine Wichmann

Chapter 6   Es tut weh

Exercise 1 1 Ich habe Zahnschmerzen. 2 Ich habe Bauchschmerzen. 3 Ich habe Kopfschmerzen. 4 Ich habe Halsschmerzen. 5 Ich habe Ohrenschmerzen. 6 Ich habe Fieber. 7 Meine Füße tun weh. 8 Ich habe Durchfall. 9 Mein Knie tut weh. 10 Ich habe Fieber.

Exercise 3 1 Mein Kopf tut weh. 2 Mein Bein tut weh. 3 Mein Fuß tut weh. 4 Meine Hand tut weh. 5 Mein Rücken tut weh. 6 Mein Arm tut weh. 7 Mein Bauch tut weh. 8 Mein Ohr tut weh. 9 Mein Knie tut weh. 10 Mein Zahn tut weh.

Exercise 4 1 Nein, das ist kein gutes Buch. 2 Nein, das ist keine schöne Frau. 3 Nein, das ist keine ruhige Straße. 4 Nein, das ist kein ruhiges Zimmer. 5 Nein, das war kein schöner Abend. 6 Nein, das war keine gute Reise. 7 Nein, das war keine ruhige Nacht. 8 Nein, das war kein schöner Ausblick.

Exercise 5 1 Nein, ich habe keine ruhige Frau. 2 Nein, ich habe kein gutes Zimmer. 3 Nein, ich habe keinen schönen Ausblick. 4 Nein, ich habe kein neues Buch. 5 Nein, ich habe keinen neuen Fußball. 6 Nein, ich habe keinen guten Doktor. 7 Nein, ich habe keine nette Schwester. 8 Nein, ich habe keine ruhige Straße.

Exercise 6 1 Frau Dr Müller 2 Neumann 3 To see the doctor 4 No 5 No 6 Tomorrow at 18.15 7 'Ich glaube, wenn es so dringend ist, dann müssen Sie ja den Notdienst anrufen'. This translates literally as 'I think, if it is so urgent, then you must telephone the emergency services'. Useful vocabulary: 'anrufen' (to telephone), 'der Notdienst' (emergency services).

Chapter 7   Was darf es sein?

Exercise 1   1 Verkäuferin: Was darf es sein?   Kundin: Ich möchte einen Rock.   Verkäuferin: Welche Größe brauchen Sie?   Kundin: Größe 40. Verkäuferin: An welches Material hatten Sie gedacht?   Kundin: Popeline. Verkäuferin: Welche Farbe möchten Sie?   Kundin: Ich möchte dunkelrot, bitte.   Verkäuferin: Der ist sehr elegant.   Kundin: Ja, er gefällt mir. Was kostet er?   2 Verkäuferin: Was darf es sein?   Kundin: Ich möchte eine Bluse.   Verkäuferin: Welche Größe brauchen Sie?   Kundin: Größe 42. Verkäuferin: An welches Material hatten Sie gedacht?   Kundin: Krepp. Verkäuferin: Welche Farbe möchten Sie?   Kundin: Ich möchte rosa, bitte. Verkäuferin: Die ist sehr elegant.   Kundin: Ja, sie gefällt mir. Was kostet sie? 3 Verkäuferin: Was darf es sein?   Kunde: Ich möchte ein Hemd. Verkäuferin: Welche Größe brauchen Sie?   Kunde: Größe 38.   Verkäuferin: An welches Material hatten Sie gedacht?   Kunde: Seide.   Verkäuferin: Welche Farbe möchten Sie?   Kunde: Ich möchte weiß, bitte.   Verkäuferin: Das ist sehr elegant.   Kunde: Ja, es gefällt mir. Was kostet es? 4 Verkäuferin: Was darf es sein?   Kunde: Ich möchte eine Jacke. Verkäuferin: Welche Größe brauchen Sie?   Kunde: Größe 46.   Verkäuferin: An welches Material hatten Sie gedacht?   Kunde: Leder.   Verkäuferin: Welche Farbe möchten Sie?   Kunde: Ich möchte dunkelbraun.   Verkäuferin: Die ist sehr elegant.   Kunde: Ja, sie gefällt mir. Was kostet sie?

Exercise 3   1 I'm only looking.   2 I'd like a pullover.   3 I don't know exactly.   4 Which material were you thinking of?   5 The blue pullover is certainly very nice.   6 I need new shoes.   7 I always wear size 40.   8 Can I try it/them on?   9 Haven't you any shoes with leather soles?   10 That's too expensive for me.

Exercise 4   1 Was kosten sie?   2 Das gefällt mir gar nicht.   3 Sind die Sohlen aus Leder?   4 Haben Sie diese Art eine Größe kleiner?   5 Was kosten die braunen Schuhe im Schaufenster?   6 Ich möchte ein Nachthemd. 7 Ich schaue mich nur um.   8 Das Hemd ist aus Seide.   9 Was kosten die Schuhe?   10 Der Pullover ist mir zu teuer.

Exercise 5   1 Der weiße Rock.   2 Die rote Hose.   3 Die schwarzen Schuhe.   4 Das lange Kleid.   5 Die braune Jacke.   6 Das hellblaue Hemd. 7 Der braune Anzug.   8 Der kurze Regenmantel.   9 Die grüne Bluse. 10 Das kleine schwarze Kleid.

Exercise 6   1 A pullover   2 Size 40   3 Blue (but it turns out that his girlfriend already has a blue one)   4 38   5 No. The shop expects a delivery the following week ('nächste Woche'), but that will be too late for the customer. He wanted to give the present that day (he says 'Ich wollte schon heute das Geschenk geben'). Useful vocabulary : 'die Lieferung' (delivery).

Chapter 8   Haben Sie Kinder?

Exercise 1   1 Pfarrer: Sagen Sie, Herr Schmidt. Sind Sie verheiratet?   Herr Schmidt: Geschieden. Pfarrer: Und haben Sie Kinder?   Herr Schmidt: Nein, ich habe keine Kinder.   Pfarrer: Es ist besser so.   2 Pfarrer: Sagen Sie, Herr Schmidt. Sind Sie verheiratet?   Herr Schmidt: Nein, ich bin verwitwet. Pfarrer: Und haben Sie Kinder?   Herr Schmidt: Ja, ich habe drei Kinder. Pfarrer: Aha.   3 Pfarrer: Sagen Sie, Herr Schmidt. Sind Sie verheiratet? Herr Schmidt: Ja, aber wir leben getrennt.   Pfarrer: Und haben Sie Kinder? Herr Schmidt: Ja, ich habe ein Kind.   Pfarrer: Aha.   4 Pfarrer: Sagen Sie, Herr Schmidt. Sind Sie verheiratet?   Herr Schmidt: Nein, ich bin nicht verheiratet.

Exercise 3   1 Ich bin Architekt.   2 Ich bin Lehrerin.   3 Ich bin Polizistin. 4 Ich bin Arzt.   5 Ich bin Studentin.   6 Ich bin Lehrer.   7 Ich bin Verkäufer.   8 Ich bin Verkäuferin.

Exercise 4   1 A job in a shop   2 6 a.m. until noon   3 DM 8.50 per hour 4 DM 8.80 per hour   5 Next Monday   6 6 a.m.

Chapter 9   Wie ist das Wetter?

Exercise 1   1 Nicht weit von Bremen.   2 Nicht weit von Hannover. 3 Nicht weit von Bielefeld.   4 Nicht weit von Koblenz.   5 Nicht weit von Frankfurt.   6 Nicht weit von Mannheim.   7 Nicht weit von Nürnberg. 8 Nicht weit von Rostock.   9 Nicht weit von Berlin.   10 Nicht weit von Erfurt.

Exercise 2   1 Kiel ist in Norddeutschland.   2 Passau ist in Süddeutschland. 3 Lübeck ist in Norddeutschland.   4 München ist in Süddeutschland. 5 Hamburg ist in Norddeutschland.   6 Augsburg ist in Süddeutschland. 7 Oldenburg ist in Norddeutschland.   8 Ulm ist in Süddeutschland. 9 Rostock ist in Norddeutschland.   10 Stralsund ist in Norddeutschland. 11 Schwerin ist in Norddeutschland.

Exercise 3   1d; 2f; 3h; 4a; 5g; 6e; 7b; 8c

Exercise 4   1 Sie kommt mit einem eleganten Kleid.   2 Er hat einen süddeutschen Akzent.   3 Es gibt eine schöne Kirche dort.   4 Mein kleiner Bruder wohnt in Hamburg.   5 Bad Reichenhall ist nicht weit von einem hohen Berg.   6 Dort gibt es ein großes Kurhaus.   7 Bei Schaffhausen ist ein großer See.   8 Die Zugspitze ist ein hoher Berg.   9 Er hat ein weißes Hemd. 10 Sie trägt einen blauen Pullover.

Exercise 5 1 Löwenbräu 2 Rostock 3 Werft 4 (c) This translates literally as 'I was last year there in the north on holiday'. 5 The island of Rügen 6 She says she will fetch him his beer.

Chapter 10 Revision tests

Test 1 Das ist meine Frau. Das ist mein Vater. Das ist meine Mutter. Das ist mein Sohn. Das ist meine Tochter. Das ist mein Onkel. Das ist meine Tante.

Test 2 Das ist unser Garten. Das ist unsere Küche. Das ist unser Schlafzimmer. Das ist unsere Garage. Das ist unser Hund. Das ist unsere Katze.

Test 3 1 Guten Morgen! 2 Prost/Zum Wohl! 3 Entschuldigen Sie bitte! 4 Viel Spaß/Viel Vergnügen! 5 Verzeihung! 6 Gute Besserung! 7 Gute Nacht! 8 Entschuldigung!/Entschuldigen Sie! 9 Entschuldigen Sie, bitte! 10 Guten Appetit!

Test 4 Hiermit bestätige ich meine Reservierung für: 1 ein Doppelzimmer mit Bad 2 ein Einzelzimmer mit Dusche 3 ein Zweibettzimmer mit Dusche 4 ein Einzelzimmer 5 ein Doppelzimmer; für die Zeit vom: 1 1. August bis zum 13. August einschließlich 2 4. April bis zum 7. April einschließlich 3 10. Juni bis zum 12. Juni einschließlich 4 10. August bis zum 17. August einschließlich 5 26. Februar bis zum 28. Februar einschließlich; Mit freundlichen Grüßen.

Test 6 1 Reisender: Wann fährt der Zug nach Freiburg ab? Angestellte: Er fährt um 9 Uhr 45 ab. Reisender: Wann kommt er in Freiburg an? Angestellte: Er kommt um 17.03 an. Reisender: Muß ich umsteigen? Angestellte: Nein, der Zug fährt direkt. 2 Reisender: Wann fährt der Zug nach Fulda ab? Angestellte: Er fährt um 11 Uhr 14 ab. Reisender: Wann kommt er in Fulda an? Angestellte: Er kommt um 13.36 an. Reisender: Muß ich umsteigen? Angestellte: Nein, der Zug fährt direkt. 3 Reisender: Wann fährt der Zug nach Basel ab? Angestellte: Er fährt um 12.10 ab. Reisender: Wann kommt er in Basel an? Angestellte: Er kommt um 17.46 an. Reisender: Muß ich umsteigen? Angestellte: Nein, der Zug fährt direkt. 4 Reisender: Wann fährt der Zug nach Freiburg ab? Angestellte: Er fährt um 15.34 ab. Reisender: Wann kommt er in Freiburg an? Angestellte: Er kommt um 17.03 an. Reisender: Muß ich umsteigen? Angestellte: Nein, der Zug fährt direkt. 5. Reisender: Wann fährt der Zug nach Karlsruhe ab? Angestellte: Er fährt um 13.37 ab. Reisender: Wann kommt er in Karlsruhe an? Angestellte: Er kommt um 16.02 an. Reisender: Muß ich umsteigen? Angestellte: Nein, der Zug fährt direkt. 6 Reisender: Wann fährt der Zug nach Basel ab? Angestellte: Er fährt um 17.04 ab. Reisender: Wann kommt er in Basel an? Angestellte: Er kommt um 17.46 an. Reisender: Muß ich umsteigen? Angestellte: Nein, der Zug

fährt direkt. 7 Reisender: Wann fährt der Zug nach Freiburg ab?
Angestellte: Er fährt um 14.42 ab. Reisender: Wann kommt er in Freiburg
an? Angestellte: Er kommt um 17.03 an. Reisender: Muß ich umsteigen?
Angestellte: Nein, der Zug fährt direkt. 8 Reisender: Wann fährt der Zug
nach Frankfurt ab? Angestellte: Er fährt um 10.00 ab. Reisender: Wann
kommt er in Frankfurt an? Angestellte: Er kommt um 14.36 an. Reisender:
Muß ich umsteigen? Angestellte: Nein, der Zug fährt direkt. 9 Reisender:
Wann fährt der Zug nach Frankfurt ab? Angestellte: Er fährt um 11 Uhr
14 ab. Reisender: Wann kommt er in Frankfurt an? Angestellte: Er kommt
um 14.36 an. Reisender: Muß ich umsteigen? Angestellte: Nein, der Zug
fährt direkt. 10 Reisender: Wann fährt der Zug nach Basel ab? Angestellte:
Er fährt um 16.03 ab. Reisender: Wann kommt er in Basel an? Angestellte:
Er kommt um 17.46 an. Reisender: Muß ich umsteigen? Angestellte:
Nein, der Zug fährt direkt.

Test 7 1 Oma ruft am Samstag an. 2 Ingrid geht am Dienstag aus.
3 Die Kinder räumen den Laden auf. 4 Mutter räumt die Spielsachen auf.
5 Peter wäscht die Teller ab. 6 Inge kauft Lebensmittel ein. 7 Helmut
wäscht am Sonntag ab. 8 Der Chef gibt seine Arbeit auf. 9 Maria schließt
den Laden ab. 10 Oma geht am Samstag aus.

Test 8 **Dialogue A** Müller: Entschuldigen Sie, bitte! Meier: Ja, bitte?
Müller: Fährt dieser Bus nach Opladen? Meier: Nach Opladen? Nein, dieser
Bus fährt nach Ludwigshafen. Müller: Welcher Bus fährt nach Opladen?
Meier: Sie brauchen die Nummer 14. **Dialogue B** Schmidt: Entschuldigen
Sie, bitte! Schüth: Ja. Kann ich Ihnen helfen? Schmidt: Fährt diese
Straßenbahn zum Schauspielhaus? Schüth: Nein, nicht zum Schauspielhaus.
Sie fährt zum Hofgarten. Schmidt: Welche Straßenbahn fährt zum
Schauspielhaus? Schüth: Sie brauchen die Nummer 1. Sie fährt zum
Schauspielhaus. Schmidt: Danke schön.

Test 9 1 Der Professor heißt Doktor Schmidt. 2 Wo ist die Tasse?
3 Hier ist das Buch. 4 Der Kaffee ist heiß. 5 Hier ist die Frau. 6 Das
Auto fährt schnell. 7 Der Mann heißt Herr Müller. 8 Die Einladung
kommt heute. 9 Das Zimmer ist groß. 10 Die Stadt ist klein.

Test 10 1 Guten Tag. 2 Guten Tag, Herr Doktor. 3 Was fehlt Ihnen
denn? 4 Mein Bein tut weh. 5 Ihr Bein? Ist es ein leichter Schmerz?
6 Nein, es ist ein stechender Schmerz. 7 Ach so, stechend. Seit wann tut es
weh? 8 Seit drei Tagen. 9 So, so. Drei Tage schon. Kein Fußball für Sie.
10 O weh.

Test 11 Sepp: Ja, mein Kopf tut weh. Ja, mein Bein tut weh. Ja, mein
Knie tut weh. Ja, mein Rücken tut weh. Ja, mein Hals tut weh. Ja, mein
Ellbogen tut weh. Ja, mein Ohr tut weh. Ja, meine Nase tut weh. Ja,
meine Schulter tut weh. Ja, mein Finger tut weh.

Test 12   1 Haben Sie dieses Material in blau?   2 Haben Sie diese Art eine Nummer kleiner?   3 Haben Sie diese Farbe in Wolle?   4 Haben Sie diese Farbe eine Nummer größer?   5 Haben Sie dieses Material in hellblau? 6 Haben Sie diese Art in Baumwolle?   7 Haben Sie diese Farbe in Polyester? 8 Haben Sie diese Art in schwarz?   9 Haben Sie diese Art in Samt? 10 Haben Sie diese Größe in weiß?

Test 13   1 Es ist sehr heiß im Sommer und es regnet im Winter.   2 Es ist sehr heiß im Sommer und es schneit im Winter.   3 Es regnet im Sommer und es regnet im Winter.   4 Es ist sehr heiß im Sommer und es ist sehr kalt im Winter.   5 Es ist sehr heiß im Sommer und es regnet im Winter.

Test 14   1 In Erfurt   2 A week   3 A single room with a bath   4 DM 160 per night   5 Breakfast and VAT   6 Room 201   7 The lift ('der Lift', also called 'der Aufzug')

Chapter 11   Ein Tisch für zwei

Exercise 1   1 A: Ja, bitte schön?   B: Einmal Eisbein mit Sauerkraut. A: Einmal Eisbein mit Sauerkraut. Möchten Sie etwas zu trinken?   B: Nein, danke.   2 A: Ja, bitte schön?   B: Zweimal Austern.   A: Zweimal Austern. B: Zweimal Seezungenfilet.   A: Zweimal Seezungenfilet   B: Zweimal Zigeunersteak.   A: Zweimal Zigeunersteak.   B: Zweimal Ananas.   A: Zweimal Ananas. Möchten Sie etwas zu trinken?   B: Eine Flasche Rheinwein, bitte.   A: Jawohl.   3 A: Ja, bitte schön?   B: Einmal Rührei mit Schinken. A: Einmal Rührei.   B: Einmal Frankfurter.   A: Einmal Frankfurter. B: Und einmal Forelle.   A: Einmal Forelle. Möchten Sie etwas zu trinken? B: Dreimal Apfelsaft, bitte.   A: Jawohl. 4 A: Bitte schön?   B: Einmal Rührei.   A: Einmal Rührei.   B: Einmal Spiegeleier mit Schinken.   A: Einmal Spiegeleier.   B: Einmal die Käseplatte.   A: Einmal die Käseplatte. Möchten Sie etwas zu trinken?   B: Zweimal Kaffee, bitte.   A: Jawohl.

Exercise 3   1 Möchten Sie auch eine Vorspeise?   2 Möchten Sie auch ein Mineralwasser?   3 Möchten Sie auch einen Cognac?   4 Möchten Sie auch eine Gulaschsuppe?   5 Möchten Sie auch eine Forelle?   6 Möchten Sie auch Salzkartoffeln?   7 Möchten Sie auch Eisbein?   8 Möchten Sie auch ein Wiener Schnitzel?   9 Möchten Sie auch eine Käseplatte?   10 Möchten Sie auch ein gemischtes Kompott?

Exercise 4   1 Wieviel Uhr ist es? Es ist ein Uhr. 2 Wieviel Uhr ist es? Es ist Mittag. 3 Wieviel Uhr ist es? Es ist fünf (Minuten) nach neun. 4 Wieviel Uhr ist es? Es ist Viertel nach sechs. 5 Wieviel Uhr ist es? Es ist fünfundzwanzig (Minuten) nach vier. 6 Wieviel Uhr ist es? Es ist halb zehn. 7 Wieviel Uhr ist es? Es ist zehn (Minuten) nach elf. 8 Wieviel Uhr ist es? Es ist zwanzig (Minuten) nach sechs. 9 Wieviel Uhr ist es? Es ist halb sieben. 10 Wieviel Uhr ist es? Es ist Viertel vor drei.

MENU

HORS D'OEUVRES

Prawn cocktail
Jellied eel
Oysters

SOUPS

Chicken soup with noodles
Goulash soup
Onion soup

EGG DISHES

Scrambled egg
Fried eggs with ham
Omelette – various

FISH DISHES

Rollmop herring
Poached trout with green salad
  and boiled potatoes
Fillet of Dover sole with French
  beans and boiled potatoes

MEAT DISHES

Pickled knuckle of pork with
  sauerkraut
'Texas' steak with chips and mixed
  salad
Veal (or pork) escalope garnished
  with mushroom sauce and chips
Veal (or pork) escalope with
  breadcrumbs garnished with fried
  egg, salad and fried potatoes
Veal (or pork) escalope garnished
  with green pepper sauce with
  onions, rice and green salad

FOR CHILDREN

Scrambled egg with ham
Two Frankfurters with chips

CHEESE

Emmenthal, butter, bread
Mixed cheese platter, butter, bread

DESSERTS

Mixed cold stewed fruit
Ice cream sundae
Pancakes
Pineapple flambé with cherry brandy

BEVERAGES

Beer Pils
    Export
Moselle wine
Rhine wine

Red wine

Sekt (German champagne)
Cognac
German brandy
Apple juice
Mineral water

Cup of coffee or tea
Pot (of coffee or tea)
OUR PRICES INCLUDE SERVICE AND VAT

Exercise 5 1 They both order the chicken soup 2 She orders Wiener
Schnitzel with chips; he has a Jägerschnitzel with fried potatoes
3 Mixed vegetables 4 Nothing 5 They both have black coffee
6 55 marks 7 3 marks

Chapter 12   Kann ich hier parken?

Exercise 1   1 Kann ich Ihr Auto borgen, bitte?   2 Kann ich Ihre Zahnbürste borgen, bitte?   3 Kann ich Ihre Zahnpasta borgen, bitte? 4 Kann ich Ihren Rasierapparat borgen, bitte?   5 Kann ich Ihre Zeitung borgen, bitte?

Exercise 2   1 Selbstverständlich   2 Auf keinen Fall   3 Aber natürlich 4 Nein, das ist unmöglich   5 Selbstverständlich   6 Nein, es tut mir leid 7 Auf keinen Fall   8 Auf keinen Fall   9 Aber natürlich 10 Selbstverständlich

Exercise 3   1 Darf ich hier parken?   2 Kann ich Ihr Fahrrad borgen, bitte? 3 Kann ich etwas Zucker borgen, bitte?   4 Kann ich das Auto nehmen, bitte? 5 Kann ich Ihre Zahnbürste borgen, bitte?

Exercise 5   1 10th row, seat number 4 (zehnte Reihe, Platznummer 4) 2 The man is not allowed into the auditorium   3 The bus   4 Ich kann Sie erst in der Pause reinlassen   5 (b) den Intendanten ('das Internat' is a boarding school, 'der Internierte' someone who is interned)   6 No. The lady says 'Der ist nicht im Haus' – he is not in (the theatre)

Chapter 13   Was sind Sie von Beruf?

Exercise 1   1 Herr Moezer ist Bäcker.   2 Frau Hacker ist Friseuse. 3 Frau Siegling ist Studentin.   4 Herr Mader ist Taxifahrer.   5 Frau Meyer ist Hausfrau.   6 Frau Bauer ist Sekretärin.   7 Frau Augustin ist Kellnerin. 8 Herr Flohr ist Polizist.   9 Herr Kahle ist Techniker. 10 Herr Löb ist Lehrer (Hauptschullehrer).

Exercise 3   1 Gefällt Ihnen die Farbe?   2 Gefällt Ihnen die Landschaft? 3 Gefällt Ihnen das Auto?   4 Gefallen Ihnen die Schuhe?   5 Gefällt Ihnen der Wind?   6 Gefällt Ihnen das Material?   7 Gefällt Ihnen das Wetter? 8 Gefällt Ihnen der Schnee?   9 Gefallen Ihnen die Geschäfte?   10 Gefällt Ihnen der Regen?

Exercise 4   1 By talking about the weather   2 Rainy   3 It is her lunch break   4 Secretary   5 Wine   6 The export section   7 She speaks English and French   8 At school (and also at the Technical School – 'die Handelsschule')   9 Back to the office

Chapter 14   Wo wohnen Sie?

Exercise 1   1 Ja, ich habe ein Wohnzimmer.   2 Ja, ich habe ein Eßzimmer. 3 Ja, ich habe eine Küche.   4 Ja, ich habe ein Badezimmer.   5 Ja, ich habe ein Schlafzimmer.   6 Ja, ich habe eine Toilette.

Exercise 2 1 Ja, ich habe ein Wohnzimmer.   2 Nein, eine Garage habe ich nicht. 3 Nein, ein Eßzimmer habe ich nicht.   4 Nein, eine Terrasse habe ich nicht.   5 Ja, ich habe eine Küche.   6 Nein, einen Balkon habe ich nicht. 7 Ja, ich habe ein Badezimmer.   8 Nein, einen Garten habe ich nicht.

Exercise 4 1 Ja, er wohnt in München.   2 Nein, er hat eine Einzimmerwohnung.   3 Ja, er hat ein Badezimmer.   4 Ja, er hat eine Küche. 5 Ja, er hat viele Bilder.   6 Antonios Onkel wohnt in Neapel (Napoli). 7 Nein, er hat ein Einzelhaus.   8 Er hat sechs Schlafzimmer. 9 Er hat zwei Gästezimmer.   10 Nein, Antonio hat eine Sozialwohnung. 11 Ja, er hat ein Eßzimmer.   12 Ja, er hat ein Badezimmer.   13 Ja, er hat eine Küche.   14 Nein, er hat einen Balkon.

Exercise 5 1 By bus   2 About ten minutes   3 One-room flat ('Einzimmerwohnung') and a balcony   4 On the third floor   5 She uses the lift ('Aufzug')   6 For some time (she says 'längere Zeit')   7 To meet again here for a coffee

Chapter 15   Interessen

Exercise 1 1 Ich tanze gern.   2 Ich wandere sehr gern.   3 Ich male wirklich sehr gern.   4 Ich lese außerordentlich gern.   5 Ich singe furchtbar gern.

Exercise 2 1 Ich koche nicht gern.   2 Ich bastele gar nicht gern.   3 Ich tanze überhaupt nicht gern.

Exercise 3 1 Nein, ich tanze nicht gern.   2 Nein, ich wandere nicht gern. 3 Ja, ich male gern.   4 Ja, ich spiele gern Karten.   5 Nein, ich fahre nicht gern Ski.   6 Ja, ich lese gern.   7 Nein, ich singe nicht gern.   8 Nein, ich reite nicht gern.

Exercise 4 1 Ja, aber Stich ist größer.   2 Ja, aber Stich ist schneller.   3 Ja, aber Stich ist gesünder.   4 Ja, aber Stich ist stärker.   5 Ja, aber Stich ist jünger.   6 Ja, aber Stich ist klüger.   7 Ja, aber Stich spielt härter.   8 Ja, aber Stich spielt besser.

Exercise 5 1 Singing   2 Baroque music   3 No, he sings in a choir ('der Chor')   4 The St Matthew Passion by Bach (the 'Matthäuspassion') 5 Next Saturday in St Jacob's Church ('St Jakobs Kirche')

Chapter 16   Wir müssen gehen

Exercise 1 1 Ich muß mein Geld mitnehmen.   2 Ich muß meine Stiefel mitnehmen.   3 Ich muß meinen Tennisschläger mitnehmen.   4 Ich muß

meine Landkarte mitnehmen. 5 Ich muß meine Eintrittskarten mitnehmen.
6 Ich muß meine Badehose mitnehmen. 7 Ich muß meinen (Reise)paß
mitnehmen. 8 Ich muß meine Zahnbürste mitnehmen. 9 Ich muß meinen
Regenschirm mitnehmen.

Exercise 2 1 Er muß Elke besuchen. 2 Er muß die Karten abholen.
3 Er muß nach Nürnberg fahren. 4 Er muß eine Kette für Elke kaufen.
5 Er muß einen Tennisschläger kaufen. 6 Er muß nach Stuttgart fahren.
7 Er muß im Bett bleiben.

Exercise 4 1 He has seen dog dirt in front of his door 2 The woman's two
poodles 3 No 4 She says her dogs have not done it 5 He threatens to
call the police

Chapter 17 Können Sie singen?

Exercise 1 1 (a) Karlheinz! Wollen wir Fußball spielen? (b) Ja, gern.
2 (a) Karlheinz! Wollen wir reiten? (b) Nein, ich kann nicht reiten.
3 (a) Karlheinz! Wollen wir Karten spielen? (b) Ja, gern. 4 (a) Karlheinz!
Wollen wir Tennis spielen? (b) Nein, ich kann nicht Tennis spielen.
5 (a) Karlheinz! Wollen wir einen Spaziergang machen? (b) Ja, gern.
6 (a) Ulrike! Wollen wir tanzen gehen? (b) Ja, gern. 7 (a) Ulrike! Wollen
wir Ski fahren? (b) Nein, ich kann nicht Ski fahren. 8 (a) Ulrike! Wollen
wir schwimmen gehen? (b) Ja, gern. 9 (a) Ulrike! Wollen wir Fußball
spielen? (b) Nein, ich kann nicht Fußball spielen. 10 (a) Ulrike! Wollen
wir Karten spielen? (b) Nein, ich kann nicht Karten spielen.

Exercise 3 1 Der Junge geht in die Schule. 2 Der Lehrer arbeitet in der
Schule. 3 Die Klasse kommt in das Klassenzimmer. 4 Die Mädchen
warten in dem Klassenzimmer. 5 Das Radio steht auf dem Tisch. 6 Ich
stelle die Milch in den Kühlschrank. 7 Das Bild hängt an der Wand. 8 Ich
halte meine Zeitung unter dem Arm. 9 Ich gehe an die Tür. 10 Ich stelle
die Tasse auf den Tisch.

Exercise 4 1 Holidays 2 That they go to Crete 3 Too hot 4 The
island of Sylt 5 Too cold 6 Too expensive and it is always raining
7 None. He has no time. He must catch his train

Chapter 18 Ich möchte reisen

Exercise 1 1 Ich möchte sie reinigen lassen. 2 Ich möchte sie reparieren
lassen. 3 Ich möchte ihn reinigen lassen. 4 Ich möchte ihn reparieren
lassen. 5 Ich möchte es reinigen lassen. 6 Ich möchte sie reinigen lassen.
7 Ich möchte sie reparieren lassen.

Exercise 3   1 Ich möchte mir die Haare waschen lassen.   2 Er will seinen Apparat reparieren lassen.   3 Elke will New York besuchen.   4 Ich möchte die Welt sehen.   5 Er möchte nach Hamburg fahren.   6 Wir müssen das Geld wechseln.   7 Wir möchten zahlen.   8 Sie muß sich ein neues Kleid machen lassen.   9 Kann ich bitte Herrn Schmidt sprechen?   10 Sie will ihren Mantel reinigen lassen.

Exercise 4   She asks for a French recipe book, a new dress, a winter coat, some new shoes and a gold necklace

Chapter 19   Gestern und vorgestern

Exercise 1   Montag – Ich bin nach Solingen gefahren.   Dienstag – Ich habe eine Armbanduhr gekauft.   Mittwoch – Ich habe eine Kette für Inge gesucht. Donnerstag – Ich bin mit Elke ins Kino gegangen.   Freitag – Ich habe Wein mit Peter getrunken.   Samstag – Ich habe Bayern-München gegen Hamburg gesehen.   Sonntag – Ich bin in die Kirche gegangen.

Exercise 3   1 Ich habe Bier getrunken.   2 Ich bin in die Stadt gegangen. 3 Er ist nach Bremen gefahren.   4 Wir sind um 8 Uhr gekommen.   5 Sie sind zu lange geblieben.   6 Sie hat ein Hemd gekauft.   7 Wir haben eine Wohnung gesucht.   8 Sie hat ihre Armbanduhr verloren.   9 Ich habe einen guten Film gesehen.   10 Sie haben Herrn Schüth getroffen.

Exercise 4   1 From Paris   2 She went straight to the office   3 Director 4 About 40   5 Financial director   6 Export director   7 8 a.m.   8 She went with Pierre Dupont   9 2 p.m. – 6 p.m.   10 She went to the opera with Pierre Dupont. They saw Don Carlos   11 In Pierre's car   12 11 a.m. 13 Yes ('der Vertrag': the contract)

Chapter 20   Revision tests

Test 1   Kellner: Guten Abend!   Sie: Guten Abend! Haben Sie einen Tisch für zwei?   Kellner: Kommen Sie, bitte.   Sie: Die Speisekarte, bitte.   Kellner: Die Speisekarte, bitte schön.   Sie: Möchten Sie eine Vorspeise?   Freund(in): Ja, bitte.   Sie: Möchten Sie Austern?   Freund(in): Austern. O ja!   Sie: Zweimal Austern, bitte.   Kellner: Zweimal Austern.   Sie: Möchten Sie das Zigeunerschnitzel?   Freund(in): Nein, danke. Ich möchte ein Jägerschnitzel. Sie: Einmal Jägerschnitzel und einmal Wiener Schnitzel.   Kellner: Jawohl. Sie: Möchten Sie etwas zu trinken?   Freund(in): O ja. Ich möchte einen Rotwein. Und Sie?   Sie: Ich möchte auch einen Rotwein. Zwei Viertel Rotwein, bitte.   Kellner: Ja.

Test 2   Customer: Guten Abend!   Head waiter: Guten Abend!   Customer: Ich möchte einen Tisch.   Head waiter: Für wie viele Personen?   Customer: Für zwei.   Head waiter: Kommen Sie, bitte.

Test 3 Customer: Guten Tag! Head waiter: Guten Tag! Customer: Ich möchte einen Tisch. Head waiter: Für wann? Customer: Für heute abend. Head waiter: Auf welchen Namen? Customer: Schmidt. Head waiter: Für wie viele Personen? Customer: Für zwei. Head waiter: Um wieviel Uhr? Customer: Um acht Uhr. Head waiter: Ist in Ordnung. Customer: Auf Wiederhören!

Test 4 Einmal Apfelkuchen Zweimal Brathähnchen Ein gekochtes Ei Zweimal Ente Dreimal Leber Einmal Leberkäs Dreimal Matjesfilet Zweimal Eisbecher Einmal Pfeffersteak Zweimal Apfelsaft Einmal Sauerkraut Dreimal Schweinefleisch

Test 5 1 Kann ich einen Tisch borgen, bitte? 2 Kann ich ein Kleid borgen, bitte? 3 Kann ich einen Stuhl borgen, bitte? 4 Kann ich einen Pullover borgen, bitte? 5 Kann ich ein Hemd borgen, bitte? 6 Kann ich eine Bluse borgen, bitte? 7 Kann ich eine Jacke borgen, bitte? 8 Kann ich eine Hose borgen, bitte? 9 Kann ich einen Regenmantel borgen, bitte? 10 Kann ich ein Nachthemd borgen, bitte?

Test 6 (assume today is Wednesday): Heute, gestern, vorgestern, morgen, übermorgen.

Test 7 1 Ja, das Wetter gefällt mir. 2 Ja, der Sonnenschein gefällt mir. 3 Nein, der Regen gefällt mir nicht. 4 Ja, der Schnee gefällt mir. 5 Nein, der Wind gefällt mir nicht. 6 Ja, die Landschaft gefällt mir. 7 Ja, das Meer gefällt mir. 8 Nein, der Nebel gefällt mir nicht. 9 Nein, der Strand gefällt mir nicht. 10 Ja, die Berge gefallen mir.

Test 8 1 Ich wohne in einem Haus. 2 Ich wohne in einer Eigentumswohnung. 3 Ich wohne in einem Einfamilienhaus. 4 Ich wohne in einem Reihenhaus. 5 Ich wohne in einem Mietshaus. 6 Ich wohne in einem Einzelhaus. 7 Ich wohne in einem Zweifamilienhaus. 8 Ich wohne in einer Wohnung. 9 Ich wohne in einer Sozialwohnung. 10 Ich wohne in einer Mietwohnung.

Test 10 1 Ich interessiere mich für Musik. 2 Ich interessiere mich für Bilder. 3 Ich interessiere mich für Bücher. 4 Ich interessiere mich für Fotografie. 5 Ich interessiere mich für Fußball. 6 Ich interessiere mich für Leichtathletik.

Test 11 1 Am Donnerstag muß er einen Tennisschläger kaufen. 2 Am Dienstag muß er nach Nürnberg fahren. 3 Am Sonntag muß er Elke besuchen. 4 Am Mittwoch muß er eine Kette für Elke kaufen. 5 Am Montag muß er die Karten abholen. 6 Am Freitag muß er nach Stuttgart fahren. 7 Am Samstag muß er im Bett bleiben.

Test 12   1 Können Sie Tennis spielen?   2 Wollen wir einen Spaziergang machen?   3 Können Sie tanzen?   4 Er kann schwimmen.   5 Sie wollen Fußball spielen.   6 Wir können Karten spielen.   7 Wollen wir nach London fahren?   8 Kann sie singen?   9 Er will nicht trinken.   10 Sie können nicht schwimmen.

Test 13   1 She cannot find it   2 The director   3 Her passport and a credit card   4 She must get her pass from her car

Translations of dialogues

The following translations give equivalents of the German dialogues.

Chapter 1   Guten Tag!

Dialogue 1

1   Secretary: Ah, Professor! Good morning (good afternoon).
Professor Hecht: Good morning, Mrs Hausmann.
    Is Mr Kirchhof there?
Secretary: Yes, just a moment.
5   Mr Kirchhof ...
    Professor Hecht is here.

    ...

Mr Kirchhof: Good morning, Professor Hecht.
Prof. Hecht: Good morning, Mr Kirchhof.
Mr Kirchhof: Please come in.
10   Prof. Hecht: Thank you.
    How are you?
Mr Kirchhof: Very well, thank you.
    Please sit down.
Prof. Hecht: Thank you
15   Mr Kirchhof: (Would you like) a cup of coffee?
Prof. Hecht: Oh yes, please.
Mr Kirchhof: Mrs Hausmann, two cups of coffee, please.
Mrs Hausmann: Certainly.
Mr Kirchhof: Now, how is your husband?
20   Prof. Hecht: Very well indeed.
Mr Kirchhof: And Andreas and Daniella?
Prof. Hecht: Very well, too.
Mr Kirchhof: And here is the catalogue.
Prof. Hecht: Yes, the catalogue.

Dialogue 2

1   Elke: Doctor Neumann! Good evening!
Doctor Neumann: Elke, good evening!
Elke: How nice.
   Do come in.
5   Dr Neumann: Thank you.
   May I introduce my wife?
Elke: Good evening, Mrs Neumann.
   Welcome!
Mrs Neumann: Good evening
10   Thank you for the invitation.
Elke: Not at all.
   This is Fritz.
Fritz: Good evening!
   My name is Löb.
15   Elke: Eckhard!
Eckhard: Elke!
Elke: You here!
   This is marvellous!
Eckhard: Elke, you are as beautiful as ever.
20   Elke: Oh, no.
Eckhard: Yes you are.
Elke: Oh yes.
   This is Fritz.
Eckhard: (My name is) Becker.
25   Fritz: Pleased to meet you.
   My name is Löb.
Eckhard: Pleased to meet you.
Elke: Excuse me!
Dr Neumann: Goodbye.
30   Thank you very much.
Elke: Not at all.
   Goodbye.

Chapter 2   Wie komme ich ...?

Dialogue 1

1   Mrs Meyer: Excuse me!
   How do I get to the Amalienstraße, please?
Pedestrian: Sorry?
Mrs Meyer: The Amalienstraße.
5   How do I get to the Amalienstraße?
Pedestrian: Now let me see, the Amalienstraße.
Mrs Meyer: Terrible!
   Quite terrible!

Pedestrian: Sorry?
10 Mrs Meyer: Everything is new here.
Pedestrian: Yes, that's right.
 To the Adriastraße, wasn't it?
Mrs Meyer: No, not the Adriastraße,
 to the Amalienstraße.
 How do I get to the Amalienstraße?
15 Pedestrian: Oh yes.
 Go straight on, then take the first street on the left.
Mrs Meyer: The first street on the left.
Pedestrian: That's Market Street.
 Go up Market Street, then you come to the Amalienstraße.

Dialogue 2

1 Elke: Excuse me!
 How do we get to Mittenwald?
Boy: Sorry?
Elke: To Mittenwald.
5 Boy: I don't know.
Elke: Thank you.
 Silly idiot!
Fritz: Excuse me!
 How do we get to Mittenwald?
10 Girl: To Mittenwald?
 Go straight on.
Fritz: Straight on.
Girl: To Garmisch.
 Turn left when you get there.
15 Fritz: Is it far?
Girl: No.
 About twenty kilometres.
Fritz: Thank you.
Girl: Keep going towards Innsbruck.
20 Fritz: Towards Innsbruck.
 Thank you.
Girl: That's all right.

Chapter 3 Ein Doppelzimmer

Dialogue 1

1 Antonio: Good evening!
Receptionist: Good evening!
Antonio: I would like to reserve a room.
Receptionist: Yes, for how long?

5   Antonio: For five nights
       From Monday to Saturday.
     Receptionist: Yes. A single room or a double room?
     Antonio: A double room.
     Receptionist: With bath or shower?
10   Antonio: With a shower.
       A quiet room, please.
     Receptionist: Yes, yes. The room is nice and quiet.
     Antonio: Good.
     Receptionist: What is the name, please?
15   Antonio: Raggi. R-A-G-G-I.
     Receptionist: Thank you very much.
     Antonio: How much is the room?
     Receptionist: It costs 120 marks a night.
     Antonio: Is that with breakfast?
20   Receptionist: Yes, that's with breakfast and VAT.
     Antonio: Thank you.
     Receptionist: That's all right. You're welcome.

Dialogue 2

1   Elke: Good afternoon!
     Receptionist: Good afternoon!
     Elke: Have you a room, please?
     Receptionist: Yes.
5   What sort of room?
     Elke: A single room.
       With bathroom.
     Receptionist: For how many nights?
     Elke: I'm staying two nights.
10   Receptionist: A single room with a bathroom.
       Yes, I can do that.
     Elke: What does the room cost?
     Receptionist: It costs 95 marks a night with breakfast.
     Elke: I'll take it.
15   Receptionist: Would you please sign the register.
       …
       Your room is on the fifth floor.
     Elke: Has the room got a view?
     Receptionist: Yes, it's got a lovely view over the Alster.
20   Elke: How nice.
     Receptionist: Have you any luggage?
     Elke: Yes, my luggage is here.
     Receptionist: Porter!

Dialogue 3

1   Receptionist: Hotel Bayerischer Hof.
      Fritz: Good afternoon!
      Have you a room available for next Saturday, please?
      Receptionist: For the 12th?
5   Fritz: Yes, for Saturday the 12th.
      Receptionist: No, I'm sorry, we're completely booked up.
      Fritz: Thank you.
      Receptionist: Not at all.

Chapter 4   Hin und zurück

Dialogue 1

1   Mrs Meyer: Good morning!
      Clerk: Good morning!
      Mrs Meyer: A second class ticket to Augsburg, please.
      Clerk: Single or return?
5   Mrs Meyer: Return please.
      How much is that?
      Clerk: Fifty-two marks.
      Mrs Meyer: What? As much as that!
      Clerk: Sorry!
10   Mrs Meyer: That's terrible!
      Clerk: There's nothing I can do about it.
      Mrs Meyer: Sixty marks.
      Clerk: 53, 54, 55, 60, thank you.
      Mrs Meyer: Thank you.
15   Fifty-two marks.
      That's terrible.
      Mrs Meyer: Excuse me!
      Information: Yes?
      Mrs Meyer: What time is the train to Augsburg?
20   Information: Augsburg ... Augsburg ....
      The train leaves at 9.27 a.m., and arrives at 10.13.
      Mrs Meyer: Thank you.
      Do I have to change?
25   Information: No. It's a through train.
      Mrs Meyer: Thank you.
      Information: You're welcome.

Dialogue 2

1   Antonio: Good morning!
      Clerk: Good morning!
      Antonio: Two second class tickets to Innsbruck, please.
      Clerk: Single or return?

5   Antonio: Single, please.
     Clerk: Two singles to Innsbruck.
       Ninety-eight marks, please.
     Antonio: Just a minute.
       A ticket to Innsbruck, too.
10   Clerk: Single?
     Antonio: No.
       Return.
     Clerk: Two singles.
       One return.
15   Is that right?
     Antonio: Yes, that's right.
     Clerk: That's 196 marks, please.
     Antonio: What time does the train leave for Innsbruck?
     Information: At 9.31.
20   Antonio: Thank you.
       Which platform?
     Information: Platform 3.
     Antonio: Thank you.
     Information: That's OK.

Chapter 5   Taxi, bitte!

Dialogue 1

1   Elke: I'd like a taxi,
       please.
     Clerk: What name?
     Elke: Kustmann.
5   Clerk: What's your address?
     Elke: Fürstenstraße 15.
     Clerk: Where do you want to go to?
     Elke: To the Nietzschestraße.
     Clerk: The taxi will be there in 10 minutes.
10   Elke: Thank you.
     Taxi Driver: Ms Kustmann?
     Elke: Yes.
     Taxi Driver: Your taxi is here.
     Elke: Nietzschestraße, please.
15   Number 30.
     Taxi Driver: All right.
       …
       Here you are.
     Elke: How much is that?
     Taxi driver: 6 marks 50.
20   Elke: Thank you.
       That's all right.

Dialogue 2

1   Mrs Meyer: Excuse me!
         Does the number 23 go to the town hall?
         Man: No, not the 23.
         Mrs Meyer: Good heavens!
5   Which bus does go to the town hall then?
         Man: You need the number 18.
         That goes to the town hall.
         Mrs Meyer: I see, thank you very much.
         The number 18.
10   Man: Yes, that goes to the town hall.
         Mrs Meyer: That's unheard of!!
         It was always the 23!!

Chapter 6   Es tut weh

Dialogue 1

1   Receptionist: Doctor Storm's surgery.
         Good morning.
         Mrs Meyer: Good morning.
         I'd like to see the doctor.
5   Receptionist: Have you got an appointment?
         Mrs Meyer: No.
         Is this morning possible?
         Receptionist: No.
         I'm sorry.
10   There's no time available this morning.
         Mrs Meyer: Oh no!
         Isn't there any time available?
         Receptionist: No.
         I'm sorry.
15   Mrs Meyer: Is this afternoon possible?
         Receptionist: Yes. Come at 4 o'clock.
         Mrs Meyer: Thank goodness!
         At 4 o'clock.
         Yes, that's all right.
20   Thank you.
         Receptionist: Goodbye.
         Mrs Meyer: Goodbye.

Dialogue 2

1   Doctor Storm: Now, what's the matter?
         Fritz: I've got a headache.
         Doctor Storm: Is that all?
         Fritz: No, doctor.

5   I've got a pain in my stomach and I've got diarrhoea.
       Doctor Storm: How long have you had diarrhoea?
       Fritz: Since yesterday.
       Doctor Storm: I'll prescribe something for the diarrhoea.
       Fritz: Thank you, doctor.

Dialogue 3

1   Doctor Storm: Now, where does it hurt?
       Antonio: Here,
           It's my back.
       Doctor Storm: Here?
5   Antonio: Ow!! Yes!
       Doctor Storm: Is it a sharp pain?
       Antonio: No.
           In the night it was a dull pain.
       Doctor Storm: I see.
10   No football for you.
       Antonio: Oh dear.

Chapter 7   Was darf es sein?

Dialogue 1

1   Saleswoman: Can I help you?
       Fritz: I'm just looking round.
       Saleswoman: Yes, of course.
       Saleswoman: Yes? Can I help you?
5   Fritz: I want a pullover.
       Saleswoman: Yes. A gentleman's or lady's pullover?
       Fritz: I'm looking for a lady's pullover.
       Saleswoman: Yes. What size does the lady take?
       Fritz: Oh, I don't know exactly.
10   Medium size, I think.
       Saleswoman: Like me?
       Fritz: Yes, about like that.
       Saleswoman: Yes, that's size 14 (40)
           What material were you thinking of?
15   Fritz: Oh yes. The material. Of course.
       Saleswoman: Wool? Cotton? Man-made?
       Fritz: Wool! Yes, wool.
       Saleswoman: I've got a lovely red pullover here.
           It's made of wool.
20   Fritz: No. She's already got a red pullover.
           Have you got this sort of thing in blue?
       Saleswoman: Has the lady got blue eyes?
       Fritz: Yes, (she has) actually.

Saleswoman: I've got a blue pullover here.

25   Fritz: Yes. The blue pullover is really very nice.
　　　What does it cost?
　Saleswoman: 90 marks.
　Fritz: I'll take it.

Dialogue 2

1   Salesman: Can I help you?
　Mrs Meyer: I need some new shoes.
　Salesman: Yes, of course.
　　　You take size $4\frac{1}{2}$ (37), I think.
5   Mrs Meyer: No. I always take size 4 (36).
　Salesman: Really?
　Mrs Meyer: How much are the brown shoes in the window?
　Salesman: They are size $4\frac{1}{2}$ (37).
　Mrs Meyer: Have you got the brown shoes a size smaller?
10   Salesman: Yes, I've got the same shoes here.
　　　But they're black.
　Mrs Meyer: Can I try them on?
　Salesman: Of course you can try them on.
　Mrs Meyer: Ow!!! That hurts!
15   　They're too small.
　Salesman: Would you like to try on the brown shoes?
　Mrs Meyer: Are the soles made of leather?
　Salesman: No. The brown shoes have got man-made soles.
20   Mrs Meyer: Man-made soles! That's terrible!
　　　I don't like that at all.
　　　Haven't you got any shoes with leather soles?
　Salesman: Certainly.
　　　Look!
25   　These blue shoes are very elegant.
　　　They are made entirely of leather.
　Mrs Meyer: What size are they?
　Salesman: Size $4\frac{1}{2}$ (37).
　Mrs Meyer: How much do they cost?
30   Salesman: They cost 225 marks.
　Mrs Meyer: What? That's too expensive!
　　　Goodbye!
　Salesman: Goodbye!
　Mrs Meyer: Disgusting! It's disgusting! 225 marks!

Chapter 8   Haben sie Kinder?

Dialogue 1

1   Antonio: Good day!
     Owner: Good day!
     Antonio: I've come about the job as a waiter.
     Owner: Oh yes.
5   Do you have any experience as a waiter?
     Antonio: No, unfortunately not.
     Owner: Hmm. Can you speak Italian?
     Antonio: Of course.
     I am Italian.
10   Owner: Oh, you are Italian.
     Where do you come from?
     Antonio: I come from Napoli.
     Owner: Napoli! Well, well, Napoli.
     I come from Benevento.
15   Antonio: That's wonderful!
     My Aunt Concetta comes from Benevento.
     Owner: No!
     Antonio: Yes, she does.
     Owner: Fantastico, fantastico!
20   When can you begin?

Dialogue 2

1   Parson: The church is very old, Mr Löb.
     Fritz: Yes, one can see that.
     Parson: Over three hundred years old.
     Fritz: Really?
5   Parson: Yes.
     Look.
     The altar is beautiful, isn't it?
     Fritz: That's true.
     It's very beautiful.
10   Parson: Riemenschneider.
     Fritz: Really.
     Tilman Riemenschneider.
     Parson: Yes.
     Tell me, Mr Löb.
15   What do you do (What are you by profession)
     if I may ask (if you don't mind my asking)?
     Fritz: I'm a teacher.

In Munich.

Parson: Really.

Are you married?

20   Fritz: Yes. That's to say, we're separated.

Parson: I'm sorry.

Fritz: Thank you.

Parson: Have you got any children?

Fritz: No, I haven't got any children.

25   Parson: Perhaps it's better that way.

Fritz: Yes, it's better that way.

Young children need a father.

Parson: That's right.

Chapter 9   Wie ist das Wetter?

Dialogue 1

1   Man: Excuse me!

Elke: Yes?

Man: I just wanted to say ...

that's a very elegant dress.

Elke: Oh, thank you.

5   That is very nice of you.

Man: You have a north German accent.

Elke: Yes. I come from Mölln.

Man: Mölln? Where is Mölln?

Elke: In North Germany.

10   Not far from Hamburg.

Man: Oh yes. Near Hamburg.

Elke: Yes. Between Hamburg and Lübeck.

Man: What is the countryside like there?

Elke: There's a large lake there,

and a very beautiful church.

15   Man: Have you still got any family there?

Elke: Yes. My brother lives in Mölln, with my parents.

Man: Oh, you've got a brother.

Elke: Yes. He's coming to Munich next week.

He's an enthusiastic skier.

20   Man: Isn't there any snow in Mölln then?

Elke: No. It rains a lot in winter.

But there's not much snow.

Man: Oh, I see.

Dialogue 2

1   Antonio: Cheers!

Girl: Cheers!

Antonio: Are you from Munich?

Girl: No. I come from Bad Reichenhall.

5   Antonio: Where is Bad Reichenhall?

Girl: Not far from Salzburg.
And you?

Antonio: I come from Naples.
But I'm a 'Münchener' now.

10   Girl: Oh, I see.

Antonio: What is there to see there,
in Bad Reichenhall?

Girl: There is a fine pump room,
and nice shops.

Antonio: And the countryside?
What is the countryside like there?

15   Girl: Oh, the countryside is wonderful!
There are high mountains.

Antonio: That's nice.

Girl: Yes. The Predigtstuhl for example.
That is a very high mountain.

20   Antonio: What's the weather like there?

Girl: It's usually nice.
There is a lot of snow in winter.

Antonio: And in summer?

Girl: It rains sometimes in summer.

25   Unfortunately.

Chapter 11   Ein Tisch für zwei

Dialogue 1

1   Owner: Blue House Restaurant.
Good morning (or good afternoon).

Fritz: Good morning!
I should like a table for this evening.

5   Owner: For how many people?

Fritz: For two.

Owner: At what time?

Fritz: At 8 o'clock.

Owner: Yes, at 8 o'clock.

10   I have a table for 8 o'clock.

Fritz: Good.

Owner: What name please?

Fritz: Löb. L – Ö – B.

Owner: Mr Löb.

15   That's all right, Mr Löb.

Fritz: Goodbye.

Owner: Goodbye.

Fritz: Good evening!

Reception: Good evening!

20   Fritz: I have reserved a table.
        Reception: For how many people?
        Fritz: For two people.
        Reception: What name, please?
        Fritz: Löb.
25   Reception: Oh, yes.
        Mr Löb.
        This way, please.

Dialogue 2

1   Fritz: Would you like a starter?
      Elke: I'd like some soup –
        some onion soup.
      Fritz: And then?
      Elke: A Texas steak.
5   And you?
        What would you like?
      Fritz: I think I'd like some soup, too –
        some goulash soup.
        And then … Texas steak as well.
      Waiter: Have you chosen?
10   Fritz: One onion soup.
        One goulash soup.
      Waiter: One onion soup.
        One goulash soup.
      Fritz: And then – two Texas steaks.
15   Elke: Without chips, please.
      Waiter: Two Texas steaks.
        One with chips.
        One without.
        Very good.
20   Fritz: Would you like something to drink?
      Elke: Yes, I'd like a quarter of red wine, please.
      Fritz: Two quarters of red wine, please.
      Waiter: Two quarters of red wine.
        Thank you.

Chapter 12   Kann ich hier parken?

Dialogue 1

1   Antonio: Excuse me!
        Excuse me!
      Policeman: Yes?
      Antonio: Can I park here?
5   Policeman: No. Sorry.
        You're not allowed to park here.

Antonio: What about over there?
　　　　Can I park over there?
Policeman: No.
10　　You're not allowed to park there either.
Antonio: Damn!
　　　　Where can I park then?
Policeman: In the multi-storey car park.
　　　　Drive to the multi-storey car park.
15　Antonio: To the car park! To the car park!
　　　　OK, to the car park.

Dialogue 2

1　Mrs Meyer: Yes?
　　　　Oh, it's you, Mr Löb.
Fritz: Good morning, Mrs Meyer!
　　　　Excuse me for disturbing you.
5　Mrs Meyer: What can I do for you?
Fritz: Mrs Meyer, my car won't start.
　　　　The battery is flat, I think.
Mrs Meyer: I'm sorry.
Fritz: Can I borrow your bicycle?
10　Mrs Meyer: My bicycle?
　　　　Yes, of course you can.
　　　　It's downstairs in the cellar.
Fritz: Thank you very much.
　　　　Oh, can I borrow the pump as well?
15　Mrs Meyer: Of course you can.
　　　　You can borrow the pump too.
Fritz: Thank you very much.
Mrs Meyer: That's quite all right.
　　　　Mind how you go.
20　Fritz: Yes, of course.

Chapter 13　Was sind Sie von Beruf?

Dialogue 1

1　Mrs Meyer: Yes?
　　　　Oh, it's you, Mr Löb.
Fritz: Good morning, Mrs Meyer.
　　　　Excuse me for disturbing you.
5　　Here is your bicycle.
Mrs Meyer: Thank you very much.
　　　　Was everything all right?
Fritz: Yes, everything was all right.
　　　　Thank you very much.
10　Mrs Meyer: You are a teacher, aren't you?

Fritz: Yes, that's right.

Mrs Meyer: Do you like your work?

Fritz: Oh yes, very much.

Mrs Meyer: When do you begin in the morning?

15   Fritz: We begin at eight o'clock.

Mrs Meyer: Oh, I see.
And when do you normally come home?

Fritz: I usually come home about two o'clock.

Mrs Meyer: How many days do you work a week?

20   Fritz: Only five.
Thank heavens!

Mrs Meyer: When I was a schoolgirl,
we had school on Saturdays too.

Fritz: Yes, we are better off.
Now, thank you very much again for the bicycle.

25   Mrs Meyer: That's quite all right, Mr Löb.
Goodbye.

Dialogue 2

1   Man: What do you do (for a living),
if you don't mind my asking?

Elke: I'm a sales assistant.

Man: Here in Munich?

Elke: Yes, at Zilling Fashions.

5   In the Leopoldstraße.

Man: Do you like the work?

Elke: Oh, yes and no.
The pay is very good (I earn very well).

Man: When do you begin work?

10   Elke: At eight o'clock.

Man: And do you have a midday break?

Elke: Yes. From twelve to one.

Man: I have a midday break from twelve to one too.

Elke: Well now!

15   Man: When do you come home in the evening?

Elke: I'm free at five o'clock.

Man: Me too.
Could I pick you up at your shop?
I have a car.

20   Perhaps we could drive out into the country.

Elke: Thank you very much.
But I have my own car.

Man: Oh, I see.

Elke: And today my boyfriend is coming at five o'clock.

25   We want to go shopping in the Viktualien Market.

Man: Oh, that's a pity.

Some other time perhaps.
Elke: Perhaps.

Chapter 14   Wo wohnen Sie?

Dialogue 1

1   Antonio: Cheers!
    Fritz: Cheers!
    Antonio: The mulled wine is nice and warm, isn't it?
    Fritz: Yes, nice and warm.
5   Antonio: Do you live here in Munich?
    Fritz: Yes, I live in the Nietzschestraße.
    Antonio: Do you live in a block of flats?
    Fritz: Yes, I have a one-room flat,
    in a large house divided up into flats.
10   Antonio: Have you only got one room?
    Fritz: Well, I have a bathroom,
    and a kitchen.
    Antonio: Anything else?
    Fritz: Apart from that I have a bed-sitting room.
    Antonio: Is the flat nice?
15   Fritz: Yes, it's small but quite nice.
    I have a lot of pictures there.
    Antonio: Pictures?
    Fritz: Yes.
    I collect pictures.
20   Antonio: Hmm, interesting.

Dialogue 2

1   Antonio: My uncle has got lots of pictures too.
    Fritz: Where does he live?
    Antonio: In Napoli.
    Fritz: Ah, in Naples.
5   Antonio: He's got a detached house.
    Fritz: That's nice.
    Antonio: He's got six bedrooms.
    and two guest-rooms.
    Fritz: Good heavens!
    Antonio: Just imagine that!
10   Six bedrooms!
    Fritz: Has he got a garden too?
    Antonio: I should say so!
    He's got trees and shrubs everywhere.
    Fritz: Very nice.
15   Antonio: As for me ...
    I've got a council flat,

in the Kaufmannsstraße.

Fritz: How many rooms have you got?

Antonio: I've got a dining-room,
and a bedroom.

Fritz: Have you got a bathroom and a kitchen?

20 Antonio: Of course!
And I've got a balcony.
That's nice.

Chapter 15   Interessen

Dialogue 1

1 Fritz: Won't you come in?

Elke: Thank you.

Fritz: This is my one-room flat.

Elke: It's very nice.

5 Fritz: It's unfortunately a bit too small.

Elke: You've got a lot of pictures.
But they are all of churches.

Fritz: Yes, I'm interested in churches.

Elke: Yes, so I see.

10 Fritz: You know,
I like photography.
I like taking pictures of churches.

Elke: Yes, so I see.

Fritz: Would you like a cup of coffee?

15 Elke: Oh yes, please.

Fritz: Look ...
this church is beautiful, isn't it?

Elke: Hmm.

Fritz: It's Romanesque.

20 Elke: Really?

Fritz: Yes. I'm very interested in Romanesque churches.
I like taking photographs of them.

Elke: Yes, so I see.

Fritz: Oh, excuse me.

25 Your coffee.
Do you take sugar?

Elke: No, thank you.

Dialogue 2

1 Student: Antonio!

Antonio: What's the matter?

Student: Nothing.
I just wanted to tell you something.

5 Antonio: Well then?

Student: As you know,
I'm interested in Italian.
Antonio: Yes, I know.
Student: And I like Italian food very much.
10   Antonio: Yes, I know that as well.
Student: Well... Yesterday I was in an Italian restaurant.
Antonio: Whereabouts?
Student: In St. Mark's Street.
15   It's called the Restaurant Giovanni.
Antonio: I don't know it.
Is it good?
Student: Well, I like pizza very much.
And the pizza was really good.
20   Antonio: Were you alone?
Student: No, Birgit was there.
She prefers cannelloni.
Antonio: Hmm. Was the cannelloni good as well?
Student: Not bad.
25   Antonio: I must go there too.
I love pizza.

Chapter 16   Wir müssen gehen

Dialogue 1

1   Elke: Fritz! Do you know what?
Fritz: No.
Elke: Herr Zilling has got tickets for Parsifal
and he can't go.
Fritz: That's bad luck.
5   Elke: For him,
but not for us.
Fritz: How's that?
Elke: Shall we take the tickets?
Fritz: What do they cost?
Elke: A hundred and sixty marks each.
10   Fritz: That's expensive.
Elke: It is Bayreuth, you know.
Fritz: Yes.
Must I put on my evening dress (i.e. dinner jacket)?
Elke: Well, that is normal.
15   I want to put on my new dress.
Fritz: Nice!
Elke: I want to wear my silk coat, too.
Fritz: Aha!
Elke: And of course my pearl necklace.
20   Fritz: When must we decide?
Elke: Oh, immediately.

We do want to go, don't we?

Fritz: Oh yes, of course we do.
When must we pick up the tickets?

Dialogue 2

1   Doctor Storm: Now, Mrs Meyer,
what's the matter with you?
Mrs Meyer: It's my head, doctor.
I keep on getting giddy.
Doctor Storm: How old are you, Mrs Meyer?
5   Mrs Meyer: I'm 75 years old.
Doctor Storm: And where do you live?
Mrs Meyer: In the Nietzschestraße.
Doctor Storm: Where is your flat?
On the ground floor?
10 Mrs Meyer: No, doctor.
On the third floor.
Doctor Storm: And you go shopping every day?
Mrs Meyer: Yes, and I fetch little Sandra from school.
Doctor Storm: Yes, yes. Now Mrs Meyer,
15 you must run about a little bit less.
When do you get up in the morning?
Mrs Meyer: At six o'clock.
Doctor Storm: You must stay in bed a bit longer,
and you must lie down for an hour every afternoon.
20 Mrs Meyer: Must I stay at home, doctor?
Doctor Storm: No, you don't need to stay at home,
but you must take these tablets.
Mrs Meyer: Must I take them in the evening?
I shan't go to sleep.
25 Doctor Storm: No, you don't need to take them in the evening.
Mrs Meyer: Thank heavens!

Chapter 17   Können Sie singen?

Dialogue 1

1   Antonio: Is this seat free?
Girl: Yes.
Antonio: Nice weather, isn't it?
Girl: Yes. Very nice.
5   Antonio: My name is Antonio.
Girl: Hmm.
...
Antonio: What's your name?
If you don't mind my asking?
Girl: Claudia.

10   Antonio: Claudia. A lovely name.
     Girl: Thank you.
     …
     Antonio: Tell me, Claudia.
          Can you play tennis?
     Girl: Yes.
15   Antonio: Good. Shall we play tennis?
     Girl: When?
     Antonio: Tomorrow, perhaps?
     Girl: Yes, I'd like to.
     Antonio: Do you play often?
20   Girl: Fairly often.
          Four or five times a week.
     Antonio: Where do you play?
     Girl: In the Carlton Club.
     Antonio: Oh?
25   Do you play well?
     Girl: Hmm, quite well.
          And you?
     Antonio: No, not very well.
          That's marvellous!!! (spoken ironically)

Dialogue 2

1   Fritz: Hello, Elke!
     Elke: It's you, Fritz!
          Come in!
     Fritz: Thank you.
5   How are you?
     Elke: Fine!
     Fritz: Elke ….
          Shall we go away at the weekend?
     Elke: Oh yes! Where to?
10   Fritz: I know a very pretty church. Near Rosenheim.
     Elke: Oh no, Fritz!
          Another church!
     Fritz: What's the matter?
15   Elke: Every time a church!
     Fritz: I'm interested in churches.
          You know that.
     Elke: But you have a different church every week.
     Fritz: I'm sorry.
20   Elke: Shall we go to Kufstein?
          We can go ski-ing there.
     Fritz: But I can't ski.
     Elke: But I can ski very well.
     Fritz: All right.

25   Let's go to Kufstein.
        Elke: Yes, you can learn.
        (On the nursery slopes.)

Chapter 18   Ich möchte reisen

Dialogue 1

1   Elke: Fritz?
        Fritz: Yes?
        Elke: It's nice here, isn't it?
        Fritz: Yes. Lovely.
5   Elke: You are really nice, you know.
        Fritz: Yes?
        ...
        Elke: Fritz?
        Fritz: Yes?
        Elke: Do you know what?
10   Fritz: No.
        Elke: I should like to go to America.
        Fritz: Really?
        Elke: Yes. I should like to see Hollywood.
        Fritz: Hollywood?
15   Elke: Yes. And I should like to visit New York.
        Fritz: Oh, New York isn't nice.
        Elke: Yes, it is!
        And I should like to go on a tramcar in San Francisco.
20   Fritz: Why do you want to go on a tramcar?
        Elke: Oh, you don't understand.
        It's so romantic in San Francisco.
        Fritz: But expensive.
        Elke: That's a typical man!!
25   You only think about money.
        I want to travel.
        I want to see the world.

Dialogue 2

1   Mrs Meyer: Leni? Do you know what?
        Inge is going to have a baby!
        Leni: No. That's wonderful!
        Where is she?
5   Mrs Meyer: In Liverpool.
        Leni: Oh yes, that's right.
        In England.
        Mrs Meyer: Of course I shall go to Liverpool.
        Leni: Yes, of course.
10   Mrs Meyer: I must have my coat cleaned.

Leni: Yes, of course.

Mrs Meyer: And I must have a new dress made.

Leni: Yes, of course.

Mrs Meyer: And then I shall need a camera.

15   I must have my old camera repaired.

Leni: Of course.

Mrs Meyer: Then I must get some money changed too.

Leni: Yes, of course.

Mrs Meyer: What sort of money do they have in England?

20   Dollars, isn't it?

Leni: No. They have pounds and pence.

Mrs Meyer: Oh yes. Of course.

Then I must have my hair washed.

Leni: Wait a minute, Irmgard.

25   When is Inge expecting her child?

Mrs Meyer: Next year.

In March.

Leni: Listen Irmgard.

You have still got lots of time.

Chapter 19   Gestern und vorgestern

Dialogue 1

1   Fritz: Good heavens!

Where have you been?

Elke: What's the matter?

My bus was late.

5   Fritz: It was late yesterday.

And today it was late again.

Elke: My bus wasn't late yesterday.

Fritz: Yes, it was!

It was thirty minutes late.

10   Elke: That's not true.

Fritz: Yes, it is true.

I was at the cinema at seven o'clock.

And you weren't there until seven thirty.

Elke: I was there on time.

15   You were simply at the cinema too early.

Fritz: And why weren't you on time the day before yesterday?

Elke: I was in the shop.

Fritz: What? Until eight o'clock?

I don't believe it!

20   Elke: I had a lot to do.

Fritz: And the boss was there too, wasn't he?

Elke: Of course.

He had a lot to do, too.

Fritz: I see. Now I understand ...!

Dialogue 2

1	Antonio:	Can I help you?
	Mrs Meyer:	Oh, I have lost my wristwatch.
	Antonio:	Here on the street?
	Mrs Meyer:	Yes, I think so.
5		I went into town.
		And I had some coffee there.
	Antonio:	Do you think you lost your watch in town?
	Mrs Meyer:	No.
		I saw it in the bus.
10	Antonio:	Have you looked at the bus stop?
	Mrs Meyer:	Yes, of course.
		I met Mrs Moezer there.
		I went to the post office with her.
	Antonio:	Do you think you lost the watch in the post office?
15	Mrs Meyer:	No, I don't think so.
	Antonio:	Have you come here straight from the post office?
	Mrs Meyer:	No. I bought some apples first.
		At Schötz's.
	Antonio:	I see. At Schötz's.
20		How long did you stay at Schötz's?
	Mrs Meyer:	Oh, not long.
		Five minutes perhaps.
	Antonio:	Have you looked in your bag?
	Mrs Meyer:	What?
25	Antonio:	Have you looked in your bag?
	Mrs Meyer:	There it is!

Grammatical summary

Grammar introduced in each chapter

1 Nouns; personal pronouns; verb 'sein' (to be); possessive adjectives; gender; singulars and plural; agreement

2 Numbers (cardinal and ordinal); the verbs 'fahren', 'gehen' and 'kommen'; regular and irregular verbs; 'zu' and 'nach'; the Umlaut

3 Days, months and dates; the verbs 'bleiben', 'haben' and 'nehmen'; expressing duration

4 Verbs with separable affixes

5 The indefinite article; 'kein'; 'nicht'; the definite article (subject and direct object); nominative and accusative case; object pronouns; 'some' or 'any'; prepositions

6 Parts of the body; predicative and attributive adjectives; adjective endings after 'ein', 'mein', 'kein', etc.

7 Regular verbs: 'suchen', 'glauben', 'brauchen'; irregular verbs: 'tragen', 'möchten'; adjective endings after 'der', 'dieser', etc.

8 Nationality; languages; adjective endings with no preceding determiner; subordinate clause word order

9 Seasons; the indirect object; the dative case (definite article, indefinite article and possessive pronouns, personal pronouns); prepositions governing the dative

11 Question forms; interrogatives; expressions of time

12 Modal verbs: 'können' and 'dürfen'; word order in sentences with modal verbs

13 Expressions of time; the use of 'gefallen' to express liking

14 Plurals of nouns

15 'Gern' and 'lieber'; comparison of adjectives

16 Modal verbs: 'wollen', 'müssen', 'brauchen nicht'

17 Modal verbs: 'wollen', 'können'; prepositions governing accusative and dative

18 Use of 'lassen' with modal verb and infinitive

19 Simple Past (or Imperfect) tense of 'haben', 'sein' and 'sagen'; Compound Past (or Perfect) tense of other verbs

A Word families

1 Cardinal numbers

The cardinal numbers are as follows:

1	ein(s)	14	vierzehn	70	siebzig
2	zwei	15	fünfzehn	80	achtzig
3	drei	16	sechzehn	90	neunzig
4	vier	17	siebzehn	100	hundert
5	fünf	18	achtzehn	120	hundert(und)-
6	sechs	19	neunzehn		zwanzig
7	sieben	20	zwanzig	221	zweihundertein-
8	acht	21	einundzwanzig		undzwanzig
9	neun	22	zweiundzwanzig	1,000	tausend
10	zehn	30	dreißig	1,101	eintausendein-
11	elf	40	vierzig		hundert(und)eins
12	zwölf	50	fünfzig	1,000,000	eine Million
13	dreizehn	60	sechzig	2,000,000	zwei Millionen

'Tausend' is not generally used in dates: 'das Jahr neunzehnhundertfünfundneunzig' (the year 1995).

There are slight irregularities in the numbers 16, 17, 30, 60 and 70. Compound numbers of hundreds, tens and units (e.g. 'zweihunderteinundzwanzig') are usually written as one word.

2 Ordinal numbers

The ordinal numbers below 20 (except those meaning first, third, seventh and eighth) are formed by adding '-t' to the corresponding cardinal number; from 20 onwards they are formed by adding '-st'. They take normal adjectival endings. When the number is a compound one, only the last part of the cardinal is changed into an ordinal:

1st	der erste	8th	der achte
2nd	der zweite	9th	der neunte
3rd	der dritte	10th	der zehnte
4th	der vierte	20th	der zwanzigste
5th	der fünfte	100th	der hundertste
6th	der sechste	101st	der hundert(und)erste
7th	der siebte	120th	der hundert(und)zwanzigste
		221st	der zweihunderteinund- zwanzigste

3 Days of the week

Sonntag	Sunday
Montag	Monday
Dienstag	Tuesday
Mittwoch	Wednesday
Donnerstag	Thursday
Freitag	Friday
Samstag/Sonnabend	Saturday

4 Parts of the body *(Plural forms are given where relevant)*

der Arm (-e)	arm	das Knie (-)	knee
der Fuß (-̈e)	foot	das Auge (-n)	eye
die Lippe (-n)	lip	das Bein (-e)	leg
die Hand (-̈e)	hand	das Ohr (-en)	ear
der Zahn (-̈e)	tooth	der Finger (-)	finger
der Kopf	head	der Zeh (-en)	toe
die Schulter (-n)	shoulder	der Ellbogen (-)	elbow
der Mund	mouth	der Bauch	stomach
die Nase	nose	der Hals	neck

5 Nouns of nationality

Nouns of nationality make their feminine form in two ways:

(i) Nouns of nationality which end in 'e' make their feminine form by changing the 'e' into 'in'. Here are some examples:

der Franzose	die Französin
der Däne	die Dänin
der Ire	die Irin
der Finne	die Finnin
der Grieche	die Griechin
der Nordire	die Nordirin
der Rumäne	die Rumänin
der Schotte	die Schottin
der Russe	die Russin
der Brite	die Britin
der Schwede	die Schwedin

(ii) Other nouns which end in 'er' make their feminine form by adding 'in'. Here are some examples:

der Engländer	die Engländerin
der Österreicher	die Österreicherin
der Belgier	die Belgierin
der Amerikaner	die Amerikanerin
der Holländer	die Holländerin
der Italiener	die Italienerin

der Norweger	die Norwegerin
der Spanier	die Spanierin
der Schweizer	die Schweizerin
der Waliser	die Waliserin

(iii) German nationality is the only exception:

der Deutsche   die Deutsche   Plural: die Deutschen

but:

ein Deutscher   eine Deutsche   Plural: Deutsche

6 Sprechen Sie Deutsch?

The German for the most common European languages is as follows:

Bulgarisch	Italienisch
Dänisch	Norwegisch
Deutsch	Polnisch
Englisch	Portugiesisch
Finnisch	Russisch
Französisch	Schwedisch
Griechisch	Spanisch
Holländisch	Tschechisch

7 The seasons

der Frühling/im Frühling	der Herbst/im Herbst
der Sommer/im Sommer	der Winter/im Winter

8 The months

Januar	Juli
Februar	August
März	September
April	Oktober
Mai	November
Juni	Dezember

B Verbs

Important points to remember

1 All infinitives end in '-en' or '-n'.
2 German does not distinguish between simple forms (I go), and continuous forms (I am going).
3 The questioning, or interrogative, form is made by putting the verb first and the subject second. There is no 'do' or 'does' in German.

9 Some important regular verbs used in Mastering German

These verbs are given in the present tense.

- *The verb* 'kommen' *(to come)*

ich komme	I come
du kommst	you come *(familiar)*
er kommt	he comes
sie kommt	she comes
wir kommen	we come
ihr kommt	you come *(familiar plural)*
Sie kommen	you come *(formal or polite)*
sie kommen	they come

- *The verb* 'gehen' *(to go)*

ich gehe	I go
du gehst	you go *(familiar)*
er geht	he goes
sie geht	she goes
wir gehen	we go
ihr geht	you go *(familiar plural)*
Sie gehen	you go *(formal or polite)*
sie gehen	they go

- *The verb* 'bleiben' *(to stay/remain)*

ich bleibe	I stay/remain
du bleibst	you stay/remain *(familiar)*
er bleibt	he stays/remains
sie bleibt	she stays/remains
wir bleiben	we stay/remain
ihr bleibt	you stay/remain *(familiar plural)*
Sie bleiben	you stay/remain *(formal or polite)*
sie bleiben	they stay/remain

- *The verb* 'suchen' *(to seek/look for)*

ich suche	I'm looking for
du suchst	you're looking for *(familiar)*
er sucht	he's looking for
sie sucht	she's looking for
wir suchen	we're looking for
ihr sucht	you're looking for *(familiar plural)*
Sie suchen	you're looking for *(formal or polite)*
sie suchen	they're looking for

- *The verb* 'glauben' *(to believe/think)*

ich glaube	I believe/think
du glaubst	you believe *(familiar)*
er glaubt	he believes
sie glaubt	she believes
wir glauben	we believes

ihr glaubt	you believe *(familiar plural)*
Sie glauben	you believe *(formal or polite)*
sie glauben	they believe

- *The verb* 'brauchen' *(to need)*

ich brauche	I need
du brauchst	you need *(familiar)*
er braucht	he needs
sie braucht	she needs
wir brauchen	we need
ihr braucht	you need *(familiar plural)*
Sie brauchen	you need *(formal or polite)*
sie brauchen	they need

10 Some important irregular verbs used in Mastering German

- *The verb* 'fahren' *(to go – by vehicle)*

ich fahre	I go
du fährst	you go *(familiar)*
er fährt	he goes
sie fährt	she goes
wir fahren	we go
ihr fahrt	you go *(familiar plural)*
Sie fahren	you go *(formal or polite)*
sie fahren	they go

- *The verb* 'nehmen' *(to take)*

ich nehme	I take
du nimmst	you take *(familiar)*
er nimmt	he takes
sie nimmt	she takes
wir nehmen	we take
ihr nehmt	you take *(familiar plural)*
Sie nehmen	you take *(formal or polite)*
sie nehmen	they take

- *The verb* 'haben' *(to have)*

ich habe	I have
du hast	you have *(familiar)*
er hat	he has
sie hat	she has
wir haben	we have
ihr habt	you have *(familiar plural)*
Sie haben	you have *(formal or polite)*
sie haben	they have

- *The verb* 'tragen' *(to wear, carry)*

| ich trage | I wear |
| du trägst | you wear *(familiar)* |

er trägt	he wears
sie trägt	she wears
wir tragen	we wear
ihr tragt	you wear *(familiar plural)*
Sie tragen	you wear *(formal or polite)*
sie tragen	they wear

11 The modal verbs

● *The verb* 'können' *('can'/to be able to)*

ich kann	I can
du kannst	you can *(familiar)*
er kann	he can
sie kann	she can
wir können	we can
ihr könnt	you can *(familiar plural)*
Sie können	you can *(formal or polite)*
sie können	they can

● *The verb* 'dürfen' *('may'/to be allowed to)*

ich darf	I may
du darfst	you may *(familiar)*
er darf	he may
sie darf	she may
wir dürfen	we may
ihr dürft	you may *(familiar plural)*
Sie dürfen	you may *(formal or polite)*
sie dürfen	they may

● *The verb* 'wollen' *(to want to)*

ich will	I want to
du willst	you want to *(familiar)*
er will	he wants to
sie will	she wants to
wir wollen	we want to
ihr wollt	you want to *(familiar plural)*
Sie wollen	you want to *(formal or polite)*
sie wollen	they want to

● *The verb* 'müssen' *('must'/to have to)*

ich muß	I must/have to
du mußt	you must/have to *(familiar)*
er muß	he must/has to
sie muß	she must/has to
wir müssen	we must/have to
ihr müßt	you must/have to *(familiar plural)*
Sie müssen	you must/have to *(formal or polite)*
sie müssen	they must/have to

- *The verb* 'brauchen nicht' *(not to have to/not to need to)*

ich brauche nicht	I don't have to/need to
du brauchst nicht	you don't have to/need to *(familiar)*
er braucht nicht	he doesn't have to/need to
sie braucht nicht	she doesn't have to/need to
wir brauchen nicht	we don't have to/need to
ihr braucht nicht	you don't have to/need to *(familiar) plural)*
Sie brauchen nicht	you don't have to/need to *(formal or polite)*
sie brauchen nicht	they don't have to/need to

- *A very important form of the verb* 'mögen' *(to like)*

ich möchte	I would like (also: I should like, etc.)
du möchtest	you would like *(familiar)*
er möchte	he would like
sie möchte	she would like
wir möchten	we would like
ihr möchtet	you would like *(familiar plural)*
Sie möchten	you would like *(formal or polite)*
sie möchten	they would like

12 The Compound Past tense, or Perfect tense, and general reference list of verbs

This contains the verbs used in *Mastering German*, and includes the fifty most frequently occurring verbs in spoken German.

Group A

The past participles of most of these verbs begin with 'ge-' and end with '-en'. Some of them change the vowel sound in the 'du' and 'er' form of the Present tense. This is indicated. Some of them change the vowel sound in the past participle. Some make their Perfect tense with 'haben', others with 'sein'.

Infinitive	Vowel change in present tense	Past participle	Meaning
bleiben		geblieben (sein)	to stay; remain
bringen		gebracht	to bring
denken		gedacht	to think
essen	i	gegessen	to eat
fahren	ä	gefahren (sein)	to go; drive
finden		gefunden	to find
geben	i	gegeben	to give
*gefallen	ä	gefallen	to like; to please
gehen		gegangen (sein)	to go
halten	ä	gehalten	to hold
heißen		gehießen	to be called
†helfen	i	geholfen	to help

kennen		gekannt	to know (someone)
kommen		gekommen (sein)	to come
laufen	äu	gelaufen (sein)	to run
lesen	ie	gelesen	to read
liegen		gelegen	to lie; recline
nehmen	i	genommen	to take
nennen		genannt	to name
reiten		geritten (sein)	to ride
schlafen	ä	geschlafen	to sleep
schwimmen		geschwommen (sein)	to swim
sehen	ie	gesehen	to see
singen		gesungen	to sing
sitzen		gesessen	to sit
sprechen	i	gesprochen	to speak
stehen		gestanden	to stand
tragen	ä	getragen	to wear; carry
treffen	i	getroffen	to meet
trinken		getrunken	to drink
tun		getan	to do
verlieren		verloren	to lose
waschen	ä	gewaschen	to wash
werden	wird	geworden (sein)	to become
wiegen		gewogen	to weigh
wissen	weiß	gewußt	to know something

* The verb 'gefallen' (to like) operates in a special way. In order to render 'I like it', one must say 'es gefällt mir', literally 'it pleases me'. Note that 'me' is rendered by 'mir' (dative case).

† The verb 'helfen' (to help) has an object in the dative case. 'He helps me' is rendered by 'er hilft mir'.

Group B

All these verbs make their past participle by dropping the '-en' at the end of the infinitive and adding '-t' (or '-et'). They are all conjugated with 'haben', except where indicated.

Infinitive	Past participle	Meaning
arbeiten	gearbeitet	to work
basteln	gebastelt	to make things as a hobby
bauen	gebaut	to build
borgen	geborgt	to borrow
brauchen	gebraucht	to need
fragen	gefragt	to ask
gehören	gehört	to belong
glauben	geglaubt	to believe

hören	gehört	to hear
kaufen	gekauft	to buy
kochen	gekocht	to cook
kriegen	gekriegt	to get
lernen	gelernt	to learn
machen	gemacht	to make, do
malen	gemalt	to paint
parken	geparkt	to park
rauchen	geraucht	to smoke
regnen (es)	geregnet	to rain
reinigen	gereinigt	to clean
reisen	gereist (sein)	to travel
sagen	gesagt	to say; tell
sammeln	gesammelt	to collect
schauen	geschaut	to look
spielen	gespielt	to play
starten	gestartet (sein)	to start
stecken	gesteckt	to put
stellen	gestellt	to put; lay
suchen	gesucht	to look for
tanzen	getanzt	to dance
träumen	geträumt	to dream
trennen	getrennt	to separate
wandern	gewandert (sein)	to go walking (hiking)
wählen	gewählt	to choose
wechseln	gewechselt	to change (money)
wohnen	gewohnt	to live
zahlen	gezahlt	to pay
zittern	gezittert	to shiver

Group C

These verbs have separable affixes, and form their past participle by placing the 'ge' between affix and stem.

Infinitve	Vowel change in present tense	Past participle	Meaning
abfahren	ä	abgefahren (sein)	to leave; depart
abholen		abgeholt	to fetch
abschließen		abgeschlossen	to lock up
abtrocknen		abgetrocknet	to dry up
abwaschen	ä	abgewaschen	to wash up
anfangen	ä	angefangen	to begin
ankommen		angekommen (sein)	to arrive
anrufen		angerufen	to telephone
anziehen		angezogen	to put on (clothes)

aufgeben	i	aufgegeben	to give up
aufräumen		aufgeräumt	to tidy up
aufstehen		aufgestanden (sein)	to get up
ausgehen		ausgegangen (sein)	to go out
einkaufen		eingekauft	to do the shopping
einschlafen	ä	einschlafen (sein)	to go to sleep
sich hinlegen		sich hingelegt	to lie down
umsteigen		umgestiegen (sein)	to change (trains)
wegfahren	ä	weggefahren (sein)	to go away
vorstellen		vorgestellt	to introduce

Group D

These verbs have no 'ge' in the past participle. They are all conjugated with 'haben'.

Infinitive	Past participle	Meaning
anprobieren	anprobiert	to try on
beginnen	begonnen	to begin
bekommen	bekommen	to get
besuchen	besucht	to visit
erwarten	erwartet	to expect
erzählen	erzählt	to tell (a story)
sich interessieren (für)	interessiert	to be interested in
reparieren	repariert	to repair
reservieren	reserviert	to reserve
telefonieren	telefoniert	to telephone
verdienen	verdient	to earn
verschreiben	verschrieben	to prescribe
verstehen	verstanden	to understand
wiederholen	wiederholt	to repeat

13 The Simple Past, or Imperfect tense

The four groups of verbs given above indicate how to form the Compound Past tense. This is the tense which you should learn to use when you want to speak or write German. There is, however, another past tense: the Simple Past tense. Some Germans use this instead of the Compound Past. At this stage of learning German it is only necessary to know how to use the Simple Past tense of the verbs 'haben', 'sein', 'sagen', 'fragen' and the modal verbs. It will, however, be useful for you to recognise the Simple Past of other verbs, if and when they are used by native speakers of German.

● *Simple Past of* 'malen' *(to paint)*
   ich mal – TE
   du mal – TEST

```
er   mal – TE
sie  mal – TE
wir  mal – TEN
ihr  mal – TET
Sie  mal – TEN
sie  mal – TEN
```

The Simple Past tense is made by adding 't' to the stem of the verb and then adding the endings as above, e.g. 'fragen – fragte' (to ask).

Some verbs make their Simple Past tense in an irregular way, adding a slightly different set of endings to the stems listed below. Here are the past tenses of 'bleiben' and 'bringen' to illustrate:

- **Simple Past of** 'bleiben' *(to stay)*   and 'bringen' *(to bring)*

ich blieb	ich brachte
du blieb – ST	du brachte – ST
er blieb	er brachte
sie blieb	sie brachte
es blieb	es brachte
wir blieb – EN	wir brachte – N
Sie blieb – EN	Sie brachte – N
ihr blieb – T	ihr brachte – T
sie blieb – EN	sie brachte – N

Infinitive	Simple Past tense
bleiben	blieb
bringen	brachte
denken	dachte
essen	aß
fahren	fuhr
finden	fand
geben	gab
gehen	ging
halten	hielt
heißen	hieß
kennen	kannte
kommen	kam
laufen	lief
lesen	las
liegen	lag
nehmen	nahm
nennen	nannte
reiten	ritt
schlafen	schlief
schwimmen	schwamm
sehen	sah
singen	sang
sitzen	saß

sprechen	sprach
stehen	stand
tragen	trug
treffen	traf
trinken	trank
tun	tat
verlieren	verlor
waschen	wusch
werden	wurde
wiegen	wog
wissen	wußte

- *Simple Past of* 'haben' *(to have)*

ich hatte	I had
du hattest	you had *(familiar)*
er hatte	he had
sie hatte	she had
es hatte	it had
wir hatten	we had
ihr hattet	you had *(familiar plural)*
Sie hatten	you had *(formal or polite)*
sie hatten	they had

- *Simple Past of* 'sein' *(to be)*

ich war	I was
du warst	you were *(familiar)*
er war	he was
sie war	she was
es war	it was
wir waren	we were
ihr wart	you were *(familiar plural)*
Sie waren	you were *(formal or polite)*
sie waren	they were

- *Simple Past of* 'sagen' *(to say)*

ich sagte	I said
du sagtest	you said *(familiar)*
er sagte	he said
sie sagte	she said
es sagte	it said
wir sagten	we said
ihr sagtet	you said *(familiar plural)*
Sie sagten	you said *(formal or polite)*
sie sagten	they said

- *Simple Past of* 'fragen' *(to ask)*

ich fragte	I asked
du fragtest	you asked *(familiar)*
er fragte	he asked

sie fragte	she asked
es fragte	it asked
wir fragten	we asked
ihr fragtet	you asked *(familiar plural)*
Sie fragten	you asked *(formal or polite)*
sie fragten	they asked

- *Simple Past of* 'können' *(to be able to)*

ich konnte	I could
du konntest	you could *(familiar)*
er konnte	he could
sie konnte	she could
es konnte	it could
wir konnten	we could
ihr konntet	you could *(familiar plural)*
Sie konnten	you could *(formal or polite)*
sie konnten	they could

- *Simple Past of* 'wollen' *(to want to)*

ich wollte	I wanted to
du wolltest	you wanted to *(familiar)*
er wollte	he wanted to
sie wollte	she wanted to
es wollte	it wanted to
wir wollten	we wanted to
ihr wolltet	you wanted to *(familiar plural)*
Sie wollten	you wanted to *(formal or polite)*
sie wollten	they wanted to

- *Simple Past of* 'müssen' *(to have to)*

ich mußte	I had to
du mußtest	you had to *(familiar)*
er mußte	he had to
sie mußte	she had to
es mußte	it had to
wir mußten	we had to
ihr mußtet	you had to *(familiar plural)*
Sie mußten	you had to *(formal or polite)*
sie mußten	they had to

- *Simple Past of* 'dürfen' *(to be allowed to)*

ich durfte	I was allowed to
du durftest	you were allowed to *(familiar)*
er durfte	he was allowed to
sie durfte	she was allowed to
es durfte	it was allowed to
wir durften	we were allowed to
ihr durftet	you were allowed to *(familiar plural)*

| Sie durften | you were allowed to *(formal or polite)* |
| sie durften | they were allowed to |

C Word order

Many sentences in this course are short phrases consisting of one or two words only. In this respect German resembles English.

When a sentence contains a verb, however, there are certain differences. Below, you will find a list of the principal sentence types used in *Mastering German*.

14 Statements

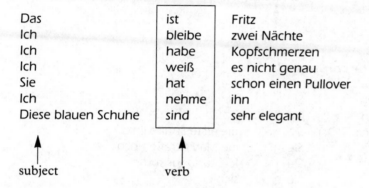

Das	ist	Fritz
Ich	bleibe	zwei Nächte
Ich	habe	Kopfschmerzen
Ich	weiß	es nicht genau
Sie	hat	schon einen Pullover
Ich	nehme	ihn
Diese blauen Schuhe	sind	sehr elegant

subject   verb

15 Questions

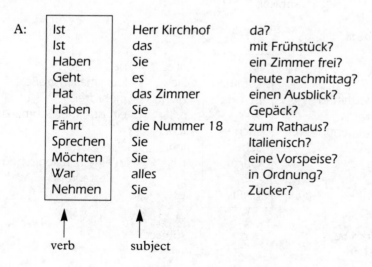

A:	Ist	Herr Kirchhof	da?
	Ist	das	mit Frühstück?
	Haben	Sie	ein Zimmer frei?
	Geht	es	heute nachmittag?
	Hat	das Zimmer	einen Ausblick?
	Haben	Sie	Gepäck?
	Fährt	die Nummer 18	zum Rathaus?
	Sprechen	Sie	Italienisch?
	Möchten	Sie	eine Vorspeise?
	War	alles	in Ordnung?
	Nehmen	Sie	Zucker?

verb   subject

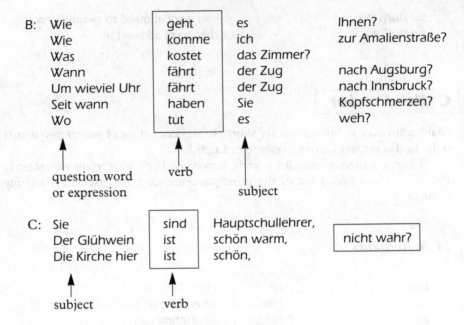

B:	Wie	geht	es	Ihnen?
	Wie	komme	ich	zur Amalienstraße?
	Was	kostet	das Zimmer?	
	Wann	fährt	der Zug	nach Augsburg?
	Um wieviel Uhr	fährt	der Zug	nach Innsbruck?
	Seit wann	haben	Sie	Kopfschmerzen?
	Wo	tut	es	weh?

question word   verb

or expression   subject

C:	Sie	sind	Hauptschullehrer,	
	Der Glühwein	ist	schön warm,	nicht wahr?
	Die Kirche hier	ist	schön,	

subject   verb

16 Orders or commands

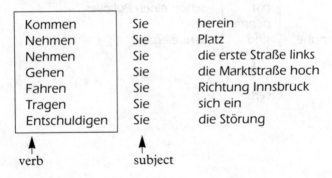

Kommen	Sie	herein
Nehmen	Sie	Platz
Nehmen	Sie	die erste Straße links
Gehen	Sie	die Marktstraße hoch
Fahren	Sie	Richtung Innsbruck
Tragen	Sie	sich ein
Entschuldigen	Sie	die Störung

verb   subject

17 Emphasis

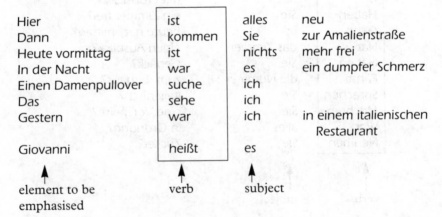

Hier	ist	alles	neu
Dann	kommen	Sie	zur Amalienstraße
Heute vormittag	ist	nichts	mehr frei
In der Nacht	war	es	ein dumpfer Schmerz
Einen Damenpullover	suche	ich	
Das	sehe	ich	
Gestern	war	ich	in einem italienischen Restaurant
Giovanni	heißt	es	

element to be   verb   subject

emphasised

18 Modal verbs

A: Statements

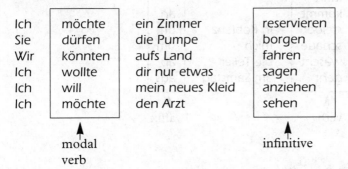

Ich	möchte	ein Zimmer	reservieren
Sie	dürfen	die Pumpe	borgen
Wir	könnten	aufs Land	fahren
Ich	wollte	dir nur etwas	sagen
Ich	will	mein neues Kleid	anziehen
Ich	möchte	den Arzt	sehen

modal verb   infinitive

B: Questions

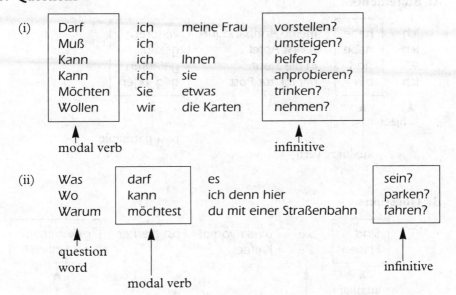

(i)

Darf	ich	meine Frau	vorstellen?
Muß	ich		umsteigen?
Kann	ich	Ihnen	helfen?
Kann	ich	sie	anprobieren?
Möchten	Sie	etwas	trinken?
Wollen	wir	die Karten	nehmen?

modal verb   infinitive

(ii)

Was	darf	es		sein?
Wo	kann	ich denn hier		parken?
Warum	möchtest	du mit einer Straßenbahn		fahren?

question word   modal verb   infinitive

C: Emphasis

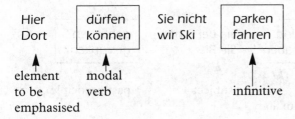

| Hier | dürfen | Sie nicht | parken |
| Dort | können | wir Ski | fahren |

element to be emphasised   modal verb   infinitive

19 Verbs with separate affixes

	verb		affix
Der Zug	fährt		ab
Der Zug	kommt		an
Sie	steigen	in Koblenz	um
Ich	schaue	mich	um
Er	wäscht	die Teller	ab
Sie	geht	am Samstag	aus

20 Compound Past (Perfect) tense

A: Statements

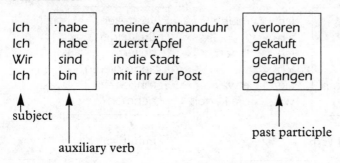

Ich	habe	meine Armbanduhr	verloren
Ich	habe	zuerst Äpfel	gekauft
Wir	sind	in die Stadt	gefahren
Ich	bin	mit ihr zur Post	gegangen

subject

auxiliary verb

past participle

B: Questions

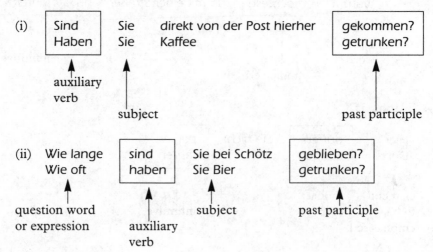

(i)

Sind	Sie	direkt von der Post hierher	gekommen?
Haben	Sie	Kaffee	getrunken?

auxiliary verb

subject

past participle

(ii)

Wie lange	sind	Sie bei Schötz	geblieben?
Wie oft	haben	Sie Bier	getrunken?

question word or expression

auxiliary verb

subject

past participle

21 Subordinate clauses

In theory, one could communicate perfectly well by using whole series of very short sentences, each containing a simple idea. This would be like a very irritating train journey on a branch line, with the train stopping at every tiny wayside halt. In order to make the language flow, two or more sentences can be combined. Here is an example from Chapter 8, Dialogue 2, line 15 (p. 83):

Was sind Sie von Beruf? Darf ich fragen? (Simple sentences)
Was sind Sie von Beruf, wenn ich fragen darf? (Combination)

Here is another example from Chapter 11, Dialogue 2, line 7 (p. 119):

Ich glaube. Ich möchte auch eine Suppe. (Simple sentences)
Ich glaube, daß ich auch eine Suppe möchte. (Combination)

In each of the above examples, one sentence is neatly combined with another. In the first case, the word 'wenn', and in the second, the word 'daß' signal that this is taking place. Frequently-used words which give this signal are:

wenn	if, whenever
daß	that
weil	because
ob	whether

If you wish to make your speech more sophisticated by using this technique, there are two vital rules to remember:

1   (Writing and Speaking) The main, or simple verb (or the modal verb, if there is one) goes to the end of the subordinate clause.

......, wenn ich fragen darf
......, daß ich auch eine Suppe möchte

2   (Writing only) The two parts of the sentence are separated by a comma.

The matter of subordinate clauses will be dealt with more thoroughly in *Mastering German 2*.

Summary

(a) The 'normal' place for the main verb is in the second position of the sentence.

(b) When the main verb comes to the beginning of a sentence, it signals a command, or a question (though a question can be introduced by a 'question word').

(c) Infinitives, affixes and past participles come at the end of the sentence.

D Comparisons

22 Comparison of adjectives

Adjectives usually make their comparative form by adding '-er'. The superlative form of the adjective is usually made by adding '-st'.

(a) Some adjectives which end in the letters '-el', '-en', '-er' usually drop the '-e' in the comparative form.

    edel   edler   der, die, das edelste   noble

(b) Adjectives which end in '-d', '-t', '-s' , 'ß' or 'z' add '-est' in the superlative form.

    heiß   heißer   der, die, das heißeste   hot

(c) Many adjectives add an Umlaut to their principal vowel in the comparative and the superlative form. This, of course, changes the pronunciation: e.g. 'groß – größer', 'alt – älter'. Here is a list of them:

arg	(bad)	dumm	(stupid)	klug	(clever)
grob	(coarse)	jung	(young)	kurz	(short)
groß	(big)	hart	(hard)	krank	(ill)
alt	(old)	kalt	(cold)	arm	(poor)
lang	(long)	schwach	(weak)	gesund	(healthy)
warm	(warm)	schwarz	(black)		
stark	(strong)	scharf	(sharp)		

(d) Some adjectives make their comparative and superlative form in an irregular way. Unfortunately, they are very popular adjectives. Here is a list of them:

gut	besser	der, die, das beste	good
hoch	höher	der, die, das höchste	high
nah(e)	näher	der, die, das nächste	near
viel	mehr	der, die, das meiste	much
wenig	weniger	der, die, das wenigste	little

(e) When adjectives in their comparative or superlative form come in front of a noun, they have to agree with the noun like ordinary adjectives. Examples:

eine klarere Aussicht	a clearer view
eine intelligentere Frau	a more intelligent woman
ein intelligenterer Mann	a more intelligent man

(f) Sometimes the superlative form of the adjective is combined with 'am'. Here are some examples:

Im Januar ist das Wetter am kältesten	The weather is coldest in January
Im Juni ist das Wetter am wärmsten	The weather is warmest in June

| Im Juni sind die Tage am längsten | In June the days are longest |

(g) This is how you can translate the word 'most':

| die meisten Bücher | most (of the) books |

(h) Notice the way that you repeat adjectives in German:

| Die Tage werden immer länger | The days are getting longer and longer |
| Die Nächte werden immer kühler | The nights are getting cooler and cooler |

(i) Here are some important expressions for making comparisons:

Peter ist (eben) so groß wie Klaus	Peter is just as big as Klaus
Klaus ist nicht so groß wie Peter	Klaus is not as big as Peter
Peter ist größer als Klaus	Peter is bigger than Klaus

23 Adverbs

Most adjectives in German can be used as *adverbs*. Here is a normal regular comparison of adverbs.

scharf	schärfer	am schärfsten	sharply
deutlich	deutlicher	am deutlichsten	clearly
klar	klarer	am klarsten	clearly

| Er spricht deutlicher als sie | He speaks more clearly than she does |
| Ich spreche am deutlichsten | I speak most clearly (of all) |

Here are some irregular comparisons of adverbs:

| bald | früher | am frühesten | soon |
| gut | besser | am besten | well |

E The cases

24 The nominative case – the case of the subject of a sentence

	Masc.	Fem.	Neut.	Plur.	
(a) **The indefinite article**	ein	eine	ein	–	(a)
(b) **The negative article**	kein	keine	kein	keine	(not a)

	Masc.	**Fem.**	**Neut.**	**Plur.**	
(c) **The possessive**	mein	meine	mein	meine	(my)
adjectives	dein	deine	dein	deine	(your)
	sein	seine	sein	seine	(his/its)
	ihr	ihre	ihr	ihre	(her/its)
	unser	unsere	unser	unsere	(our)
	euer	eu(e)re	euer	eu(e)re	(your)
	Ihr	Ihre	Ihr	Ihre	(your)
	ihr	ihre	ihr	ihre	(their)
(d) **The definite article**	der	die	das	die	(the)

(e) Adjective endings

(i) After 'ein/mein', etc.:

ein –er + *noun*   eine –e + *noun*   ein –es + *noun*
meine –en + *noun* (plural)

(ii) After 'der/dieser', etc.:

der –e + *noun*   die –e + *noun*   das –e + *noun*
die –en + *noun* (plural)

(f) The personal pronouns

Sing.		**Plur.**	
ich	I	wir	we
du	you	ihr	you *(familiar)*
Sie	you	Sie	you *(formal or polite)*
er	he/it		
sie	she/it	sie	they
es	it		

25 The accusative case – the case of the direct object of a sentence

	Masc.	**Fem.**	**Neut.**	**Plur.**	
(a) **The indefinite article**	einen	eine	ein	–	(a)
(b) **The negative article**	keinen	keine	kein	keine	(not a)
(c) **The possessive**	meinen	meine	mein	meine	(my)
adjectives	deinen	deine	dein	deine	(your)

	Masc.	Fem.	Neut.	Plur.	
	seinen	seine	sein	seine	(his/its)
	ihren	ihre	ihr	Ihre	(her/its)
	unseren	unsere	unser	unsere	(our)
	eu(e)ren	eu(e)re	euer	eu(e)re	(your)
	Ihren	Ihre	Ihr	Ihre	(your)
	ihren	ihre	ihr	ihre	(their)
(d) **The definite article**	den	die	das	die	(the)

(e) Adjective endings

(i) After 'einen/meinen', etc.:

einen –en + *noun*   eine –e + *noun*   ein –es + *noun*

meine –en + *noun* (plural)

(ii) After den/diesen, etc.:

den –en + *noun*   die –e + *noun*   das –e + *noun*

die –en + *noun* (plural)

(f) The personal pronouns

Sing.		**Plur.**	
mich	me	uns	us
dich	you	euch	you *(familiar)*
Sie	you	Sie	you *(formal or polite)*
ihn	him/it		
sie	her/it	sie	them
es	it		

26 The genitive case – the case with which certain relationships of one noun to another are conveyed

	Masc.	Fem.	Neut.	Plur.	
(a) **The indefinite article**	eines	einer	eines	–	(of a)
(b) **The negative article**	keines	keiner	keines	keiner	(of no)
(c) **The possessive adjectives**	meines	meiner	meines	meiner	(of my)
	deines	deiner	deines	deiner	(of your)
	seines	seiner	seines	seiner	(of his/its)
	ihres	ihrer	ihres	ihrer	(of her/its)
	unseres	unserer	unseres	unserer	(of our)

	Masc.	Fem.	Neut.	Plur.	
	eu(e)res	eu(e)rer	eu(e)res	eu(e)rer	(of your)
	Ihres	Ihrer	Ihres	ihrer	(of your)
	ihres	ihrer	ihres	ihrer	(of their)

(d) **The definite article**   des   der   des   der   (of the)

(e) Adjective endings

(i) After 'eines/meines', etc.:

eines –en + *noun* –(e)s   einer –en + *noun*   eines –en + *noun* –(e)s

meiner –en + *noun* (plural)

(ii) After 'des/dieses', etc.:

des –en + *noun* –(e)s   der –en + *noun*   des –en + *noun* –(e)s

der –en + *noun* (plural)

N.B. When the genitive case is used in the masculine and neuter singular the noun itself is marked.

(a) If the noun ends in '-s', '-ß', '-x', '-tz', then the marker is /es/
   e.g. des Hauses, des Flußes, des Platzes.

(b) When nouns end in '-ld', '-lg', '-nd', '-sch', '-st', then most German-speakers prefer the marker /es/ in order to avoid having too full a mouthful of consonants
   e.g. des Windes, des Landes, des Bildes.

(c) Single-syllable nouns are treated in the same way, with /es/
   e.g. des Tages, des Buches, des Kopfes.

(d) However, if the noun ends in '-el', '-em', '-en', '-er', then the marker is only /s/
   e.g. des Onkels, des Koffers, des Reifens.

(e) The same goes for nouns ending in '-chen', '-lein'
   e.g. des Mädchens, des Fräuleins.

(f) Also for nouns ending in '-ig', '-ing', '-ling'
   e.g. des Herings, des Frühlings.

(g) German-speakers also prefer the short /s/ marker when nouns end with a vowel or diphthong
   e.g. des Tees, des Schnees, des Baus, des Heus

or when a noun ends with a vowel + /h/
   e.g. des Schuhs.

Meanings of the genitive case

The genitive can show *possession* or *belonging*,
   e.g. Ottos Buch (Otto's book), die Frau meines Bruders (my brother's wife)

Do you see the similarity with English? Easy, isn't it?

The genitive can show that one thing is *part of* another,

e.g. ein Drittel des Weges (a third of the way); zwei seiner Bücher (two of his books).

The genitive can show possession of a *quality, property or characteristics,*

e.g. zweiter Klasse ((of the) second class); die Intelligenz der Frau (the woman's intelligence); die Schönheit des Mannes (the man's beauty).

27 *The dative case – the case of the* indirect object *of a sentence*

	Masc.	**Fem.**	**Neut.**	**Plur.**	
(a) **The indefinite article**	einem	einer	einem	–	(a)
(b) **The negative article**	keinem	keiner	keinem	keinen	(not a)
(c) **The possessive adjectives**	meinem	meiner	meinem	meinen	(my)
	deinem	deiner	deinem	deinen	(your)
	seinem	seiner	seinem	seinen	(his/its)
	ihrem	ihrer	ihrem	ihren	(her/ist)
	unserem	unserer	unserem	unseren	(our)
	eu(e)rem	eu(e)rer	eu(e)rem	eu(e)ren	(your)
	Ihrem	Ihrer	Ihrem	Ihren	(your)
	ihrem	ihrer	ihrem	ihren	(their)
(d) **The definite article**	dem	der	dem	den	(the)

(e) Adjective endings

(i) After 'einem/meinem', etc.:

einem –en + *noun* einer –en + *noun* einem –en + *noun*
meinen –en + *noun* (plural)

(ii) After 'dem/diesem', etc.:

dem –en + *noun* der –en + *noun* dem –en + *noun*
den –en + *noun* (plural)

(f) The personal pronouns

Sing.		**Plur.**	
mir	me	uns	us
dir	you	euch	you *(familiar)*
Ihnen	you	Ihnen	you *(formal or polite)*

Sing.		Plur.	
ihm	him/it		
ihr	her/it	ihnen	them
ihm	it		

N.B.   Nouns in the dative plural end in '-n' or '-en', except those which end in '-s'.

28 Possessive adjectives

<u>Mein</u> Mann
<u>Meine</u> Frau

The following are the possessive adjectives with the corresponding personal pronouns:

ich	I		mein	my
du	you *(familiar)*		dein	your *(familiar)*
er	he/it		sein	his/its
sie	she/it		ihr	her/its
es	it		sein	its
wir	we		unser	our
ihr	you *(familiar)*		euer	your *(familiar)*
Sie	you *(polite)*		Ihr	your *(polite)*
sie	they		ihr	their

This is how *possessive adjectives* agree with *nouns*.

Masc.

mein Mann	my husband
dein Mann	your husband
sein Garten	his garden
ihr Mann	her husband
sein Garten	its garden
unser Garten	our garden
euer Garten	your garden
Ihr Mann	your husband
ihr Garten	their garden

Fem.

meine Frau	my wife
deine Frau	your wife
seine Frau	his wife
ihre Zeitung	her newspaper
seine Küche	its kitchen
unsere Küche	our kitchen
eu(e)re Küche	your kitchen
Ihre Zeitung	your newspaper
ihre Straße	their street

Neut.

mein Auto	my car
dein Auto	your car
sein Auto	his car
ihr Auto	her car
sein Fenster	its window
unser Haus	our house
euer Haus	your house
Ihr Haus	your house
ihr Haus	their house

Plur.

meine Schuhe	my shoes
deine Schuhe	your shoes
seine Schuhe	his shoes
ihre Schuhe	her shoes
seine Zimmer	its rooms
unsere Autos	our cars
eu(e)re Freunde	your friends
Ihre Freunde	your friends
ihre Freunde	their friends

29 The indefinite article

	Masc.	Fem.	Neut.
nominative	ein	eine	ein
accusative	einen	eine	ein
genitive	eines	einer	eines
dative	einem	einer	einem

All these words mean 'a' or 'an'. The 'nominative case' is used for the subject of the sentence, and the 'accusative case' is used for the direct object of the sentence.

Examples of direct objects:

Haben Sie ein Zimmer? (das Zimmer)	Have you got a room?
Ich möchte einen Kaffee (der Kaffee)	I'd like a coffee

You do not use the indefinite article when you want to indicate somebody's profession:

Er ist Professor	He is a professor
Sie ist Sekretärin	She is a secretary

There is no direct object after the verb 'sein' (to be).

30 Negative ('not a ...')

The negative form of 'ein', meaning 'not a', is 'kein'.

Er ist kein Freund	He is not a friend
Nein, sie ist keine Sekretärin	No, she is not a secretary

Schmidt: Eine Tasse Kaffee?
Müller: Ja, bitte.
Schmidt: Ugh! Das ist kein Kaffee. Das ist Tee!

31 The definite article

	Masc.	Fem.	Neut.	Plur.
nominative	der	die	das	die
accusative	den	die	das	die
genitive	des	der	des	der
dative	dem	der	dem	den

The nominative case is used for the subject of the sentence and the accusative case is used for the direct object of the sentence.

The dative case is used for the indirect object of a sentence.

(a) Contractions of the definite article

The definite article is often contracted with certain prepositions. E.g. 'an das' – 'ans', 'auf das' – 'aufs', 'in das' – 'ins', 'um das' – 'ums', 'in dem' – 'im', 'zu der' – 'zur', 'zu dem' – 'zum'.

(b) Definite article with countries, geographical features and streets

die Schweiz	Switzerland
der Rhein	the Rhine
die Donau	the Danube
die Weser	the Weser
die Elbe	the Elbe
die Mozartstraße	Mozart Street

(c) The definite article is not used when two nouns are closely connected in one idea

Stadt und Land	town and country
Hand in Hand	hand in hand
Wind und Wetter	wind and weather

32 Adjective endings (1)

Agreement of the adjective after the words 'der', 'die' or 'das' (also after 'dieser', 'diese', 'dieses') – *nominative case*. The adjective is part of the subject of the sentence:

Der blaue Pullover ist sehr schön.
Die blauen Schuhe sind sehr elegant.

Agreement of the adjective after the words 'den', 'die' or 'das' (also after 'diesen', 'diese', 'dieses') – *accusative case*:

Haben Sie die blauen Schuhe?
Ich habe die gleichen Schuhe.

Agreement of the adjective in a phrase introduced by a preposition governing the *dative case*:

Er kommt aus der schönen Stadt Bonn.
Wir fahren mit dem alten Taxi.

Sing.	Masc.	Fem.	Neut.
nominative	der rote Rock	die schöne Bluse	das weiße Hemd
accusative	den roten Rock	die schöne Bluse	das weiße Hemd
genitive	des roten Rocks	der schönen Bluse	des weißen Hemdes
dative	dem roten Rock	der schönen Bluse	dem weißen Hemd

Plural.	Masc.	Fem.	Neut.
nominative	die rot**en** Röcke	die schön**en** Blusen	die weiß**en** Hemden
accusative	die rot**en** Röcke	die schön**en** Blusen	die weiß**en** Hemden
genitive	der rot**en** Röcke	der schön**en** Blusen	der weiß**en** Hemden
dative	den rot**en** Röcken	den schön**en** Blusen	den weiß**en** Hemden

33 Adjective endings (2)

Agreement of the adjective after the words 'ein', 'kein', 'mein', 'unser', etc. – *nominative case*. The adjective is part of the subject of the sentence:

Ein <u>guter</u> Wein kostet viel Geld.
Mein <u>altes</u> Fahrrad ist kaputt.

The adjective is part of the direct object of a sentence, or agrees with a preposition governing the *accusative case*:

Ich habe einen <u>neuen</u> Mantel gekauft.
Wir gehen eine <u>alte</u> Straße entlang.

The adjective is part of the indirect object of a sentence, or agrees with a preposition governing the *dative case*:

Er gibt seiner <u>schönen</u> Sekretärin eine Kette.
Er kommt mit seinem <u>alten</u> Koffer.

Sing.	Masc.	Fem.	Neut.
nominative	ein gut**er** Wein	eine schön**e** Kette	ein alt**es** Auto
accusative	einen gut**en** Wein	eine schön**e** Kette	ein alt**es** Auto
genitive	eines gut**en** Weines	einer schön**en** Kette	eines alt**en** Autos
dative	einem gut**en** Wein	einer schön**en** Kette	einem alt**en** Auto

Plur.	Masc.	Fem.	Neut.
nominative	meine alt**en** Schuhe	meine schön**en** Blusen	unsere alt**en** Autos
accusative	meine alt**en** Schuhe	meine schön**en** Blusen	unsere alt**en** Autos
genitive	meiner alt**en** Schuhe	meiner schön**en** Blusen	unserer alt**en** Autos
dative	meinen alt**en** Schuhen	meinen schön**en** Blusen	unseren alt**en** Autos

34 Adjective endings (3)

Sometimes adjectives occur by themselves. That is to say, they are not preceded by the words 'der' or 'dieser', or by the words 'ein', 'mein', 'kein', etc. In these cases the adjective is declined somewhat differently. The endings are set out for you overleaf:

Sing.	Masc.	Fem.	Neut.
	good wine	good milk	good beer
nominative	gut<u>er</u> Wein	gut<u>e</u> Milch	gut<u>es</u> Bier
accusative	gut<u>en</u> Wein	gut<u>e</u> Milch	gut<u>es</u> Bier
genitive	gut<u>en</u> Weines	gut<u>er</u> Milch	gut<u>en</u> Bieres
dative	gut<u>em</u> Wein	gut<u>er</u> Milch	gut<u>em</u> Bier
Plur.			
nominative	gut<u>e</u> Weine	schön<u>e</u> Blusen	rot<u>e</u> Hemden
accusative	gut<u>e</u> Weine	schön<u>e</u> Blusen	rot<u>e</u> Hemden
genitive	gut<u>er</u> Weine	schön<u>er</u> Blusen	rot<u>er</u> Hemden
dative	gut<u>en</u> Weinen	schön<u>en</u> Blusen	rot<u>en</u> Hemden

35 Prepositions governing the accusative case

The following prepositions make the definite or indefinite article occur in the accusative case:

durch	through
entlang	along
für	for
gegen	against
ohne	without
um	round

Durch
Der Fußball geht durch das
   Fenster.

The football goes through the
   window

Sie geht durch den Zug

She goes through the train

Entlang
Wir gehen die Straße entlang
Er kommt den Korridor entlang

We go along the street
He comes along the corridor

Note that the word entlang comes after the noun.

Für
Hier ist ein Brief für den Chef
Ich kaufe einen Pullover für das
   Kind

Here is a letter for the boss
I buy a pullover for the child

Gegen
Ich habe nichts gegen
   den Plan

I have nothing against the
   plan

Ohne
Ich komme ohne meinen Mantel
Sie schwimmt ohne eine
   Bademütze

I'm coming without my coat
She is swimming without a bathing
   cap

Um

Wir sitzen um den Tisch	We're sitting round the table
Er geht um das Rathaus	He goes round the town hall

36 Prepositions governing the dative case

The following *prepositions* govern the dative case

aus	out of/from
außer	beside/except
bei	near/with/among
gegenüber	opposite
mit	with
nach	to/after/according/to
seit	since
von	about
zu	to/at

Aus
generally means 'out of', 'from':

(a) to express movement from a place

Er kommt aus dem Zimmer	He comes out of the room

(b) to express origin referring to time, place or material

Glas aus der Römerzeit	glass from Roman times
Er kommt aus Hamburg	He comes from Hamburg
Das Haus ist aus Stein	The house is made of stone

(c) to express a cause – special phrases

aus diesem Grund	for this reason
aus Versehen	by mistake

Außer
generally means 'outside', 'out of', 'beyond', 'except':

außer Gefahr	out of danger
außer Frage	out of the question
außer sich	beside oneself (e.g. with joy)
außer Zweifel	beyond doubt
außer Kontrolle	beyond control
alle außer mir	everyone except me

Bei

(a) generally means 'by', 'near', 'beside':

Mölln bei Hamburg	Mölln near Hamburg

(b) it means 'at the house of' or 'living with'

Er wohnt bei seinen Eltern	He lives with his parents

(c) it means 'with' or 'on', referring to persons

Ich habe kein Geld bei mir	I have no money with me, or on me

(d) other phrases

beim Frühstück	at breakfast
beim Mittagessen	at lunch
bei Tisch	at table
bei diesem Wetter	in this weather
bei dieser Gelegenheit	on this occasion
bei der Arbeit	at work

Gegenüber

Das Rathaus ist gegenüber dem Theater	The town hall is opposite the theatre
Wir sind gegenüber der Post	We're opposite the post office

Mit

(a) generally means 'with', 'by'

Kommen Sie mit?	Are you coming (with me)?

(b) it means 'by', referring to means of transport

mit dem Zug	by train
mit dem Auto	by car
mit dem Rad	by bicycle

Nach

(a) means 'to' with the names of places

nach Berlin	to Berlin
nach Deutschland	to Germany

(b) means 'after'

nach 10 Minuten	after 10 minutes
nach einer halben Stunde	after half an hour

(c) means 'according to'

Nach seinem Brief ist er krank	According to his letter he is ill
nach meiner Meinung (or meiner Meinung nach)	in my opinion
nach Belieben	as desired

(d) other phrases

nach Hause gehen (fahren)	to go home
nach oben	upwards or upstairs
nach außen	outwards or outside

Seit

(a) generally means 'since'

seit Weihnachten	since Christmas
seit Ostern	since Easter

(b) it also means 'for'

seit 10 Jahren	for 10 years
Ich wohne seit 10 Jahren in Hamburg	I have lived in Hamburg for 10 years

Note that the present tense is used. And note that the expression of time comes *before* that of place.

Von

(a) it means 'of', or 'about', or 'concerning'

Ich spreche von ihm	I'm speaking about him
Ich spreche von ihr	I'm speaking about her

(b) it means 'by', e.g. written by

Hamlet von Shakespeare	Hamlet by Shakespeare

(c) it means 'from'

von Jahr zu Jahr	from year to year
von Zeit zu Zeit	from time to time

Note that the English word 'of' is sometimes omitted in German:

zwei Glas Milch	two glasses of milk
eine Menge Leute	a crowd of people
eine Tasse Tee	a cup of tea
die Stadt London	the town of London
die Firma Schmidt	the firm of Smith
der Monat Januar	the month of January

Zu

(a) it means 'to', when used with the names of places, or buildings in a town

Ich gehe zum Rathaus	I'm going to the town hall
Er geht zur Haltestelle	He's going to the bus stop

(b) it means 'at' with the names of seasons

zu Weihnachten	at Christmas
zu Ostern	at Easter

(c) it means 'at' referring to prices

Fleisch zu 11 Mark das Pfund	meat at 11 marks a pound

(d) it means 'for' referring to purpose

zu diesem Zweck	for this purpose
zum Beispiel	for example

(e) other phrases

zu Fuß	on foot
zum zweiten Mal	for the second time
zum dritten Mal	for the third time
zu Ende	at an end
zu Hause	at home

37 Prepositions governing either the accusative or the dative case

an	by/on/at/to
auf	on
hinter	behind
in	in
neben	beside/near
über	over/above
unter	under
vor	in front of/before
zwischen	between

When they occur with a verb which indicates *position*, they govern the dative.
When they occur with a verb which indicates *movement towards* something, they govern the accusative.

An with the dative
generally means 'at', 'near', 'by the side of'

Er sitzt an dem Tisch	He is sitting at the table
Das Bild hängt an der Wand	The picture is hanging on the wall
Er steht an dem Fenster	He is standing at the window

An with the accusative
generally means 'at', 'to'

Er setzt sich an den Tisch	He sits down at the table
Er hängt das Bild an die Wand	He hangs the picture on the wall
Er geht an das Fenster	He goes to the window

Auf with the dative
generally means 'on', 'on top of'

Das Buch liegt auf dem Tisch	The book is on the desk

In a number of idioms, auf means 'in' or 'at'

auf der Straße	in the street
auf dem Markt	at the market
auf dem Land	in the country

Auf with the accusative
generally means 'on', 'on top of'

Er stellt die Tasse auf den Tisch	He puts the cup on the table
Er stellt das Radio auf den Stuhl	He puts the radio on the chair

Auf also means 'for' when it refers to future time

Er fährt auf drei Tage nach Hamburg	He is going to Hamburg for three days

Hinter means 'behind'

Er steht hinter der Tür	He is standing behind the door
Er geht hinter die Tür	He goes behind the door

In with the dative
generally means 'in', referring to time or place

Das Geld ist in meiner Tasche	The money is in my pocket
Das Radio ist im Wohnzimmer	The radio is in the living room

In also has a number of other meanings

in der Schule	at school
in der Kirche	at church
im Alter von ...	at the age of ...
im ersten Stock	on the first floor
im großen und ganzen	on the whole
im Gegenteil	on the contrary
heute in acht Tagen	a week today

In with the accusative
generally means 'into'

Er steckt das Geld in seine Tasche	He puts the money into his pocket
Er fährt das Auto in die Garage	He drives the car into the garage

Other meanings

Er geht in die Kirche	He goes to church
Sie fährt in die Stadt	She drives to town
Wir gehen ins Theater	We go to the theatre

Neben generally means 'beside', 'by', 'at the side of'

Er steht neben der Tür	He is standing by the door
Er stellt den Stuhl neben die Tür	He puts the chair beside the door

Über with the dative
generally means 'over', 'above'

Über dem Berg sind Wolken	There are clouds over the mountain

Über with the accusative
generally means 'over', 'across'

Er geht über die Straße	He goes across the street
Sie schwimmt über den Fluß	She swims across the river

Other meanings

Das Päckchen wiegt über 500 Gramm	The packet weighs more than 500 grams
Der Zug fährt über München	The train goes via Munich

Unter with the dative
generally means 'under', 'among', 'amid'

Öl ist unter dem Auto	There is oil under the car
Du bist unter Freunden	You are among friends

Other meanings

Das Päckchen wiegt unter 500 Gramm	The packet weighs less than 500 grams
unter dieser Bedingung	on this condition
unter diesen Umständen	under these circumstances

Unter with the accusative
generally means 'under', 'among'

Der Ball rollt unter das Auto	The ball rolls underneath the car
Die Katze läuft unter den Tisch	The cat runs under the table

Vor with the dative
generally means 'before' (referring to time or place), 'in front of'

vor dem Krieg	before the war
Er steht vor dem Haus	He stands in front of the house

Other meanings

vor zwei Tagen	two days ago
vor langer Zeit	a long time ago
Sie zittert vor Kälte	She is shivering with cold

Vor with the accusative
generally means 'before', 'in front of'

Sie kommt vor die Klasse	She comes in front of the class
Er springt vor das Auto	He jumps in front of the car

Zwischen means 'between'

Das Fahrrad ist zwischen dem Bus und dem Auto	The bicycle is between the bus and the car
Er fährt das Auto zwischen die Polizisten	He drives the car between the policemen

38 Prepositions governing the genitive case

Außerhalb means 'outside'

außerhalb des Hauses	outside the house

Diesseits means 'on this side'

    diesseits des Flußes   on this side of the river

Jenseits means 'on that side'

    jenseits des Flußes   on that side of the river

Innerhalb means 'inside'

    innerhalb des Hauses   inside the house

Während means 'while' or 'during'

    während des Winters   during the winter
    während des Spiels   during the game

Wegen means 'on account of', or 'because of'

    wegen des Wetters   on account of the weather/
                                          because of the weather
    wegen des Unfalls   on account of the accident/
                                          because of the accident

Trotz means 'in spite of'

    trotz des Wetters   in spite of the weather

(N.B. 'trotz' can also govern the dative case; 'trotz dem Wetter')

Money, weights and measures

German, Austrian and Swiss money

German currency

Mark = DM; Pfennig = Pf; DM 1 = 100Pf.
DM 2,72 = zwei Mark zweiundsiebzig Pfennig.

Coins (Münzen)

DM – ,01	ein Pfennig
DM – ,05	fünf Pfennig
DM – ,10	zehn Pfennig
DM – ,50	fünfzig Pfennig
DM 1, –	eine Mark
DM 2, –	zwei Mark
DM 5, –	fünf Mark

Notes (Banknoten)

DM 10, –	zehn Mark
DM 20, –	zwanzig Mark
DM 50, –	fünfzig Mark
DM 100, –	hundert Mark
DM 500, –	fünfhundert Mark

Austrian currency

100 Groschen = 1 Schilling.

Coins

2 Groschen
5 Groschen
10 Groschen
50 Groschen
1 Schilling
5 Schillinge
10 Schillinge

Notes

20 Schillinge
50 Schillinge
100 Schillinge
500 Schillinge
1000 Schillinge

Swiss currency

100 Centimes = 1 Franc.
In German you say 'Rappen' for centimes and 'Franken' for francs.

Coins	Notes
5 Rappen	10 Franken
10 Rappen	20 Franken
20 Rappen	50 Franken
1/2 Franke	100 Franken
1 Franke	1000 Franken
2 Franken	
5 Franken	

Distances

1 mile = 1.6 kilometres   1,6 Kilometer = 1 Meile

Miles	10	20	30	40	50	60	70	80	90	100	Meilen
Kilometres	16	32	48	64	80	96	112	128	144	160	Kilometer

Lengths and sizes

General clothes sizes (including chest/hip measurements)

UK	USA	Germany	Europe	ins	cms
8	6	34	36	30/32	76/81
10	8	36	38	32/34	81/86
12	10	38	40	34/36	86/91
14	12	40	42	36/38	91/97
16	14	42	44	38/40	97/102
18	16	44	46	40/42	102/107
20	18	46	48	42/44	107/112
22	20	48	50	44/46	112/117
24	22	50	52	46/48	117/122
26	24	52	54	48/50	122/127

Waist measurements

(ins) UK/USA

22	24	26	28	30	32	34	36	38	40	42	44	46	48	50

(cms) Europe

56	61	66	71	76	81	86	91	97	102	107	112	117	122	127

Shoes

UK
3 3½ 4 4½ 5 5½ 6 6½ 7 7½ 8 8½ 9 10 11 12

USA
4½ 5 5½ 6 6½ 7 7½ 8 8½ 9 9½ 10 10½ 11½ 12½ 13½

Europe
36   37   38   39   40   41   42 43 44 45

Weights

Some very approximate equivalents – 'Gramm' (g) (grams) and 'Kilogramm' (Kg) (kilograms):

1000 Gramm (1000 g)	1 Kilogramm (1 Kilo/kg)
1 oz	25 Gramm (g)
4 oz	100/125 Gramm
8 oz	225 Gramm
1 pound (16 oz)	450 Gramm
1 pound 2 oz	500 Gramm (½ Kilogramm)
2 pounds 4 oz	1 Kilogramm (1 Kilo/kg)
1 stone	6 Kilogramm

Body weight

Body weight in Europe is measured in kilograms ('Kilogramm'). Some approximate equivalents:

Pounds	Stones	Kilograms
28	2	12½
42	3	19
56	4	25
70	5	31½
84	6	38
98	7	44
112	8	50½
126	9	56½
140	10	63
154	11	69½
168	12	75½
182	13	82
196	14	88

Liquid measures

Petrol and oil are measured in litres ('Liter') as are most other liquids, including milk. Wine is sometimes sold in litre bottles, but more frequently in bottles containing ¾ litre.

Some approximate equivalents:

1 pint = 0.57 Liter (litres)		1 gallon = 4.55 litres	
UK measures	**Liter (litres)**	**UK measures**	**Liter (litres)**
1 pint	= 0.57		
		4.4 gallons	= 20
		5.5 gallons	= 25
1.7 pints	= 1	6.6 gallons	= 30
1.1 gallons	= 5	7.7 gallons	= 35
2.2 gallons	= 10	8.8 gallons	= 40
3.3 gallons	= 15	9.9 gallons	= 45

Temperature

	Fahrenheit (F)	Grad Celsius (C) Centigrade
Boiling point	212°	100°
	104°	40°
Body temperature	98.4°	36.9°
	86°	30°
	68°	20°
	59°	15°
	50°	10°
Freezing point	32°	0°
	23°	−5°
	0°	−18°

(Convert Fahrenheit to Celsius by subtracting 32 and multiplying by 5/9. Convert Celsius to Fahrenheit by multiplying by 9/5 and adding 32.)

Some useful hints and tips

Visiting a German-speaking country means going into a different culture with different ways of doing things. This can sometimes be a problem, even if you know German quite well. You might like to know, therefore, of two publications which are specially prepared for prospective visitors to Germany. One is called *Treffpunkt Deutschland*, and the other is called *Glückliche Ferientage in Deutschland*. This second publication appears in English under the title *Happy Days in Germany*. Both can be obtained by sending a postcard to the German Tourist Office, Beethovenstraße 69, 60325 Frankfurt or from its nearest branch. Many large towns also prepare brochures with useful tips and town plans, some specially designed for young people who wish to visit Germany. Frankfurt produces a brochure called *16 bis 36* and Munich produces a brochure called *Young People's Guide to Munich*. These and similar brochures can be obtained by writing to the local tourist office. You should write to the 'Verkehrsamt der Stadt' (plus name of town).

Telephoning

The cheapest local call ('Ortsgespräch') costs 30 Pfennig. You can make international telephone calls from many public call boxes. Those accepting coins are called Münzfernsprecher. Many call boxes accept phone cards (Telefonkarten); they are labelled 'Mit Karte'. The cards come in different denominations and function as in the UK.

Stamps

Generally speaking in Germany you can buy stamps only in post offices. They are not usually available in souvenir shops. In Austria you can buy stamps with your postcards in Austria Tabak shops.

Shopping hours

Shops, chemists and also travel agencies are usually open from Monday to Friday from 9 a.m. until 6 or 6.30 p.m. though most close for lunch. On Saturdays they are usually open only until midday or 2 o'clock, though many places now have 'langer Samstag' on the first Saturday of each month and throughout December, when shops stay open during the afternoon. When shops are closed, you can buy certain things in petrol stations, newspaper kiosks, and railway stations.

Banking hours

Banks are open from 9 to 12 a.m. and from 2 until 4 p.m. They are closed on Saturdays. You can sometimes find currency-exchange kiosks in stations and airports.

Public transport

Most towns have a comprehensive system of trams, buses, underground railways and suburban railways. It is worthwhile making enquiries about tickets. Frequently you can travel right through a whole city with one ticket. Taxis are fairly expensive.

Reductions

If you have an international pupils' or students' card, there are often special reductions for the theatre, museums, mountain railways and city sightseeing tours.

How to eat cheaply

Look out for snack bars. They will be called Imbiß or Imbißstube. It's worth knowing that many butchers' shops often have a small table and chair where you can go to eat freshly cooked sausage. You can eat fairly cheaply in the cafeterias of large department stores, and you can go into university restaurants to eat. You simply have to buy a meal ticket as German students do. If you are in country areas, it's worth looking out for small guest-houses. Don't forget to ask for German specialities.

Travelling

You can hitchhike in Germany, but not on the motorway. If you wish to travel long distances, you must take care to find a car before it reaches the motorway. It is allowed, however, to thumb a lift at the entries and exits to motorways. Girls are advised not to go hitchhiking alone. It is interesting to note that the first letter or letters of German registration numbers indicate the town where that car is registered.

There is a system in Germany of arranging to travel with somebody who is proposing to make a motorway journey. You give your name to a central office and say where you want to travel to, and the office puts you in touch with someone who is going to make a journey. You often have to wait one or two days until your name comes to the top of the list, but it is cheap and safe. You should look up 'Mitfahrer-Zentrale' in the telephone directory.

Rail travel

Inter Rail is available up to the age of 26 years. The ticket is valid for one month in twenty-one different countries of Europe.

'Tramper-Monats-Ticket' is available up to the age of 26 years, and valid for one month in Germany. It allows you to travel throughout Germany.

'Junior-Paß' is available up to the age of 26 years, and is valid for one year in Germany. The ticket allows you to buy rail tickets at half price.

Car rental

You have to be over 21 to hire a car. It is also possible to rent bicycles at more than 200 railway stations. You can leave your bicycle at the station of your destination. The cost includes insurance.

Staying in Germany

There are about 600 Youth Hostels (JH) in Germany. You need a valid international Youth Hostel Membership Card, which you can obtain either in your own country or by writing to the Deutscher Jugendherbergsverband (DJH) in Detmold. For the high season it's advisable to make a booking as early as possible. In the most popular tourist areas it's even necessary to book up a year in advance. Information about German Youth Hostels can be obtained from DJH, Bülowstraße 26, 32756 Detmold.

You can also stay at the YMCA ('CVJM-Jugendheim'); guest-houses for young people ('Jugendgästehäuser', 'Jugendhotels'); small overnight huts in the alps ('Hütten der Alpenvereine'). There are camping sites ('Camping-plätze'), and many private rooms and small guest-houses ('Pensionen'). Information about all these places can best be obtained by writing to the 'Verkehrsamt' of the town you wish to visit. One of the cheapest and most interesting ways of staying overnight is in the equivalent of bed and breakfast. Look out for the sign: 'Fremdenzimmer'.

Emergencies

If you are ill and cannot find a hospital, go to the nearest telephone kiosk or telephone directory and look for 'Ärztlicher Notdienst'. This service is manned around the clock. In an emergency you could also try the Red Cross ('Rotes Kreuz'), or the Social Assistance Centre at railway stations ('Bahnhofsmission'). However, the best thing to do is to insure yourself against illness before travelling abroad.

If you lose your money or passport, you should report the matter to the nearest police station ('Polizeirevier') or to the British Embassy or Consulate. Directory enquiries in the German telephone system is found by dialling 118 or 0118. In large cities, the police can be contacted by dialling 110. If you break down on the motorway, there are yellow emergency telephones at the roadside.

A few things to see

Here are one or two ideas to whet your appetite. They are the sort of things which many tourists would not think of doing:

Berlin – a stroll through the artists' quarter in Kreuzberg.
Munich – visit the fruit and vegetable market (Viktualienmarkt) in the early morning; or go for a trip on a raft on the river Isar.
Hamburg – visit the fish market at 4 o'clock in the morning.

See some of the beautiful old towns, which have retained their ancient appearance, or been beautifully restored. For example: Freiburg with its cathedral, Bamberg with its cathedral, Passau with its three rivers (the Danube, the Inn and the Ilz), Nuremberg with its medieval castle.

Parts of Germany are already well-known for their beautiful landscapes, such as Bavaria, the Black Forest, the Rhine and Lake Constance (the Bodensee). There are, however, many other beautiful parts of Germany which are less well-known, such as the Bavarian Forest (der bayerische Wald) with its virgin forest, or the Valley of the river Tauber in Franconia or the Hohenloher Land in Württemberg with its many castles. Then there are the beautiful areas of the Odenwald, the Spessart, the Rhön, the Eiffel, the Lüneburg Heath and the Frisian islands (Halligen). Instead of taking a boat trip on the Rhine, why not try the river Weser? Instead of visiting Heidelberg and Rothenburg ob der

Tauber, why not go to see Schwäbisch Hall, Bad Wimpfen on the river Neckar, or the tiny forgotten town of Wolframs-Eschenbach in Franconia, with its old town wall still intact? Celle on the Lüneburg Heath and Regensburg on the Danube are well worth a visit, both for their beauty and for their historic interest.

These are, of course, only one or two of the many attractive places you could visit in Germany. The experienced and adventurous traveller, equipped with a copy of *Mastering German*, cannot fail to have a delightful holiday by taking the byroads and discovering the beautiful sights which Germany has to offer. Always try to speak a few words of German, and you will instantly make friends.

Signs on public display

ABFAHRT	Departures
ABTEILUNG	Department
ACHTUNG	Take care
ADAC	German equivalent of AA/RAC
AN	On (switches, etc.)
ANKUNFT	Admissions/Arrivals
ANLIEGER FREI	Access only (i.e. only if your destination is in this street)
AN SONN- UND FEIERTAGEN FREI	No charge Sundays and Bank Holidays
APOTHEKE	Dispensing chemist
ARZT	Doctor
AUFZUG	Lift
AUS	Off (switches, etc.)
AUSFAHRT	Exit (driving)
AUSGANG	Exit
AUSKUNFT	Enquiries
AUSSER BETRIEB	Not in use
AUSVERKAUF	Sale
AUTOBAHN	Motorway
AUTOBAHNKREUZ	Motorway interchange
BAHNSTEIG	Platform
BAUSTELLE	Building site; road works ahead
BEI VERSAGEN KNOPF DRÜCKEN	Press button to get money back
BESETZT	Engaged; no vacancies; occupied
BETRETEN VERBOTEN	Keep out; no trespassing
BITTE MOTOR ABSCHALTEN	Please switch engine off
DAMEN	Ladies; Ladies' Room
DURCHGEHEND	Continuously
EIN	In
EINBAHNSTRASSE	One-way street
EINFAHRT	Way in (driving)
EINFAHRT FREIHALTEN	Do not obstruct entrance
EINGANG	Entrance

EINORDNEN	Get in lane
EINTRITT	Admission
EMPFANG	Reception
ERDGESCHOSS	Ground floor
ERSATZTEILE	Spare parts
FAHRPLAN	Timetable
FAHRSPUR GESPERRT	Lane closed
FAHRSTUHL	Lift
FAMILIENNAME	Last name
FESTHALTEN	Hold tight
FLUG	Flight
FRAUEN	Women
FREI	Vacant
FREMDENZIMMER	Room to let (Bed and breakfast)
FUNDBÜRO	Lost property office
GASTHAUS	Inn; pub
GASTHOF	Inn; pub
GEFAHR	Danger
GEPÄCKABGABE	Left luggage
GESCHLOSSEN	Closed
GRENZÜBERGANG	Frontier
HABEN SIE IHREN SCHLÜSSEL ABGEGEBEN?	Have you handed in your key?
HAUPTBAHNHOF	Main station (in a city)
HEISSE GETRÄNKE	Hot drinks
HERREN	Gentlemen; Gents
KASSE	Cash desk; till
KEIN AUSGANG	No way out
KEINE DURCHFAHRT	No thoroughfare
KEINE EINFAHRT	No access
KEIN EINGANG	Exit only; No entry
KEIN TRINKWASSER	Not drinking water
KOSTENPFLICHTIG	At owner's expense
LANGSAM	Slow
LEBENSGEFAHR	Danger
LKW	Lorries
MÄNNER	Men
MOTOR ABSTELLEN	Switch off engine
MÜNZEINWURF	Insert coin
MÜNZEN	Coins
MÜNZRÜCKGABE	Reject coins
MÜNZWECHSLER	Coin change
NICHT ANGREIFEN	Do not touch
NICHT BERÜHREN	Do not touch
NICHT RAUCHEN	Do not smoke
NICHTRAUCHER	Non-smoker
NICHT RESERVIERT	Unreserved
NICHT ÜBERHOLEN	No overtaking
NOTAUSGANG	Emergency exit; fire exit
NUR FÜR RASIERAPPARATE	Shavers only
NUR MIT SONDERGENEHMIGUNG	Permit holders only

OBEN/UNTEN	(This side) up; down
OFFEN (TÄGLICH) (BIS)	Open (daily) (till)
ÖFFNUNGSZEITEN	Opening hours
PARKPLATZ	Parking
PARKZEIT 30 MINUTEN	Waiting limited to 30 minutes
PKW	Cars
PLATZ	Seat
PLATZRESERVIERUNG	Seat reservations
POLIZEI	Police
POSTAMT	Post Office
PRAKT. ARZT	Doctor
PRIVATPARKPLATZ	Private parking only
RASTPLATZ	Lay-by
RASTSTÄTTE	Services (on the motorway)
REINIGUNG	Cleaners
REISEBÜRO	Travel office
REISEFÜHRER	Guide
REPARATUREN	Repairs
RESERVIERT	Reserved
RESERVIERUNGEN	Reservations
ROLLSPLITT	Loose chippings
RÜCKGABEKNOPF	Press to reject
RUHETAG	Rest day (closed)
RUNDFAHRT	Tour
SB-TANKSTELLE	Self-service petrol station
SCHLÜSSELFÄCHER	Left luggage lockers
SCHNELLDIENST	While you wait
SCHWIMMBAD	Swimming pool
SCHWIMMEN UND BADEN VERBOTEN	No bathing; no swimming
SELBSTBEDIENUNG	Self-service
SELBST TANKEN	Self-service (petrol)
SONDERANGEBOTE	Bargains; special offers
SPARKASSE	Bank
SPEISEKARTE	Menu
SPRECHSTUNDEN	Surgery hours
SPRECHZEITEN	Surgery hours
STADTMITTE	Town centre
TAGESAUSFLÜGE	Day excursions
TANKSTELLE	Petrol station; service area
TREPPE	Stairs
TRINKWASSER	Drinking water
TÜRE SCHLIESSEN	Close door (firmly)
TÜREN SCHLIESSEN AUTOMATISCH	Doors close automatically
ÜBERNACHTUNG UND FRÜHSTÜCK	Bed and breakfast
UMKLEIDERAUM	Changing room
UMLEITUNG	Diversion
UNFALL	Accident
UNTERFÜHRUNG	Subway
UNTERKUNFT	Accommodation

VERBOTEN	Prohibited
VERKAUFS- UND KUNDENDIENST	Sales and service
VERKEHRSAMT	Tourist office
VORFAHRT BEACHTEN	Give way: major road ahead
VORSICHT	Caution
WARME KÜCHE (DURCHGEHEND)	Hot meals (served all day)
WARNUNG	Warning
WARTERAUM	Waiting area
WARTEZIMMER	Waiting room
WECHSEL	Exchange
ZAHNARZT	Dentist
ZEITUNGEN	Newspapers
ZENTRUM	Town centre
ZIMMER FREI	Room to let
ZIMMERNACHWEIS	Accommodation bureau
ZIMMER ZU VERMIETEN	Rooms to let
ZUBEHÖR	Accessories
ZUFAHRT	Access
ZUSCHLAG	Additional charge

Bibliography

Books recommended for improving your spoken German

Breakthrough German, Macmillan Press

Get by in German, BBC Publications

A small book with lots of useful vocabulary

Survive: German, Longman.

Grammars

Martin Durrell, *Hammer's German Grammar and Usage* (2nd Edition, Hodder & Stoughton, 1991). A thorough and valuable book for the advanced student.
Harrap's German Grammar, Harrap. Thorough and clear.
A Grammar of Contemporary German, Hueber. Adapted from the original German.

Hints and tips about Germany

Treffpunkt Deutschland, German Tourist Office, Beethovenstraße 69, 60325 Frankfurt.
Glückliche Ferientage in Deutschland (Happy Days in Germany), German Tourist Office, Beethovenstraße 69, 60325 Frankfurt.

Dictionaries

Collins *German Dictionary* (one volume).
Harrap's *German Mini Dictionary*.
The Pocket Oxford-Duden German Dictionary (OUP and Dudenverlag)

Further information about learning German may be obtained from the Centre for Information on Language Teaching and Research, 20 Bedfordbury, London, WC2N 4LB, and from the Goethe Institute, 50 Princes Gate, Exhibition Road, London SW7 2PH or in Manchester, York or Glasgow.

Macmillan Master Series

Accounting
Advanced English Language
Arabic
Astronomy
Banking
Basic Management
Biology
British Politics
Business Communication
Business Law
Business Microcomputing
C Programming
Catering Science
Catering Theory
Chemistry
COBOL Programming
Commerce
Computer Programming
Computers
Databases
Economic and Social History
Economics
Electrical Engineering
Electronic and Electrical
    calculations
Electronics
English as a Foreign Language
English Grammar
English Language
English Literature
English Spelling
French
French 2
German

German 2
Hairdressing
Human Biology
Italian
Italian 2
Japanese
Manufacturing
Marketing
Mathematics
Mathematics for Electrical and
    Electronic Engineering
Modern British History
Modern European History
Modern World History
Pascal Programming
Philosophy
Photography
Physics
Psychology
Pure Mathematics
Restaurant Service
Science
Secretarial Procedures
Social Welfare
Sociology
Spanish
Spanish 2
Spreadsheets
Statistics
Study Skills
Word Processing